FREE Study Skills DVD Offer

Dear Customer,

Thank you for your purchase from Mometrix! We consider it an honor and privilege that you have purchased our product and want to ensure your satisfaction.

As a way of showing our appreciation and to help us better serve you, we have developed a Study Skills DVD that we would like to give you for <u>FREE</u>. **This DVD covers our "best practices" for studying for your exam, from using our study materials to preparing for the day of the test.**

All that we ask is that you email us your feedback that would describe your experience so far with our product. Good, bad or indifferent, we want to know what you think!

To get your **FREE Study Skills DVD**, email <u>freedvd@mometrix.com</u> with "FREE STUDY SKILLS DVD" in the subject line and the following information in the body of the email:

    a. The name of the product you purchased.

    b. Your product rating on a scale of 1-5, with 5 being the highest rating.

    c. Your feedback. It can be long, short, or anything in-between, just your impressions and experience so far with our product. Good feedback might include how our study material met your needs and will highlight features of the product that you found helpful.

    d. Your full name and shipping address where you would like us to send your free DVD.

If you have any questions or concerns, please don't hesitate to contact me directly.

Thanks again!

Sincerely,

Jay Willis
Vice President
<u>jay.willis@mometrix.com</u>
1-800-673-8175

NYSTCE

ALST — Academic Literacy Skills Test (202)

SECRETS

Study Guide
Your Key to Exam Success

NYSTCE Exam Review for the
New York State Teacher Certification Examinations

Published by
Mometrix Test Preparation
NYSTCE Exam Secrets Test Prep Team

Written and edited by the NYSTCE Exam Secrets Test Prep Staff

Printed in the United States of America

This paper meets the requirements of ANSI/NISO Z39.48-1992 (Permanence of Paper).

Mometrix offers volume discount pricing to institutions. For more information or a price quote, please contact our sales department at sales@mometrix.com or 888-248-1219.

ISBN 13: 978-1-5167-0302-9
ISBN 10: 1-5167-0302-2

Dear Future Exam Success Story:

Congratulations on your purchase of our study guide. Our goal in writing our study guide was to cover the content on the test, as well as provide insight into typical test taking mistakes and how to overcome them.

Standardized tests are a key component of being successful, which only increases the importance of doing well in the high-pressure high-stakes environment of test day. How well you do on this test will have a significant impact on your future, and we have the research and practical advice to help you execute on test day.

The product you're reading now is designed to exploit weaknesses in the test itself, and help you avoid the most common errors test takers frequently make.

How to use this study guide

We don't want to waste your time. Our study guide is fast-paced and fluff-free. We suggest going through it a number of times, as repetition is an important part of learning new information and concepts.

First, read through the study guide completely to get a feel for the content and organization. Read the general success strategies first, and then proceed to the content sections. Each tip has been carefully selected for its effectiveness.

Second, read through the study guide again, and take notes in the margins and highlight those sections where you may have a particular weakness.

Finally, bring the manual with you on test day and study it before the exam begins.

Your success is our success

We would be delighted to hear about your success. Send us an email and tell us your story. Thanks for your business and we wish you continued success.

Sincerely,

Mometrix Test Preparation Team

Need more help? Check out our flashcards at: http://MometrixFlashcards.com/NYSTCE

TABLE OF CONTENTS

Top 20 Test Taking Tips

1. Carefully follow all the test registration procedures
2. Know the test directions, duration, topics, question types, how many questions
3. Setup a flexible study schedule at least 3-4 weeks before test day
4. Study during the time of day you are most alert, relaxed, and stress free
5. Maximize your learning style; visual learner use visual study aids, auditory learner use auditory study aids
6. Focus on your weakest knowledge base
7. Find a study partner to review with and help clarify questions
8. Practice, practice, practice
9. Get a good night's sleep; don't try to cram the night before the test
10. Eat a well balanced meal
11. Know the exact physical location of the testing site; drive the route to the site prior to test day
12. Bring a set of ear plugs; the testing center could be noisy
13. Wear comfortable, loose fitting, layered clothing to the testing center; prepare for it to be either cold or hot during the test
14. Bring at least 2 current forms of ID to the testing center
15. Arrive to the test early; be prepared to wait and be patient
16. Eliminate the obviously wrong answer choices, then guess the first remaining choice
17. Pace yourself; don't rush, but keep working and move on if you get stuck
18. Maintain a positive attitude even if the test is going poorly
19. Keep your first answer unless you are positive it is wrong
20. Check your work, don't make a careless mistake

Reading

Understanding Literature

Reading literature is a different experience than reading non-fiction works. Our imagination is more active as we review what we have read, imagine ourselves as characters in the novel, and try to guess what will happen next. Suspense, surprise, fantasy, fear, anxiety, compassion, and a host of other emotions and feelings may be stirred by a provocative novel.

Reading longer works of fiction is a cumulative process. Some elements of a novel have a great impact, while others may go virtually unnoticed. Therefore, as novels are read with a critical eye to language, it is helpful to perceive and identify larger patterns and movements in the work as a whole. This will benefit the reader by placing characters and events in perspective, and will enrich the reading experience greatly. Novels should be savored rather than gulped. Careful reading and thoughtful analysis of the major themes of the novel are essential to a clear understanding of the work.

One of the most important skills in reading comprehension is the identification of **topics** and **main ideas.** There is a subtle difference between these two features. The topic is the subject of a text, or what the text is about. The main idea, on the other hand, is the most important point being made by the author. The topic is usually expressed in a few words at the most, while the main idea often needs a full sentence to be completely defined. As an example, a short passage might have the topic of penguins and the main idea *Penguins are different from other birds in many ways*. In most nonfiction writing, the topic and the main idea will be stated directly, often in a sentence at the very beginning or end of the text. When being tested on an understanding of the author's topic, the reader can quickly *skim* the passage for the general idea, stopping to read only the first sentence of each paragraph. A paragraph's first sentence is often (but not always) the main topic sentence, and it gives you a summary of the content of the paragraph. However, there are cases in which the reader must figure out an unstated topic or main idea. In these instances, the student must read every sentence of the text, and try to come up with an overarching idea that is supported by each of those sentences.

> **Review Video:** Topics and Main Ideas
> *Visit* **mometrix.com/academy** *and enter* **Code: 110792**

While the main idea is the overall premise of a story, **supporting details** provide evidence and backing for the main point. In order to show that a main idea is correct, or valid, the author needs to add details that prove their point. All texts contain details, but they are only classified as supporting details when they serve to reinforce some larger point. Supporting details are most commonly found in informative and persuasive texts. In some cases, they will be clearly indicated with words like *for example* or *for instance*, or they will be enumerated with words like *first, second,* and *last.* However, they may not be indicated with special words. As a reader, it is important to consider whether the author's supporting details really back up his or her main point.

Supporting details can be factual and correct but still not relevant to the author's point. Conversely, supporting details can seem pertinent but be ineffective because they are based on opinion or assertions that cannot be proven.

> ➤ **Review Video:** Supporting Details
> *Visit **mometrix.com/academy** and enter **Code: 655186***

An example of a main idea is: "Giraffes live in the Serengeti of Africa." A supporting detail about giraffes could be: "A giraffe uses its long neck to reach twigs and leaves on trees." The main idea gives the general idea that the text is about giraffes. The supporting detail gives a specific fact about how the giraffes eat.

As opposed to a main idea, themes are seldom expressed directly in a text, so they can be difficult to identify. A **theme** is an issue, an idea, or a question raised by the text. For instance, a theme of William Shakespeare's *Hamlet* is indecision, as the title character explores his own psyche and the results of his failure to make bold choices. A great work of literature may have many themes, and the reader is justified in identifying any for which he or she can find support. One common characteristic of themes is that they raise more questions than they answer. In a good piece of fiction, the author is not always trying to convince the reader, but is instead trying to elevate the reader's perspective and encourage him to consider the themes more deeply. When reading, one can identify themes by constantly asking what general issues the text is addressing. A good way to evaluate an author's approach to a theme is to begin reading with a question in mind (for example, how does this text approach the theme of love?) and then look for evidence in the text that addresses that question.

> ➤ **Review Video:** Theme
> *Visit **mometrix.com/academy** and enter **Code: 732074***

Purposes for Writing

In order to be an effective reader, one must pay attention to the author's **position** and purpose. Even those texts that seem objective and impartial, like textbooks, have some sort of position and bias. Readers need to take these positions into account when considering the author's message. When an author uses emotional language or clearly favors one side of an argument, his position is clear. However, the author's position may be evident not only in what he writes, but in what he doesn't write. For this reason, it is sometimes necessary to review some other texts on the same topic in order to develop a view of the author's position. If this is not possible, then it may be useful to acquire a little background personal information about the author. When the only source of information is the text, however, the reader should look for language and argumentation that seems to indicate a particular stance on the subject.

> ➤ **Review Video:** Author's Position
> *Visit **mometrix.com/academy** and enter **Code: 355405***

Identifying the **purpose** of an author is usually easier than identifying her position. In most cases, the author has no interest in hiding his or her purpose. A text that is meant to entertain, for instance, should be obviously written to please the reader. Most narratives, or stories, are written to entertain, though they may also inform or persuade. Informative texts are easy to identify as well. The most difficult purpose of a text to identify is persuasion, because the author has an interest in making this purpose hard to detect. When a person knows that the author is trying to convince him, he is automatically more wary and skeptical of the argument. For this reason persuasive texts often try to establish an entertaining tone, hoping to amuse the reader into agreement, or an informative tone, hoping to create an appearance of authority and objectivity.

An author's purpose is often evident in the organization of the text. For instance, if the text has headings and subheadings, if key terms are in bold, and if the author makes his main idea clear from the beginning, then the likely purpose of the text is to inform. If the author begins by making a claim and then makes various arguments to support that claim, the purpose is probably to persuade. If the author is telling a story, or is more interested in holding the attention of the reader than in making a particular point or delivering information, then his purpose is most likely to entertain. As a reader, it is best to judge an author on how well he accomplishes his purpose. In other words, it is not entirely fair to complain that a textbook is boring: if the text is clear and easy to understand, then the author has done his job. Similarly, a storyteller should not be judged too harshly for getting some facts wrong, so long as he is able to give pleasure to the reader.

> **Review Video: Purpose**
> *Visit **mometrix.com/academy** and enter **Code: 516955***

The author's purpose for writing will affect his writing style and the response of the reader. In a **persuasive essay**, the author is attempting to change the reader's mind or convince him of something he did not believe previously. There are several identifying characteristics of persuasive writing. One is opinion presented as fact. When an author attempts to persuade the reader, he often presents his or her opinions as if they were fact. A reader must be on guard for statements that sound factual but which cannot be subjected to research, observation, or experiment. Another characteristic of persuasive writing is emotional language. An author will often try to play on the reader's emotion by appealing to his sympathy or sense of morality. When an author uses colorful or evocative language with the intent of arousing the reader's passions, it is likely that he is attempting to persuade. Finally, in many cases a persuasive text will give an unfair explanation of opposing positions, if these positions are mentioned at all.

> **Review Video: Persuasion and Persuasive Essays**
> *Visit **mometrix.com/academy** and enter **Code: 302658***

An **informative text** is written to educate and enlighten the reader. Informative texts are almost always nonfiction, and are rarely structured as a story. The intention of an informative text is to deliver information in the most comprehensible way possible, so the structure of the text is likely to be very clear. In an informative text, the thesis statement is often in the first sentence. The author may use some colorful language, but is likely to put more emphasis on clarity and precision. Informative essays do not typically appeal to the emotions. They often contain facts and figures, and rarely include the opinion of the author. Sometimes a persuasive essay can resemble an informative essay, especially if the author maintains an even tone and presents his or her views as if they were established fact.

> **Review Video: Informative Text**
> *Visit **mometrix.com/academy** and enter **Code: 422759***

The success or failure of an author's intent to **entertain** is determined by those who read the author's work. Entertaining texts may be either fiction or nonfiction, and they may describe real or imagined people, places, and events. Entertaining texts are often narratives, or stories. A text that is written to entertain is likely to contain colorful language that engages the imagination and the emotions. Such writing often features a great deal of figurative language, which typically enlivens its subject matter with images and analogies. Though an entertaining text is not usually written to persuade or inform, it may accomplish both of these tasks. An entertaining text may appeal to the reader's emotions and cause him or her to think differently about a particular subject. In any case, entertaining texts tend to showcase the personality of the author more so than do other types of writing.

➢ **Review Video: Entertainment Texts**
*Visit **mometrix.com/academy** and enter **Code:** 201386*

When an author intends to **express feelings,** she may use colorful and evocative language. An author may write emotionally for any number of reasons. Sometimes, the author will do so because she is describing a personal situation of great pain or happiness. Sometimes an author is attempting to persuade the reader, and so will use emotion to stir up the passions. It can be easy to identify this kind of expression when the writer uses phrases like *I felt* and *I sense*. However, sometimes the author will simply describe feelings without introducing them. As a reader, it is important to recognize when an author is expressing emotion, and not to become overwhelmed by sympathy or passion. A reader should maintain some detachment so that he or she can still evaluate the strength of the author's argument or the quality of the writing.

➢ **Review Video: Express Feelings**
*Visit **mometrix.com/academy** and enter **Code:** 335296*

In a sense, almost all writing is descriptive, insofar as it seeks to describe events, ideas, or people to the reader. Some texts, however, are primarily concerned with **description**. A descriptive text focuses on a particular subject, and attempts to depict it in a way that will be clear to the reader. Descriptive texts contain many adjectives and adverbs, words that give shades of meaning and create a more detailed mental picture for the reader. A descriptive text fails when it is unclear or vague to the reader. On the other hand, however, a descriptive text that compiles too much detail can be boring and overwhelming to the reader. A descriptive text will certainly be informative, and it may be persuasive and entertaining as well. Descriptive writing is a challenge for the author, but when it is done well, it can be fun to read.

➢ **Review Video: Descriptive Texts**
*Visit **mometrix.com/academy** and enter **Code:** 170644*

Writing Devices

Authors will use different stylistic and writing devices to make their meaning more clearly understood. One of those devices is comparison and contrast. When an author describes the ways in which two things are alike, he or she is **comparing** them. When the author describes the ways in which two things are different, he or she is **contrasting** them. The "compare and contrast" essay is one of the most common forms in nonfiction. It is often signaled with certain words: a comparison may be indicated with such words as *both*, *same*, *like*, *too*, and *as well*; while a contrast may be indicated by words like *but*, *however*, *on the other hand*, *instead*, and *yet*. Of course, comparisons and contrasts may be implicit without using any such signaling language. A single sentence may both compare and contrast. Consider the sentence *Brian and Sheila love ice cream, but Brian prefers vanilla and Sheila prefers strawberry*. In one sentence, the author has described both a similarity (love of ice cream) and a difference (favorite flavor).

> ➤ **Review Video:** <u>Compare and Contrast</u>
> *Visit **mometrix.com/academy** and enter **Code: 798319***

One of the most common text structures is **cause and effect**. A cause is an act or event that makes something happen, and an effect is the thing that happens as a result of that cause. A cause-and-effect relationship is not always explicit, but there are some words in English that signal causality, such as *since*, *because*, and *as a result*. As an example, consider the sentence *Because the sky was clear, Ron did not bring an umbrella*. The cause is the clear sky, and the effect is that Ron did not bring an umbrella. However, sometimes the cause-and-effect relationship will not be clearly noted. For instance, the sentence *He was late and missed the meeting* does not contain any signaling words, but it still contains a cause (he was late) and an effect (he missed the meeting). It is possible for a single cause to have multiple effects, or for a single effect to have multiple causes. Also, an effect can in turn be the cause of another effect, in what is known as a cause-and-effect chain.

> ➤ **Review Video:** <u>Cause and Effect</u>
> *Visit **mometrix.com/academy** and enter **Code: 428037***

Authors often use analogies to add meaning to the text. An **analogy** is a comparison of two things. The words in the analogy are connected by a certain, often undetermined relationship. Look at this analogy: moo is to cow as quack is to duck. This analogy compares the sound that a cow makes with the sound that a duck makes. Even if the word 'quack' was not given, one could figure out it is the correct word to complete the analogy based on the relationship between the words 'moo' and 'cow'. Some common relationships for analogies include synonyms, antonyms, part to whole, definition, and actor to action.

Another element that impacts a text is the author's point of view. The **point of view** of a text is the perspective from which it is told. The author will always have a point of view about a story before he draws up a plot line. The author will know what events they want to take place, how they want the characters to interact, and how the story will resolve. An author will also have an opinion on the topic, or series of events, which is presented in the story, based on their own prior experience and beliefs. The two main points of view that authors use are first person and third person. If the narrator of the story is also the main character, or *protagonist*, the text is written in first-person point of view. In first person, the author writes with the word *I*. Third-person point of view is probably the most common point of view that authors use. Using third person, authors refer to each character using the words *he* or *she.* In third-person omniscient, the narrator is not a character in the story and tells the story of all of the characters at the same time.

> ➤ **Review Video:** <u>Point of View</u>
> *Visit **mometrix.com/academy** and enter **Code: 383336***

A good writer will use **transitional words** and phrases to guide the reader through the text. You are no doubt familiar with the common transitions, though you may never have considered how they operate. Some transitional phrases (*after, before, during, in the middle of*) give information about time. Some indicate that an example is about to be given (*for example, in fact, for instance*). Writers use them to compare (*also, likewise*) and contrast (*however, but, yet*). Transitional words and phrases can suggest addition (*and, also, furthermore, moreover*) and logical relationships (*if, then, therefore, as a result, since*). Finally, transitional words and phrases can demarcate the steps in a process (*first, second, last*). You should incorporate transitional words and phrases where they will orient your reader and illuminate the structure of your composition.

> ➤ **Review Video: Transitional Words and Phrases**
> *Visit **mometrix.com/academy** and enter **Code: 197796***

Types of Passages

A **narrative** passage is a story. Narratives can be fiction or nonfiction. However, there are a few elements that a text must have in order to be classified as a narrative. To begin with, the text must have a plot. That is, it must describe a series of events. If it is a good narrative, these events will be interesting and emotionally engaging to the reader. A narrative also has characters. These could be people, animals, or even inanimate objects, so long as they participate in the plot. A narrative passage often contains figurative language, which is meant to stimulate the imagination of the reader by making comparisons and observations. A metaphor, which is a description of one thing in terms of another, is a common piece of figurative language. *The moon was a frosty snowball* is an example of a metaphor: it is obviously untrue in the literal sense, but it suggests a certain mood for the reader. Narratives often proceed in a clear sequence, but they do not need to do so.

> ➤ **Review Video: Narratives**
> *Visit **mometrix.com/academy** and enter **Code: 953005***

An **expository** passage aims to inform and enlighten the reader. It is nonfiction and usually centers around a simple, easily defined topic. Since the goal of exposition is to teach, such a passage should be as clear as possible. It is common for an expository passage to contain helpful organizing words, like *first, next, for example*, and *therefore*. These words keep the reader oriented in the text. Although expository passages do not need to feature colorful language and artful writing, they are often more effective when they do. For a reader, the challenge of expository passages is to maintain steady attention. Expository passages are not always about subjects in which a reader will naturally be interested, and the writer is often more concerned with clarity and comprehensibility than with engaging the reader. For this reason, many expository passages are dull. Making notes is a good way to maintain focus when reading an expository passage.

> ➤ **Review Video: Expository Passages**
> *Visit **mometrix.com/academy** and enter **Code: 114851***

A **technical** passage is written to describe a complex object or process. Technical writing is common in medical and technological fields, in which complicated mathematical, scientific, and engineering ideas need to be explained simply and clearly. To ease comprehension, a technical passage usually proceeds in a very logical order. Technical passages often have clear headings and subheadings, which are used to keep the reader oriented in the text. It is also common for these passages to break sections up with numbers or letters. Many technical passages look more like an outline than a piece of prose. The amount of jargon or difficult vocabulary will vary in a technical passage depending on the intended audience. As much as possible, technical passages try to avoid language that the reader will have to research in order to understand the message. Of course, it is not always possible to avoid jargon.

> ➤ **Review Video: Technical Passages**
> *Visit **mometrix.com/academy** and enter **Code: 198064***

A **persuasive** passage is meant to change the reader's mind or lead her into agreement with the author. The persuasive intent may be obvious, or it may be quite difficult to discern. In some cases, a persuasive passage will be indistinguishable from an informative passage: it will make an assertion and offer supporting details. However, a persuasive passage is more likely to make claims based on opinion and to appeal to the reader's emotions. Persuasive passages may not describe alternate positions and, when they do, they often display significant bias. It may be clear that a persuasive passage is giving the author's viewpoint, or the passage may adopt a seemingly objective tone. A persuasive passage is successful if it can make a convincing argument and win the trust of the reader.

A persuasive essay will likely focus on one central argument, but it may make many smaller claims along the way. These are subordinate arguments with which the reader must agree if he or she is going to agree with the central argument. The central argument will only be as strong as the subordinate claims. These claims should be rooted in fact and observation, rather than subjective judgment. The best persuasive essays provide enough supporting detail to justify claims without overwhelming the reader. Remember that a fact must be susceptible to independent verification: that is, it must be something the reader could confirm. Also, statistics are only effective when they take into account possible objections. For instance, a statistic on the number of foreclosed houses would only be useful if it was taken over a defined interval and in a defined area. Most readers are wary of statistics, because they are so often misleading. If possible, a persuasive essay should always include references so that the reader can obtain more information. Of course, this means that the writer's accuracy and fairness may be judged by the inquiring reader.

Opinions are formed by emotion as well as reason, and persuasive writers often appeal to the feelings of the reader. Although readers should always be skeptical of this technique, it is often used in a proper and ethical manner. For instance, there are many subjects that have an obvious emotional component, and therefore cannot be completely treated without an appeal to the emotions. Consider an article on drunk driving: it makes sense to include some specific examples that will alarm or sadden the reader. After all, drunk driving often has serious and tragic consequences. Emotional appeals are not appropriate, however, when they attempt to mislead the reader. For instance, in political advertisements it is common to emphasize the patriotism of the preferred candidate, because this will encourage the audience to link their own positive feelings about the country with their opinion of the candidate. However, these ads often imply that the other candidate is unpatriotic, which in most cases is far from the truth. Another common and improper emotional appeal is the use of loaded language, as for instance referring to an avidly religious person as a "fanatic" or a passionate environmentalist as a "tree hugger." These terms introduce an emotional component that detracts from the argument.

> ➤ **Review Video: Persuasion and Persuasive Essays**
> *Visit **mometrix.com/academy** and enter **Code: 302658***

History and Culture

Historical context has a profound influence on literature: the events, knowledge base, and assumptions of an author's time color every aspect of his or her work. Sometimes, authors hold opinions and use language that would be considered inappropriate or immoral in a modern setting, but that was acceptable in the author's time. As a reader, one should consider how the historical context influenced a work and also how today's opinions and ideas shape the way modern readers read the works of the past. For instance, in most societies of the past, women were treated as second-class citizens. An author who wrote in 18th-century England might sound sexist to modern readers, even if that author was relatively feminist in his time. Readers should not have to excuse the faulty assumptions and prejudices of the past, but they should appreciate that a person's thoughts and words are, in part, a result of the time and culture in which they live or lived, and it is perhaps unfair to expect writers to avoid all of the errors of their times.

> ➢ **Review Video:** Historical Context
> *Visit* **mometrix.com/academy** *and enter* **Code: 169770**

Even a brief study of world literature suggests that writers from vastly different cultures address similar themes. For instance, works like the *Odyssey* and *Hamlet* both tackle the individual's battle for self-control and independence. In every culture, authors address themes of personal growth and the struggle for maturity. Another universal theme is the conflict between the individual and society. In works as culturally disparate as *Native Son*, the *Aeneid*, and *1984*, authors dramatize how people struggle to maintain their personalities and dignity in large, sometimes oppressive groups. Finally, many cultures have versions of the hero's (or heroine's) journey, in which an adventurous person must overcome many obstacles in order to gain greater knowledge, power, and perspective. Some famous works that treat this theme are the *Epic of Gilgamesh*, Dante's *Divine Comedy*, and *Don Quixote*.

Authors from different genres (for instance poetry, drama, novel, short story) and cultures may address similar themes, but they often do so quite differently. For instance, poets are likely to address subject matter obliquely, through the use of images and allusions. In a play, on the other hand, the author is more likely to dramatize themes by using characters to express opposing viewpoints. This disparity is known as a dialectical approach. In a novel, the author does not need to express themes directly; rather, they can be illustrated through events and actions. In some regional literatures, like those of Greece or England, authors use more irony: their works have characters that express views and make decisions that are clearly disapproved of by the author. In Latin America, there is a great tradition of using supernatural events to illustrate themes about real life. In China and Japan, authors frequently use well-established regional forms (haiku, for instance) to organize their treatment of universal themes.

Responding to Literature

When reading good literature, the reader is moved to engage actively in the text. One part of being an active reader involves making predictions. A **prediction** is a guess about what will happen next. Readers are constantly making predictions based on what they have read and what they already know. Consider the following sentence: *Staring at the computer screen in shock, Kim blindly reached over for the brimming glass of water on the shelf to her side.* The sentence suggests that Kim is agitated and that she is not looking at the glass she is going to pick up, so a reader might predict that she is going to knock the glass over. Of course, not every prediction will be accurate: perhaps Kim will pick the glass up cleanly. Nevertheless, the author has certainly created the expectation that the water might be spilled. Predictions are always subject to revision as the reader acquires more information.

Test-taking tip: To respond to questions requiring future predictions, the student's answers should be based on evidence of past or present behavior.

> ➤ **Review Video: Predictions**
> *Visit mometrix.com/academy and enter Code:* **310671**

Readers are often required to understand text that claims and suggests ideas without stating them directly. An **inference** is a piece of information that is implied but not written outright by the author. For instance, consider the following sentence: *Mark made more money that week than he had in the previous year.* From this sentence, the reader can infer that Mark either has not made much money in the previous year or made a great deal of money that week. Often, a reader can use information he or she already knows to make inferences. Take as an example the sentence *When his coffee arrived, he looked around the table for the silver cup.* Many people know that cream is typically served in a silver cup, so using their own base of knowledge they can infer that the subject of this sentence takes his coffee with cream. Making inferences requires concentration, attention, and practice.

Test-taking tip: While being tested on his ability to make correct inferences, the student must look for contextual clues. An answer can be *true* but not *correct*. The contextual clues will help you find the answer that is the best answer out of the given choices. Understand the context in which a phrase is stated. When asked for the implied meaning of a statement made in the passage, the student should immediately locate the statement and read the context in which it was made. Also, look for an answer choice that has a similar phrase to the statement in question.

> ➤ **Review Video: Inferences**
> *Visit mometrix.com/academy and enter Code:* **379203**

A reader must be able to identify a text's **sequence**, or the order in which things happen. Often, and especially when the sequence is very important to the author, it is indicated with signal words like *first*, *then*, *next*, and *last*. However, sometimes a sequence is merely implied and must be noted by the reader. Consider the sentence *He walked in the front door and switched on the hall lamp.* Clearly, the man did not turn the lamp on before he walked in the door, so the implied sequence is that he first walked in the door and then turned on the lamp. Texts do not always proceed in an orderly sequence from first to last: sometimes, they begin at the end and then start over at the beginning. As a reader, it can be useful to make brief notes to clarify the sequence.

> ➤ **Review Video: Sequence**
> Visit *mometrix.com/academy* and enter *Code:* **994384**

In addition to inferring and predicting things about the text, the reader must often **draw conclusions** about the information he has read. When asked for a *conclusion* that may be drawn, look for critical "hedge" phrases, such as *likely*, *may*, *can*, *will often*, among many others. When you are being tested on this knowledge, remember that question writers insert these hedge phrases to cover every possibility. Often an answer will be wrong simply because it leaves no room for exception. Extreme positive or negative answers (such as always, never, etc.) are usually not correct. The reader should not use any outside knowledge that is not gathered from the reading passage to answer the related questions. Correct answers can be derived straight from the reading passage.

> ➤ **Review Video: Identifying a Logical Conclusion**
> Visit *mometrix.com/academy* and enter *Code:* **157215**

Literary Genres

Literary genres refer to the basic generic types of poetry, drama, fiction, and nonfiction. Literary genre is a method of classifying and analyzing literature. There are numerous subdivisions within genre, including such categories as novels, novellas, and short stories in fiction. Drama may also be subdivided into comedy, tragedy, and many other categories. Poetry and nonfiction have their own distinct divisions.

Genres often overlap, and the distinctions among them are blurred, such as that between the nonfiction novel and docudrama, as well as many others. However, the use of genres is helpful to the reader as a set of understandings that guide our responses to a work. The generic norm sets expectations and forms the framework within which we read and evaluate a work. This framework will guide both our understanding and interpretation of the work. It is a useful tool for both literary criticism and analysis.

> ➤ **Review Video: Literary Genres**
> Visit *mometrix.com/academy* and enter *Code:* **587617**

Fiction is a general term for any form of literary narrative that is invented or imagined rather than being factual. For those individuals who equate fact with truth, the imagined or invented character of fiction tends to render it relatively unimportant or trivial among the genres. Defenders of fiction are quick to point out that the fictional mode is an essential part of being. The ability to imagine or discuss what-if plots, characters, and events is clearly part of the human experience.

Prose is derived from the Latin and means "straightforward discourse." Prose fiction, although having many categories, may be divided into three main groups:

- **Short stories**: a fictional narrative, the length of which varies, usually under 20,000 words. Short stories usually have only a few characters and generally describe one major event or insight. The short story began in magazines in the late 1800s and has flourished ever since.
- **Novels**: a longer work of fiction, often containing a large cast of characters and extensive plotting. The emphasis may be on an event, action, social problems, or any experience. There is now a genre of nonfiction novels pioneered by Truman Capote's *In Cold Blood* in the 1960s. Novels may also be written in verse.
- **Novellas**: a work of narrative fiction longer than a short story but shorter than a novel. Novellas may also be called short novels or novelettes. They originated from the German tradition and have become common forms in all of the world's literature.

Many elements influence a work of prose fiction. Some important ones are:

- Speech and dialogue: Characters may speak for themselves or through the narrator. Dialogue may be realistic or fantastic, depending on the author's aim.
- Thoughts and mental processes: There may be internal dialogue used as a device for plot development or character understanding.
- Dramatic involvement: Some narrators encourage readers to become involved in the events of the story, whereas others attempt to distance readers through literary devices.
- Action: This is any information that advances the plot or involves new interactions between the characters.
- Duration: The time frame of the work may be long or short, and the relationship between described time and narrative time may vary.
- Setting and description: Is the setting critical to the plot or characters? How are the action scenes described?
- Themes: This is any point of view or topic given sustained attention.
- Symbolism: Authors often veil meanings through imagery and other literary constructions.

Fiction is much wider than simply prose fiction. Songs, ballads, epics, and narrative poems are examples of non-prose fiction. A full definition of fiction must include not only the work itself but also the framework in which it is read. Literary fiction can also be defined as not true rather than nonexistent, as many works of historical fiction refer to real people, places, and events that are treated imaginatively as if they were true. These imaginary elements enrich and broaden literary expression.

When analyzing fiction, it is important for the reader to look carefully at the work being studied. The plot or action of a narrative can become so entertaining that the language of the work is ignored. The language of fiction should not simply be a way to relate a plot—it should also yield many insights to the judicious reader. Some prose fiction is based on the reader's engagement with the language rather than the story. A studious reader will analyze the mode of expression as well as the narrative. Part of the reward of reading in this manner is to discover how the author uses different language to describe familiar objects, events, or emotions. Some works focus the reader on an author's unorthodox use of language, whereas others may emphasize characters or storylines. What happens in a story is not always the critical element in the work. This type of reading may be difficult at first but yields great rewards.

The **narrator** is a central part of any work of fiction, and can give insight about the purpose of the work and its main themes and ideas. The following are important questions to address to better understand the voice and role of the narrator and incorporate that voice into an overall understanding of the novel:

- Who is the narrator of the novel? What is the narrator's perspective, first person or third person? What is the role of the narrator in the plot? Are there changes in narrators or the perspective of narrators?
- Does the narrator explain things in the novel, or does meaning emerge from the plot and events? The personality of the narrator is important. She may have a vested interest in a character or event described. Some narratives follow the time sequence of the plot, whereas others do not. A narrator may express approval or disapproval about a character or events in the work.
- Tone is an important aspect of the narration. Who is actually being addressed by the narrator? Is the tone familiar or formal, intimate or impersonal? Does the vocabulary suggest clues about the narrator?

> **Review Video: The Narrator**
> *Visit mometrix.com/academy and enter Code:* **416375**

A **character** is a person intimately involved with the plot and development of the novel. Development of the novel's characters not only moves the story along but will also tell the reader a lot about the novel itself. There is usually a physical description of the character, but this is often omitted in modern and postmodern novels. These works may focus on the psychological state or motivation of the character. The choice of a character's name may give valuable clues to his role in the work.

Characters are said to be flat or round. Flat characters tend to be minor figures in the story, changing little or not at all. Round characters (those understood from a well-rounded view) are more central to the story and tend to change as the plot unfolds. Stock characters are similar to flat characters, filling out the story without influencing it.

Modern literature has been greatly affected by Freudian psychology, giving rise to such devices as the interior monologue and magical realism as methods of understanding characters in a work. These give the reader a more complex understanding of the inner lives of the characters and enrich the understanding of relationships between characters.

> **Review Video: Characters**
> *Visit mometrix.com/academy and enter Code:* **429493**

Another important genre is that of **drama**: a play written to be spoken aloud. The drama is in many ways inseparable from performance. Reading drama ideally involves using imagination to visualize and re-create the play with characters and settings. The reader stages the play in his imagination, watching characters interact and developments unfold. Sometimes this involves simulating a theatrical presentation; other times it involves imagining the events. In either case, the reader is imagining the unwritten to re-create the dramatic experience. Novels present some of the same problems, but a narrator will provide much more information about the setting, characters, inner dialogues, and many other supporting details. In drama, much of this is missing, and we are required to use our powers of projection and imagination to taste the full flavor of the dramatic work. There are many empty spaces in dramatic texts that must be filled by the reader to fully appreciate the work.

When reading drama in this way, there are some advantages over watching the play performed (though there is much criticism in this regard):

- Freedom of point of view and perspective: Text is free of interpretations of actors, directors, producers, and technical staging.
- Additional information: The text of a drama may be accompanied by notes or prefaces placing the work in a social or historical context. Stage directions may also provide relevant information about the author's purpose. None of this is typically available at live or filmed performances.
- Study and understanding: Difficult or obscure passages may be studied at leisure and supplemented by explanatory works. This is particularly true of older plays with unfamiliar language, which cannot be fully understood without an opportunity to study the material.

Critical elements of drama, especially when it is being read aloud or performed, include dialect, speech, and dialogue. Analysis of speech and dialogue is important in the critical study of drama. Some playwrights use speech to develop their characters. Speeches may be long or short, and written in as normal prose or blank verse. Some characters have a unique way of speaking which illuminates aspects of the drama. Emphasis and tone are both important, as well. Does the author make clear the tone in which lines are to be spoken, or is this open to interpretation? Sometimes there are various possibilities in tone with regard to delivering lines.

> **Review Video: Drama**
> Visit *mometrix.com/academy* and enter *Code:* **416097**

Dialect is any distinct variety of a language, especially one spoken in a region or part of a country. The criterion for distinguishing dialects from languages is that of mutual understanding. For example, people who speak Dutch cannot understand English unless they have learned it. But a speaker from Amsterdam can understand one from Antwerp; therefore, they speak different dialects of the same language. This is, however, a matter of degree; there are languages in which different dialects are unintelligible.

Dialect mixtures are the presence in one form of speech with elements from different neighboring dialects. The study of speech differences from one geographical area to another is called dialect geography. A dialect atlas is a map showing distribution of dialects in a given area. A dialect continuum shows a progressive shift in dialects across a territory, such that adjacent dialects are understandable, but those at the extremes are not.

Dramatic dialogue can be difficult to interpret and changes depending upon the tone used and which words are emphasized. Where the stresses, or meters, of dramatic dialogue fall can determine meaning. Variations in emphasis are only one factor in the manipulability of dramatic speech. Tone is of equal or greater importance and expresses a range of possible emotions and feelings that cannot be readily discerned from the script of a play. The reader must add tone to the words to understand the full meaning of a passage. Recognizing tone is a cumulative process as the reader begins to understand the characters and situations in the play. Other elements that influence the interpretation of dialogue include the setting, possible reactions of the characters to the speech, and possible gestures or facial expressions of the actor. There are no firm rules to guide the interpretation of dramatic speech. An open and flexible attitude is essential in interpreting dramatic dialogue.

> **Review Video: Dialogue, Paradox and Dialect**
> Visit *mometrix.com/academy* and enter *Code:* **684341**

Action is a crucial element in the production of a dramatic work. Many dramas contain little dialogue and much action. In these cases, it is essential for the reader to carefully study stage directions and visualize the action on the stage. Benefits of understanding stage directions include knowing which characters are on the stage at all times, who is speaking to whom, and following these patterns through changes of scene.

Stage directions also provide additional information, some of which is not available to a live audience. The nature of the physical space where the action occurs is vital, and stage directions help with this. The historical context of the period is important in understanding what the playwright was working with in terms of theaters and physical space. The type of staging possible for the author is a good guide to the spatial elements of a production.

> ➢ **Review Video:** Action and Stage Directions
> *Visit **mometrix.com/academy** and enter **Code: 539974***

Asides and soliloquies are devices that authors use in plot and character development. **Asides** indicate that not all characters are privy to the lines. This may be a method of advancing or explaining the plot in a subtle manner. **Soliloquies** are opportunities for character development, plot enhancement, and to give insight to characters' motives, feelings, and emotions. Careful study of these elements provides a reader with an abundance of clues to the major themes and plot of the work.

> ➢ **Review Video:** Monologue, Soliloquy, and Dramatic Irony
> *Visit **mometrix.com/academy** and enter **Code: 649777***

Art, music, and literature all interact in ways that contain many opportunities for the enrichment of all of the arts. Students could apply their knowledge of art and music by creating illustrations for a work or creating a musical score for a text. Students could discuss the meanings of texts and decide on their illustrations, or a score could amplify the meaning of the text.

Understanding the art and music of a period can make the experience of literature a richer, more rewarding experience. Students should be encouraged to use the knowledge of art and music to illuminate the text. Examining examples of dress, architecture, music, and dance of a period may be helpful in a fuller engagement of the text. Much of period literature lends itself to the analysis of the prevailing taste in art and music of an era, which helps place the literary work in a more meaningful context.

Opinions, Facts, and Fallacies

Critical thinking skills are mastered through understanding various types of writing and the different purposes that authors have for writing the way they do. Every author writes for a purpose. Understanding that purpose, and how they accomplish their goal, will allow you to critique the writing and determine whether or not you agree with their conclusions.

Readers must always be conscious of the distinction between fact and opinion. A **fact** can be subjected to analysis and can be either proved or disproved. An **opinion**, on the other hand, is the author's personal feeling, which may not be alterable by research, evidence, or argument. If the author writes that the distance from New York to Boston is about two hundred miles, he is stating a fact. But if he writes that New York is too crowded, then he is giving an opinion, because there is no objective standard for overpopulation. An opinion may be indicated by words like *believe*, *think*, or *feel*. Also, an opinion may be supported by facts: for instance, the author might give the population density of New York as a reason for why it is overcrowded. An opinion supported by fact tends to be more convincing. When authors support their opinions with other opinions, the reader is unlikely to be moved.

Facts should be presented to the reader from reliable sources. An opinion is what the author thinks about a given topic. An opinion is not common knowledge or proven by expert sources, but it is information that the author believes and wants the reader to consider. To distinguish between fact and opinion, a reader needs to look at the type of source that is presenting information, what information backs-up a claim, and whether or not the author may be motivated to have a certain point of view on a given topic. For example, if a panel of scientists has conducted multiple studies on the effectiveness of taking a certain vitamin, the results are more likely to be factual than if a company selling a vitamin claims that taking the vitamin can produce positive effects. The company is motivated to sell its product, while the scientists are using the scientific method to prove a theory. If the author uses words such as "I think...", the statement is an opinion.

> **Review Video: Fact or Opinion**
> Visit *mometrix.com/academy* and enter *Code:* **614191**

In their attempt to persuade, writers often make mistakes in their thinking patterns and writing choices. It's important to understand these so you can make an informed decision. Every author has a point of view, but when an author ignores reasonable counterarguments or distorts opposing viewpoints, she is demonstrating a **bias**. A bias is evident whenever the author is unfair or inaccurate in his or her presentation. Bias may be intentional or unintentional, but it should always alert the reader to be skeptical of the argument being made. It should be noted that a biased author may still be correct. However, the author will be correct in spite of her bias, not because of it. A **stereotype** is like a bias, except that it is specifically applied to a group or place. Stereotyping is considered to be particularly abhorrent because it promotes negative generalizations about people. Many people are familiar with some of the hateful stereotypes of certain ethnic, religious, and cultural groups. Readers should be very wary of authors who stereotype. These faulty assumptions typically reveal the author's ignorance and lack of curiosity.

> **Review Video: Bias and Stereotype**
> Visit *mometrix.com/academy* and enter *Code:* **412908**

Sometimes, authors will **appeal to the reader's emotion** in an attempt to persuade or to distract the reader from the weakness of the argument. For instance, the author may try to inspire the pity of the reader by delivering a heart-rending story. An author also might use the bandwagon approach, in which he suggests that his opinion is correct because it is held by the majority. Some authors resort to name-calling, in which insults and harsh words are delivered to the opponent in an attempt to distract. In advertising, a common appeal is the testimonial, in which a famous person endorses a product. Of course, the fact that a celebrity likes something should not really mean anything to the reader. These and other emotional appeals are usually evidence of poor reasoning and a weak argument.

> **Review Video: Appeal to the Reader's Emotions**
> Visit *mometrix.com/academy* and enter *Code:* **163442**

Certain *logical fallacies* are frequent in writing. A logical fallacy is a failure of reasoning. As a reader, it is important to recognize logical fallacies, because they diminish the value of the author's message. The four most common logical fallacies in writing are the false analogy, circular reasoning, false dichotomy, and overgeneralization. In a **false analogy**, the author suggests that two things are similar, when in fact they are different. This fallacy is often committed when the author is attempting to convince the reader that something unknown is like something relatively familiar. The author takes advantage of the reader's ignorance to make this false comparison. One example might be the following statement: *Failing to tip a waitress is like stealing money out of somebody's wallet*. Of course, failing to tip is very rude, especially when the service has been good, but people are not arrested for failing to tip as they would for stealing money from a wallet. To compare stingy diners with thieves is a false analogy.

> ➤ **Review Video:** False Analogy
> *Visit mometrix.com/academy and enter Code:* **944550**

Circular reasoning is one of the more difficult logical fallacies to identify, because it is typically hidden behind dense language and complicated sentences. Reasoning is described as circular when it offers no support for assertions other than restating them in different words. Put another way, a circular argument refers to itself as evidence of truth. A simple example of circular argument is when a person uses a word to define itself, such as saying *Niceness is the state of being nice*. If the reader does not know what *nice* means, then this definition will not be very useful. In a text, circular reasoning is usually more complex. For instance, an author might say *Poverty is a problem for society because it creates trouble for people throughout the community*. It is redundant to say that poverty is a problem because it creates trouble. When an author engages in circular reasoning, it is often because he or she has not fully thought out the argument, or cannot come up with any legitimate justifications.

> ➤ **Review Video:** Circular Reasoning
> *Visit mometrix.com/academy and enter Code:* **136169**

One of the most common logical fallacies is the **false dichotomy**, in which the author creates an artificial sense that there are only two possible alternatives in a situation. This fallacy is common when the author has an agenda and wants to give the impression that his view is the only sensible one. A false dichotomy has the effect of limiting the reader's options and imagination. An example of a false dichotomy is the statement *You need to go to the party with me, otherwise you'll just be bored at home*. The speaker suggests that the only other possibility besides being at the party is being bored at home. But this is not true, as it is perfectly possible to be entertained at home, or even to go somewhere other than the party. Readers should always be wary of the false dichotomy: when an author limits alternatives, it is always wise to ask whether he is being valid.

> ➤ **Review Video:** False Dichotomy
> *Visit mometrix.com/academy and enter Code:* **910480**

Overgeneralization is a logical fallacy in which the author makes a claim that is so broad it cannot be proved or disproved. In most cases, overgeneralization occurs when the author wants to create an illusion of authority, or when he is using sensational language to sway the opinion of the reader. For instance, in the sentence *Everybody knows that she is a terrible teacher*, the author makes an assumption that cannot really be believed. This kind of statement is made when the author wants to create the illusion of consensus when none actually exists: it may be that most people have a negative view of the teacher, but to say that *everybody* feels that way is an exaggeration. When a reader spots overgeneralization, she should become skeptical about the argument that is being made, because an author will often try to hide a weak or unsupported assertion behind authoritative language.

> ➤ **Review Video:** <u>Overgeneralization</u>
> Visit *mometrix.com/academy* and enter *Code:* **249659**

Two other types of logical fallacies are **slippery slope** arguments and **hasty generalizations**. In a slippery slope argument, the author says that if something happens, it automatically means that something else will happen as a result, even though this may not be true. (i.e., just because you study hard does not mean you are going to ace the test). "Hasty generalization" is drawing a conclusion too early, without finishing analyzing the details of the argument. Writers of persuasive texts often use these techniques because they are very effective. In order to **identify logical fallacies**, readers need to read carefully and ask questions as they read. Thinking critically means not taking everything at face value. Readers need to critically evaluate an author's argument to make sure that the logic used is sound.

> ➤ **Review Video:** <u>Logical Fallacies</u>
> Visit *mometrix.com/academy* and enter *Code:* **644845**

Organization of the Text

The way a text is organized can help the reader to understand more clearly the author's intent and his conclusions. There are various ways to organize a text, and each one has its own purposes and uses.

> ➤ **Review Video:** <u>Organizational Methods to Structure Text</u>
> Visit *mometrix.com/academy* and enter *Code:* **606263**

Some nonfiction texts are organized to **present a problem** followed by a solution. In this type of text, it is common for the problem to be explained before the solution is offered. In some cases, as when the problem is well known, the solution may be briefly introduced at the beginning. The entire passage may focus on the solution, and the problem will be referenced only occasionally. Some texts will outline multiple solutions to a problem, leaving the reader to choose among them. If the author has an interest or an allegiance to one solution, he may fail to mention or may describe inaccurately some of the other solutions. Readers should be careful of the author's agenda when reading a problem-solution text. Only by understanding the author's point of view and interests can one develop a proper judgment of the proposed solution.

> ➤ **Review Video:** <u>Present a Problem</u>
> Visit *mometrix.com/academy* and enter *Code:* **789155**

Authors need to organize information logically so the reader can follow it and locate information within the text. Two common organizational structures are cause and effect and chronological order. When using **chronological order**, the author presents information in the order that it happened. For example, biographies are written in chronological order; the subject's birth and childhood are presented first, followed by their adult life, and lastly by the events leading up to the person's death.

> ➤ **Review Video:** <u>Chronology</u>
> Visit *mometrix.com/academy* and enter *Code:* **804598**

In **cause and effect**, an author presents one thing that makes something else happen. For example, if one were to go to bed very late, they would be tired. The cause is going to bed late, with the effect of being tired the next day.

It can be tricky to identify the cause-and-effect relationships in a text, but there are a few ways to approach this task. To begin with, these relationships are often signaled with certain terms. When an author uses words like *because*, *since*, *in order*, and *so*, she is likely describing a cause-and-effect relationship. Consider the sentence, "He called her because he needed the homework." This is a simple causal relationship, in which the cause was his need for the homework and the effect was his phone call. Not all cause-and-effect relationships are marked in this way, however. Consider the sentences, "He called her. He needed the homework." When the cause-and-effect relationship is not indicated with a keyword, it can be discovered by asking why something happened. He called her: why? The answer is in the next sentence: He needed the homework.

Persuasive essays, in which an author tries to make a convincing argument and change the reader's mind, usually include cause-and-effect relationships. However, these relationships should not always be taken at face value. An author frequently will assume a cause or take an effect for granted. To read a persuasive essay effectively, one needs to judge the cause-and-effect relationships the author is presenting. For instance, imagine an author wrote the following: "The parking deck has been unprofitable because people would prefer to ride their bikes." The relationship is clear: the cause is that people prefer to ride their bikes, and the effect is that the parking deck has been unprofitable. However, a reader should consider whether this argument is conclusive. Perhaps there are other reasons for the failure of the parking deck: a down economy, excessive fees, etc. Too often, authors present causal relationships as if they are fact rather than opinion. Readers should be on the alert for these dubious claims.

> ➤ **Review Video:** <u>Cause and Effect</u>
> *Visit **mometrix.com/academy** and enter **Code: 428037***

Thinking critically about ideas and conclusions can seem like a daunting task. One way to make it easier is to understand the basic elements of ideas and writing techniques. Looking at the way different ideas relate to each other can be a good way for the reader to begin his analysis. For instance, sometimes writers will write about two different ideas that are in opposition to each other. The analysis of these opposing ideas is known as **contrast**. Contrast is often marred by the author's obvious partiality to one of the ideas. A discerning reader will be put off by an author who does not engage in a fair fight. In an analysis of opposing ideas, both ideas should be presented in their clearest and most reasonable terms. If the author does prefer a side, he should avoid indicating this preference with pejorative language. An analysis of opposing ideas should proceed through the major differences point by point, with a full explanation of each side's view. For instance, in an analysis of capitalism and communism, it would be important to outline each side's view on labor, markets, prices, personal responsibility, etc. It would be less effective to describe the theory of communism and then explain how capitalism has thrived in the West. An analysis of opposing views should present each side in the same manner.

Many texts follow the **compare-and-contrast** model, in which the similarities and differences between two ideas or things are explored. Analysis of the similarities between ideas is called comparison. In order for a comparison to work, the author must place the ideas or things in an equivalent structure. That is, the author must present the ideas in the same way. Imagine an author wanted to show the similarities between cricket and baseball. The correct way to do so would be to summarize the equipment and rules for each game. It would be incorrect to summarize the equipment of cricket and then lay out the history of baseball, since this would make it impossible for the reader to see the similarities. It is perhaps too obvious to say that an analysis of similar ideas should emphasize the similarities. Of course, the author should take care to include any differences that must be mentioned. Often, these small differences will only reinforce the more general similarity.

> ➤ **Review Video: <u>Compare and Contrast</u>**
> *Visit **mometrix.com/academy** and enter **Code: 798319***

Drawing Conclusions

Authors should have a clear purpose in mind while writing. Especially when reading informational texts, it is important to understand the logical conclusion of the author's ideas. **Identifying this logical conclusion** can help the reader understand whether he agrees with the writer or not. Identifying a logical conclusion is much like making an inference: it requires the reader to combine the information given by the text with what he already knows to make a supportable assertion. If a passage is written well, then the conclusion should be obvious even when it is unstated. If the author intends the reader to draw a certain conclusion, then all of his argumentation and detail should be leading toward it.

One way to approach the task of drawing conclusions is to make brief notes of all the points made by the author. When these are arranged on paper, they may clarify the logical conclusion. Another way to approach conclusions is to consider whether the reasoning of the author raises any pertinent questions. Sometimes it will be possible to draw several conclusions from a passage, and on occasion these will be conclusions that were never imagined by the author. It is essential, however, that these conclusions be supported directly by the text.

> ➤ **Review Video: <u>Identifying a Logical Conclusion</u>**
> *Visit **mometrix.com/academy** and enter **Code: 157215***

The term **text evidence** refers to information that supports a main point or points in a story, and can help lead the reader to a conclusion. Information used as *text evidence* is precise, descriptive, and factual. A main point is often followed by supporting details that provide evidence to back-up a claim. For example, a story may include the claim that winter occurs during opposite months in the Northern and Southern hemispheres. *Text evidence* based on this claim may include countries where winter occurs in opposite months, along with reasons that winter occurs at different times of the year in separate hemispheres (due to the tilt of the Earth as it rotates around the sun).

Readers interpret text and respond to it in a number of ways. Using textual support helps defend your response or interpretation because it roots your thinking in the text. You are interpreting based on information in the text and not simply your own ideas. When crafting a response, look for important quotes and details from the text to help bolster your argument. If you are writing about a character's personality trait, for example, use details from the text to show that the character acted in such a way. You can also include statistics and facts from a nonfiction text to strengthen your response. For example, instead of writing, "A lot of people use cell phones," use statistics to provide the exact number. This strengthens your argument because it is more precise.

> ➤ **Review Video: <u>Text Evidence</u>**
> *Visit **mometrix.com/academy** and enter **Code: 538095***

The text used to support an argument can be the argument's downfall if it is not credible. A text is **credible**, or believable, when the author is knowledgeable and objective, or unbiased. The author's motivations for writing the text play a critical role in determining the credibility of the text and must be evaluated when assessing that credibility. The author's motives should be for the dissemination of information. The purpose of the text should be to inform or describe, not to persuade. When an author writes a persuasive text, he has the motivation that the reader will do what they want. The extent of the author's knowledge of the topic and their motivation must be evaluated when assessing the credibility of a text. Reports written about the Ozone layer by an environmental scientist and a hairdresser will have a different level of credibility.

> ➢ **Review Video: Credible**
> *Visit **mometrix.com/academy** and enter **Code: 580162***

After determining your own opinion and evaluating the credibility of your supporting text, it is sometimes necessary to communicate your ideas and findings to others. When **writing a response to a text**, it is important to use elements of the text to support your assertion or defend your position. Using supporting evidence from the text strengthens the argument because the reader can see how in depth the writer read the original piece and based their response on the details and facts within that text. Elements of text that can be used in a response include: facts, details, statistics, and direct quotations from the text. When writing a response, one must make sure they indicate which information comes from the original text and then base their discussion, argument, or defense around this information.

> ➢ **Review Video: Writing a Response to the Text**
> *Visit **mometrix.com/academy** and enter **Code: 689859***

A reader should always be drawing conclusions from the text. Sometimes conclusions are implied from written information, and other times the information is **stated directly** within the passage. It is always more comfortable to draw conclusions from information stated within a passage, rather than to draw them from mere implications. At times an author may provide some information and then describe a counterargument. The reader should be alert for direct statements that are subsequently rejected or weakened by the author. The reader should always read the entire passage before drawing conclusions. Many readers are trained to expect the author's conclusions at either the beginning or the end of the passage, but many texts do not adhere to this format.

> ➢ **Review Video: Conclusions that are Stated Directly**
> *Visit **mometrix.com/academy** and enter **Code: 260315***

Drawing conclusions from information implied within a passage requires confidence on the part of the reader. **Implications** are things the author does not state directly, but which can be assumed based on what the author does say. For instance, consider the following simple passage: "I stepped outside and opened my umbrella. By the time I got to work, the cuffs of my pants were soaked." The author never states that it is raining, but this fact is clearly implied. Conclusions based on implication must be well supported by the text. In order to draw a solid conclusion, a reader should have multiple pieces of evidence, or, if he only has one, must be assured that there is no other possible explanation than his conclusion. A good reader will be able to draw many conclusions from information implied by the text, which enriches the reading experience considerably.

As an aid to drawing conclusions, the reader should be adept at **outlining** the information contained in the passage; an effective outline will reveal the structure of the passage, and will lead to solid conclusions. An effective outline will have a title that refers to the basic subject of the text, though it need not recapitulate the main idea. In most outlines, the main idea will be the first major section. It will have each major idea of the passage established as the head of a category. For instance, the most common outline format calls for the main ideas of the passage to be indicated with Roman numerals. In an effective outline of this kind, each of the main ideas will be represented by a Roman numeral and none of the Roman numerals will designate minor details or secondary ideas. Moreover, all supporting ideas and details should be placed in the appropriate place on the outline. An outline does not need to include every detail listed in the text, but it should feature all of those that are central to the argument or message. Each of these details should be listed under the appropriate main idea.

> ➢ **Review Video:** <u>Outlining</u>
> *Visit **mometrix.com/academy** and enter **Code:** 584445*

It is also helpful to **summarize** the information you have read in a paragraph or passage format. This process is similar to creating an effective outline. To begin with, a summary should accurately define the main idea of the passage, though it does not need to explain this main idea in exhaustive detail. It should continue by laying out the most important supporting details or arguments from the passage. All of the significant supporting details should be included, and none of the details included should be irrelevant or insignificant. Also, the summary should accurately report all of these details. Too often, the desire for brevity in a summary leads to the sacrifice of clarity or veracity. Summaries are often difficult to read, because they omit all of graceful language, digressions, and asides that distinguish great writing. However, if the summary is effective, it should contain much the same message as the original text.

> ➢ **Review Video:** <u>Summarizing Text</u>
> *Visit **mometrix.com/academy** and enter **Code:** 332936*

Paraphrasing is another method the reader can use to aid in comprehension. When paraphrasing, one puts what they have read into their own words, rephrasing what the author has written to make it their own, to "translate" all of what the author says to their own words, including as many details as they can.

Informational Sources

Informational sources often come in short forms like a memo or recipe, or longer forms like books, magazines, or journals. These longer sources of information each have their own way of organizing information, but there are some similarities that the reader should be aware of.

Most books, magazines, and journals have a **table of contents** at the beginning. This helps the reader find the different parts of the book. The table of contents is usually found a page or two after the title page in a book, and on the first few pages of a magazine. However, many magazines now place the table of contents in the midst of an overabundance of advertisements, because they know readers will have to look at the ads as they search for the table.

The standard orientation for a table of contents is the sections of the book listed along the left side, with the initial page number for each along the right. It is common in a book for the prefatory material (preface, introduction, etc.) to be numbered with Roman numerals. The contents are always listed in order from the beginning of the book to the end.

> ➤ **Review Video:** Table of Contents
> *Visit* **mometrix.com/academy** *and enter* **Code: 940585**

A nonfiction book will also typically have an **index** at the end so that the reader can easily find information about particular topics. An index lists the topics in alphabetical order. The names of people are listed with the last name first. For example, *Adams, John* would come before *Washington, George*. To the right of the entry, the relevant page numbers are listed. When a topic is mentioned over several pages, the index will often connect these pages with a dash. For instance, if the subject is mentioned from pages 35 to 42 and again on 53, then the index entry will be labeled as *35-42, 53*. Some entries will have subsets, which are listed below the main entry, indented slightly, and placed in alphabetical order. This is common for subjects that are discussed frequently in the book. For instance, in a book about Elizabethan drama, William Shakespeare will likely be an important topic. Beneath Shakespeare's name in the index, there might be listings for *death of, dramatic works of, life of*, etc. These more specific entries help the reader refine his search.

> ➤ **Review Video:** Index
> *Visit* **mometrix.com/academy** *and enter* **Code: 654228**

Many informative texts, especially textbooks, use **headings** and **subheadings** for organization. Headings and subheadings are typically printed in larger and bolder fonts, and are often in a different color than the main body of the text. Headings may be larger than subheadings. Also, headings and subheadings are not always complete sentences. A heading announces the topic that will be addressed in the text below. Headings are meant to alert the reader to what is about to come. Subheadings announce the topics of smaller sections within the entire section indicated by the heading. For instance, the heading of a section in a science textbook might be *AMPHIBIANS*, and within that section might be subheadings for *Frogs, Salamanders*, and *Newts*. Readers should always pay close attention to headings and subheadings, because they prime the brain for the information that is about to be delivered, and because they make it easy to go back and find particular details in a long text.

> ➤ **Review Video:** Headings and Sub-Headings
> *Visit* **mometrix.com/academy** *and enter* **Code: 643919**

Reference Materials

Knowledge of reference materials such as dictionaries, encyclopedias, and manuals are vital for any reader. **Dictionaries** contain information about words. A standard dictionary entry begins with a pronunciation guide for the word. The entry will also give the word's part of speech: that is, whether it is a noun, verb, adjective, etc. A good dictionary will also include the word's origins, including the language from which it is derived and its meaning in that language. This information is known as the word's etymology.

Dictionary entries are in alphabetical order. Many words have more than one definition, in which case the definitions will be numbered. Also, if a word can be used as different parts of speech, its various definitions in those different capacities may be separated. A sample entry might look like this:

WELL: (adverb) 1. in a good way (noun) 1. a hole drilled into the earth.

The correct definition of a word will vary depending on how it is used in a sentence. When looking up a word found while reading, the best way to determine the relevant definition is to substitute the dictionary's definitions for the word in the text, and select the definition that seems most appropriate.

➢ **Review Video: Dictionaries**
*Visit **mometrix.com/academy** and enter **Code:** 302080*

Encyclopedias used to be the best source for general information on a range of common subjects. Many people took pride in owning a set of encyclopedias, which were often written by top researchers. Now, encyclopedias largely exist online. Although they no longer have a preeminent place in general scholarship, these digital encyclopedias now often feature audio and video clips. A good encyclopedia remains the best place to obtain basic information about a well-known topic. There are also specialty encyclopedias that cover more obscure or expert information. For instance, there are many medical encyclopedias that contain the detail and sophistication required by doctors. For a regular person researching a subject like ostriches, Pennsylvania, or the Crimean War, an encyclopedia is a good source.

A **thesaurus** is a reference book that gives synonyms of words. It is different from a dictionary because a thesaurus does not give definitions, only lists of synonyms. A thesaurus can be helpful in finding the meaning of an unfamiliar word when reading. If the meaning of a synonym is known, then the meaning of the unfamiliar word will be known. The other time a thesaurus is helpful is when writing. Using a thesaurus helps authors to vary their word choice.

➢ **Review Video: Thesaurus**
*Visit **mometrix.com/academy** and enter **Code:** 391773*

A **database** is an informational source that has a different format than a publication or a memo. They are systems for storing and organizing large amounts of information. As personal computers have become more common and accessible, databases have become ever more present. The standard layout of a database is as a grid, with labels along the left side and the top. The horizontal rows and vertical columns that make up the grid are usually numbered or lettered, so that a particular square within the database might have a name like A3 or G5. Databases are good for storing information that can be expressed succinctly. They are most commonly used to store numerical data, but they also can be used to store the answers to yes-no questions and other brief data points. Information that is ambiguous (that is, has multiple possible meanings) or difficult to express in a few words is not appropriate for a database.

Often, a reader will come across a word that he does not recognize. The reader needs to know how to identify the definition of a word from its context. This means defining a word based on the words around it and the way it is used in a sentence. For instance, consider the following sentence: *The elderly scholar spent his evenings hunched over arcane texts that few other people even knew existed.* The adjective *arcane* is uncommon, but the reader can obtain significant information about it based on its use here. Based on the fact that few other people know of their existence, the reader can assume that arcane texts must be rare and only of interest to a few people. And, because they are being read by an elderly scholar, the reader can assume that they focus on difficult academic subjects. Sometimes, words can even be defined by what they are not. For instance, consider the following sentence: *Ron's fealty to his parents was not shared by Karen, who disobeyed their every command.* Because someone who disobeys is not demonstrating *fealty*, the word can be inferred to mean something like obedience or respect.

When conducting research, it is important to depend on reputable **primary sources**. A primary source is the documentary evidence closest to the subject being studied. For instance, the primary sources for an essay about penguins would be photographs and recordings of the birds, as well as accounts of people who have studied penguins in person. A secondary source would be a review of a movie about penguins or a book outlining the observations made by others. A primary source should be credible and, if it is on a subject that is still being explored, recent. One way to assess the credibility of a work is to see how often it is mentioned in other books and articles on the same subject. Just by reading the works cited and bibliographies of other books, one can get a sense of what are the acknowledged authorities in the field.

The Internet was once considered a poor place to find sources for an essay or article, but its credibility has improved greatly over the years. Still, students need to exercise caution when performing research online. The best sources are those affiliated with established institutions, like universities, public libraries, and think tanks. Most newspapers are available online, and many of them allow the public to browse their archives. Magazines frequently offer similar services. When obtaining information from an unknown website, however, one must exercise considerably more caution. A website can be considered trustworthy if it is referenced by other sites that are known to be reputable. Also, credible sites tend to be properly maintained and frequently updated. A site is easier to trust when the author provides some information about him or herself, including some credentials that indicate expertise in the subject matter.

Organizing and Understanding Graphic Information

Two of the most common ways to organize ideas from a text, paraphrasing and summarizing, are verbal ways to organize data. Ideas from a text can also be organized using **graphic organizers**. A graphic organizer is a way to simplify information and just take key points from the text. A graphic organizer such as a timeline may have an event listed for a corresponding date on the timeline, whereas an outline may have an event listed under a key point that occurs in the text. Each reader needs to create the type of graphic organizer that works the best for him or her in terms of being able to recall information from a story. Examples include a *spider-map,* which takes a main idea from the story and places it in a bubble, with supporting points branching off the main idea, an *outline,* useful for diagramming the main and supporting points of the entire story, and a *Venn diagram,* which classifies information as separate or overlapping.

These graphic organizers can also be used by authors to enliven their presentation or text, but this may be counterproductive if the graphics are confusing or misleading. A graph should strip the author's message down to the essentials. It should have a clear title, and should be in the appropriate format. Authors may elect to use tables, line or bar graphs, or pie charts to illustrate their message. Each of these formats is correct for different types of data. The graphic should be large enough to read, and should be divided into appropriate categories.

For instance, if the text is about the differences between federal spending on the military and on the space program, a pie chart or a bar graph would be the most effective choices. The pie chart could show each type of spending as a portion of total federal spending, while the bar graph would be better for directly comparing the amounts of money spent on these two programs.

In most cases, the work of interpreting information presented in graphs, tables, charts, and diagrams is done for the reader. The author will usually make explicit his or her reasons for presenting a certain set of data in such a way. However, an effective reader will avoid taking the author's claims for granted. Before considering the information presented in the graphic, the reader should consider whether the author has chosen the correct format for presentation, or whether the author has omitted variables or other information that might undermine his case. Interpreting the graphic itself is essentially an exercise in spotting trends. On a graph, for instance, the reader should be alert for how one variable responds to a change in the other. If education level increases, for example, does income increase as well? The same can be done for a table. Readers should be alert for values that break or exaggerate a trend; these may be meaningless outliers or indicators of a change in conditions.

When a reader is required to draw conclusions from the information presented in graphs, tables, charts, or diagrams, it is important to limit these conclusions to the terms of the graphic itself. In other words, the reader should avoid extrapolating from the data to make claims that are not supportable. As an example, consider a graph that compares the price of eggs to the demand. If the price and demand rise and fall together, a reader would be justified in saying that the demand for eggs and the price are tied together. However, this simple graph does not indicate which of these variables causes the other, so the reader would not be justified in concluding that the price of eggs raises or lowers the demand. In fact, demand could be tied to all sorts of other factors not included in this chart.

> ➤ **Review Video: <u>Graphic Organizers</u>**
> *Visit **mometrix.com/academy** and enter **Code: 919468***

Types of Tables and Charts

Tables are presented in a standard format so that they will be easy to read and understand. At the top of the table, there will be a title. This will be a short phrase indicating the information the table or graph intends to convey. The title of a table could be something like "Average Income for Various Education Levels" or "Price of Milk Compared to Demand." A table is composed of information laid out in vertical columns and horizontal rows. Typically, each column will have a label. If "Average Income for Various Education Levels" was placed in a table format, the two columns could be labeled "Education Level" and "Average Income." Each location on the table is called a cell. Cells are defined by their column and row (e.g., second column, fifth row). The table's information is placed in these cells.

> ➤ **Review Video: <u>Tables</u>**
> *Visit **mometrix.com/academy** and enter **Code: 769453***

Like a table, a **graph** will typically have a title on top. This title may simply state the identities of the two axes: e.g., "Income vs. Education." However, the title may also be something more descriptive, like "A comparison of average income with level of education." In any case, bar and line graphs are laid out along two perpendicular lines, or axes. The vertical axis is called the y-axis, and the horizontal axis is called the x-axis. It is typical for the x-axis to be the independent variable and the y-axis to be the dependent variable. The independent variable is the one manipulated by the researcher or whoever put together the graph. In the above example, the independent variable would be "level of education," since the maker of the graph will define these values (high school, college, master's degree, etc.). The dependent value is not controlled by the researcher.

When selecting a graph format, it is important to consider the intention and the structure of the presentation. A bar graph, for instance, is appropriate for displaying the relations between a series of distinct quantities that are on the same scale. For instance, if one wanted to display the amount of money spent on groceries during the months of a year, a bar graph would be appropriate. The vertical axis would represent values of money, and the horizontal axis would identify the bar representing each month. A line graph also requires data expressed in common units, but it is better for demonstrating the general trend in that data. If the grocery expenses were plotted on a line graph instead of a bar graph, there would be more emphasis on whether the amount of money spent rose or fell over the course of the year. Whereas a bar graph is good for showing the relationships between the different values plotted, the line graph is good for showing whether the values tended to increase, decrease, or remain stable.

> **Review Video: Graphs**
> *Visit **mometrix.com/academy** and enter **Code: 916096***

A **line graph** is a type of graph that is typically used for measuring trends over time. It is set up along a vertical and a horizontal axis. The variables being measured are listed along the left side and the bottom side of the axes. Points are then plotted along the graph, such that they correspond with their values for each variable. For instance, imagine a line graph measuring a person's income for each month of the year. If the person earned $1500 in January, there would be a point directly above January, perpendicular to the horizontal axis, and directly to the right of $1500, perpendicular to the vertical axis. Once all of the lines are plotted, they are connected with a line from left to right. This line provides a nice visual illustration of the general trends. For instance, using the earlier example, if the line sloped up, it would be clear that the person's income had increased over the course of the year.

> **Review Video: Line Graph**
> *Visit **mometrix.com/academy** and enter **Code: 480147***

The **bar graph** is one of the most common visual representations of information. Bar graphs are used to illustrate sets of numerical data. The graph has a vertical axis, along which numbers are listed, and a horizontal axis, along which categories, words, or some other indicators are placed. One example of a bar graph is a depiction of the respective heights of famous basketball players: the vertical axis would contain numbers ranging from five to eight feet, and the horizontal axis would contain the names of the players. The length of the bar above the player's name would illustrate his height, as the top of the bar would stop perpendicular to the height listed along the left side. In this representation, then, it would be easy to see that Yao Ming is taller than Michael Jordan, because Yao's bar would be higher.

> **Review Video: Bar Graph**
> *Visit **mometrix.com/academy** and enter **Code: 226729***

A **pie chart**, also known as a circle graph, is useful for depicting how a single unit or category is divided. The standard pie chart is a circle within which wedges have been cut and labeled. Each of these wedges is proportional in size to its part of the whole. For instance, consider a pie chart representing a student's budget. If the student spends half her money on rent, then the pie chart will represent that amount with a line through the center of the pie. If she spends a quarter of her money on food, there will be a line extending from the edge of the circle to the center at a right angle to the line depicting rent. This illustration would make it clear that the student spends twice as much money on rent as she does on food. The pie chart is only appropriate for showing how a whole is divided.

A pie chart is effective at showing how a single entity is divided into parts. They are not effective at demonstrating the relationships between parts of different wholes. For example, it would not be as helpful to use a pie chart to compare the respective amounts of state and federal spending devoted to infrastructure, since these values are only meaningful in the context of the entire budget.

> **Review Video: Pie Chart**
*Visit **mometrix.com/academy** and enter **Code: 895285***

Plot lines are another way to visual represent information. Every plot line follows the same stages. One can identify each of these stages in every story they read. These stages are: the introduction, rising action, conflict, climax, falling action, and resolution. The introduction tells the reader what the story will be about and sets up the plot. The rising action is what happens that leads up to the conflict, which is some sort of problem that arises, with the climax at its peak. The falling action is what happens after the climax of the conflict. The resolution is the conclusion and often has the final solution to the problem in the conflict. A plot line looks like this:

> **Review Video: Plot Line**
*Visit **mometrix.com/academy** and enter **Code: 944011***

Determining Word Meaning

An understanding of the basics of language is helpful, and often vital, to understanding what you read. The term *structural analysis* refers to looking at the parts of a word and breaking it down into its different components to determine the word's meaning. Parts of a word include prefixes, suffixes, and the root word. By learning the meanings of prefixes, suffixes, and other word fundamentals, you can decipher the meaning of words which may not yet be in your vocabulary. Prefixes are common letter combinations at the beginning of words, while suffixes are common letter combinations at the end. The main part of the word is known as the root. Visually, it would look like this: prefix + root word + suffix. Look first at the individual meanings of the root word, prefix and/or suffix. Using knowledge of the meaning(s) of the prefix and/or suffix to see what information it adds to the root. Even if the meaning of the root is unknown, one can use knowledge of the prefix's and/or suffix's meaning(s) to determine an approximate meaning of the word. For example, if one sees the word *uninspired* and does not know what it means, they can use the knowledge that *un-* means 'not' to know that the full word means "not inspired." Understanding the common prefixes and suffixes can illuminate at least part of the meaning of an unfamiliar word.

> **Review Video:** <u>Determining Word Meanings</u>
> *Visit **mometrix.com/academy** and enter **Code: 894894***

Below is a list of common prefixes and their meanings:

Prefix	Definition	Examples
a	in, on, of, up, to	abed, afoot
a-	without, lacking	atheist, agnostic
ab-	from, away, off	abdicate, abjure
ad-	to, toward	advance
am-	friend, love	amicable, amatory
ante-	before, previous	antecedent, antedate
anti-	against, opposing	antipathy, antidote
auto-	self	autonomy, autobiography
belli-	war, warlike	bellicose
bene-	well, good	benefit, benefactor
bi-	two	bisect, biennial
bio-	life	biology, biosphere
cata-	down, away, thoroughly	catastrophe, cataclysm
chron-	time	chronometer, synchronize
circum-	around	circumspect, circumference
com-	with, together, very	commotion, complicate
contra-	against, opposing	contradict, contravene
cred-	belief, trust	credible, credit
de-	from	depart
dem-	people	demographics, democracy
dia-	through, across, apart	diameter, diagnose
dis-	away, off, down, not	dissent, disappear
epi-	upon	epilogue
equi-	equal, equally	equivalent
ex-	out	extract
for-	away, off, from	forget, forswear
fore-	before, previous	foretell, forefathers
homo-	same, equal	homogenized
hyper-	excessive, over	hypercritical, hypertension
hypo-	under, beneath	hypodermic, hypothesis
in-	in, into	intrude, invade
in-	not, opposing	incapable, ineligible
inter-	among, between	intercede, interrupt
intra-	within	intramural, intrastate
magn-	large	magnitude, magnify

mal-	bad, poorly, not	malfunction
micr-	small	microbe, microscope
mis-	bad, poorly, not	misspell, misfire
mono-	one, single	monogamy, monologue
mor-	die, death	mortality, mortuary
neo-	new	neolithic, neoconservative
non-	not	nonentity, nonsense
ob-	against, opposing	objection
omni-	all, everywhere	omniscient
ortho-	right, straight	orthogonal, orthodox
over-	above	overbearing
pan-	all, entire	panorama, pandemonium
para-	beside, beyond	parallel, paradox
per-	through	perceive, permit
peri-	around	periscope, perimeter
phil-	love, like	philosophy, philanthropic
poly-	many	polymorphous, polygamous
post-	after, following	postpone, postscript
pre-	before, previous	prevent, preclude
prim-	first, early	primitive, primary
pro-	forward, in place of	propel, pronoun
re-	back, backward, again	revoke, recur
retro-	back, backward	retrospect, retrograde
semi-	half, partly	semicircle, semicolon
sub-	under, beneath	subjugate, substitute
super-	above, extra	supersede, supernumerary
sym-	with, together	sympathy, symphony
trans-	across, beyond, over	transact, transport
ultra-	beyond, excessively	ultramodern, ultrasonic, ultraviolet
un-	not, reverse of	unhappy, unlock
uni-	one	uniform, unity
vis-	to see	visage, visible

Below is a list of common suffixes and their meanings:

Suffix	Definition	Examples
-able	able to, likely	capable, tolerable
-age	process, state, rank	passage, bondage
-ance	act, condition, fact	acceptance, vigilance
-arch	to rule	monarch
-ard	one that does excessively	drunkard, wizard
-ate	having, showing	separate, desolate
-ation	action, state, result	occupation, starvation
-cy	state, condition	accuracy, captaincy
-dom	state, rank, condition	serfdom, wisdom

-en	cause to be, become	deepen, strengthen
-er	one who does	teacher
-esce	become, grow, continue	convalesce, acquiesce
-esque	in the style of, like	picturesque, grotesque
-ess	feminine	waitress, lioness
-fic	making, causing	terrific, beatific
-ful	full of, marked by	thankful, zestful
-fy	make, cause, cause to have	glorify, fortify
-hood	state, condition	manhood, statehood
-ible	able, likely, fit	edible, possible, divisible
-ion	action, result, state	union, fusion
-ish	suggesting, like	churlish, childish
-ism	act, manner, doctrine	barbarism, socialism
-ist	doer, believer	monopolist, socialist
-ition	action, state, result	sedition, expedition
-ity	state, quality, condition	acidity, civility
-ize	make, cause to be, treat with	sterilize, mechanize, criticize
-less	lacking, without	hopeless, countless
-like	like, similar	childlike, dreamlike
-logue	type of written/spoken language	prologue
-ly	like, of the nature of	friendly, positively
-ment	means, result, action	refreshment, disappointment
-ness	quality, state	greatness, tallness
-or	doer, office, action	juror, elevator, honor
-ous	marked by, given to	religious, riotous
-ship	the art or skill of	statesmanship
-some	apt to, showing	tiresome, lonesome
-th	act, state, quality	warmth, width
-tude	quality, state, result	magnitude, fortitude
-ty	quality, state	enmity, activity
-ward	in the direction of	backward, homeward

When defining words in a text, words often have a meaning that is more than the dictionary definition. The **denotative** meaning of a word is the literal meaning. The **connotative** meaning goes beyond the denotative meaning to include the emotional reaction a word may invoke. The connotative meaning often takes the denotative meaning a step further due to associations which the reader makes with the denotative meaning. The reader can differentiate between the denotative and connotative meanings by first recognizing when authors use each meaning. Most non-fiction, for example, is fact-based, the authors not using flowery, figurative language. The reader can assume that the writer is using the denotative, or literal, meaning of words. In fiction, on the other hand, the author may be using the connotative meaning. Connotation is one form of figurative language. The reader should use context clues to determine if the author is using the denotative or connotative meaning of a word.

> **Review Video:** Denotative and Connotative Meanings
> Visit **mometrix.com/academy** and enter **Code: 736707**

Readers of all levels will encounter words with which they are somewhat unfamiliar. The best way to define a word in **context** is to look for nearby words that can help. For instance, unfamiliar nouns are often accompanied by examples that furnish a definition. Consider the following sentence: "Dave arrived at the party in hilarious garb: a leopard-print shirt, buckskin trousers, and high heels." If a reader was unfamiliar with the meaning of garb, he could read the examples and quickly determine that the word means "clothing." Examples will not always be this obvious. For instance, consider this sentence: "Parsley, lemon, and flowers were just a few of items he used as garnishes." Here, the possibly unfamiliar word *garnishes* is exemplified by parsley, lemon, and flowers. Readers who have eaten in a few restaurants will probably be able to identify a garnish as something used to decorate a plate.

In addition to looking at the context of a passage, readers can often use contrasts to define an unfamiliar word in context. In many sentences, the author will not describe the unfamiliar word directly, but will instead describe the opposite of the unfamiliar word. Of course, this provides information about the word the reader needs to define. Consider the following example: "Despite his intelligence, Hector's low brow and bad posture made him look obtuse." The author suggests that Hector's appearance was opposite to his actual intelligence. Therefore, *obtuse* must mean unintelligent or stupid. Here is another example: "Despite the horrible weather, we were beatific about our trip to Alaska." The word *despite* indicates that the speaker's feelings were at odds with the weather. Since the weather is described as "horrible," *beatific* must mean something good.

In some cases, there will be very few contextual clues to help a reader define the meaning of an unfamiliar word. When this happens, one strategy the reader may employ is substitution. A good reader will brainstorm some possible synonyms for the given word, and then substitute these words into the sentence. If the sentence and the surrounding passage continue to make sense, the substitution has revealed at least some information about the unfamiliar word. Consider the sentence, "Frank's admonition rang in her ears as she climbed the mountain." A reader unfamiliar with *admonition* might come up with some substitutions like "vow," "promise," "advice," "complaint," or "compliment." All of these words make general sense of the sentence, though their meanings are diverse. The process has suggested, however, that an admonition is some sort of message. The substitution strategy is rarely able to pinpoint a precise definition, but can be effective as a last resort.

It is sometimes possible to define an unfamiliar word by looking at the descriptive words in the context. Consider the following sentence: "Fred dragged the recalcitrant boy kicking and screaming up the stairs." *Dragged*, *kicking*, and *screaming* all suggest that the boy does not want to go up the stairs. The reader may assume that *recalcitrant* means something like unwilling or protesting. In that example, an unfamiliar adjective was identified. It is perhaps more typical to use description to define an unfamiliar noun, as in this sentence: "Don's wrinkled frown and constantly shaking fist identified him as a curmudgeon of the first order." Don is described as having a "wrinkled frown and constantly shaking fist," suggesting that a *curmudgeon* must be a grumpy old man. Contrasts do not always provide detailed information about the unfamiliar word, but they at least give the reader some clues.

When a word has more than one meaning, it can be tricky to determine how it is being used in a given sentence. Consider the verb *cleave*, which bizarrely can mean either "join" or "separate." When a reader comes upon this word, she will have to select the definition that makes the most sense. So, take as an example the following sentence: "The birds cleaved together as they flew from the oak tree." Immediately, the presence of the word *together* should suggest that in this sentence *cleave* is being used to mean "*join*." A slightly more difficult example would be the sentence, "Hermione's knife cleaved the bread cleanly." It doesn't make sense for a knife to join bread together, so the word must be meant to indicate separation. Discovering the meaning of a word with multiple meanings requires the same tricks as defining an unknown word: looking for contextual clues and evaluating substituted words.

> ➢ **Review Video:** Context
> *Visit **mometrix.com/academy** and enter **Code: 613660***

Literary Devices

Understanding how words relate to each other can often add meaning to a passage. This is explained by understanding **synonyms** (words that mean the same thing) and **antonyms** (words that mean the opposite of one another). As an example, *dry* and *arid* are synonyms, and *dry* and *wet* are antonyms. There are many pairs of words in English that can be considered synonyms, despite having slightly different definitions. For instance, the words *friendly* and *collegial* can both be used to describe a warm interpersonal relationship, so it would be correct to call them synonyms. However, *collegial* (kin to *colleague*) is more often used in reference to professional or academic relationships, while *friendly* has no such connotation. Nevertheless, it would be appropriate to call these words synonyms. If the difference between the two words is too great, however, they may not be called synonyms. *Hot* and *warm* are not synonyms, for instance, because their meanings are too distinct. A good way to determine whether two words are synonyms is to substitute one for the other and see if the sentence means the same thing. Substituting *warm* for *hot* in a sentence would convey a different meaning.

> ➢ **Review Video:** Synonyms and Antonyms
> *Visit **mometrix.com/academy** and enter **Code: 105612***

Antonyms are opposites. *Light* and *dark*, *up* and *down*, *right* and *left*, *good* and *bad*: these are all sets of antonyms. It is important to distinguish between antonyms and pairs of words that are simply different. *Black* and *gray*, for instance, are not antonyms because gray is not the opposite of black. *Black* and *white*, on the other hand, are antonyms. Not every word has an antonym. For instance, many nouns do not. What would be the antonym of *chair*, after all? On a standardized test, the questions related to antonyms are more likely to concern adjectives. Remember that adjectives are words that describe a noun. Some common adjectives include *red*, *fast*, *skinny*, and *sweet*. Of these four examples, only *red* lacks a group of obvious antonyms.

There are many types of language devices that authors use to convey their meaning in a more descriptive or interesting way. Understanding these concepts will help you understand what you read. These types of devices are called *figurative language* – language that goes beyond the literal meaning of the words. **Descriptive language** that evokes imagery in the reader's mind is one type of figurative language. **Exaggeration** is also one type of figurative language. Also, when you compare two things, you are using figurative language.

Similes and **metaphors** are ways of comparing things, and both are types of figurative language commonly found in poetry. An example of figurative language (a simile in this case) is: "The child howled like a coyote when her mother told her to pick up the toys." In this example, the child's howling is compared to that of a coyote. Figurative language is descriptive in nature and helps the reader understand the sound being made in this sentence.

> ➤ **Review Video: Simile**
> Visit **mometrix.com/academy** and enter **Code: 642949**

Alliteration is a stylistic device, or literary technique, in which successive words (more strictly, stressed syllables) begin with the same sound or letter. Alliteration is a frequent tool in poetry but it is also common in prose, particularly to highlight short phrases. Especially in poetry, it contributes to euphony of the passage, lending it a musical air. It may act to humorous effect. Alliteration draws attention to itself, which may be a good or a bad thing. Authors should be conscious of the character of the sound to be repeated. In the above example, a *th* sound is somewhat difficult to make quickly in four consecutive words, so the phrase conveys a little of the difficulty of moving through tall grass. If the author is indeed trying to suggest this difficulty, then the alliteration is a success. Consider, however, the description of eyes as "glassy globes of glitter." This is definitely alliteration, since the initial *gl* sound is used three times. However, one might question whether this awkward sound is appropriate for a description of pretty eyes. The phrase is not especially pleasant to the ear, and therefore is probably not effective as alliteration. Related to alliteration are *assonance*, the repetition of vowel sounds, and *consonance*, the repetition of consonant sounds.

> ➤ **Review Video: Alliteration**
> Visit **mometrix.com/academy** and enter **Code: 462837**

A **figure of speech**, sometimes termed a rhetorical figure or device, or elocution, is a word or phrase that departs from straightforward, literal language. Figures of speech are often used and crafted for emphasis, freshness of expression, or clarity. However, clarity may also suffer from their use.

Note that not all theories of meaning necessarily have a concept of "literal language" (see literal and figurative language). Under theories that do not, figure of speech is not an entirely coherent concept. As an example of the figurative use of a word, consider the sentence, "I am going to crown you." It may mean:
- I am going to place a literal crown on your head.
- I am going to symbolically exalt you to the place of kingship.
- I am going to punch you in the head with my clenched fist.
- I am going to put a second checker on top of your checker to signify that it has become a king.

> ➤ **Review Video: Figure of Speech**
> Visit **mometrix.com/academy** and enter **Code: 111295**

A **metaphor** is a type of figurative language in which the writer equates one thing with a different thing. For instance, in the sentence "The bird was an arrow arcing through the sky," the arrow is serving as a metaphor for the bird. The point of a metaphor is to encourage the reader to think about the thing being described in a different way. Using this example, we are being asked to envision the bird's flight as being similar to the arc of an arrow, so we will imagine it to be swift, bending, etc. Metaphors are a way for the author to describe without being direct and obvious.

Metaphors are a more lyrical and suggestive way of providing information. Note that the thing to which a metaphor refers will not always be mentioned explicitly by the author. For instance, consider the following description of a forest in winter: "Swaying skeletons reached for the sky and groaned as the wind blew through them." The author is clearly using *skeletons* as a metaphor for leafless trees. This metaphor creates a spooky tone while inspiring the reader's imagination.

> **Review Video: Metaphor**
> Visit **mometrix.com/academy** and enter **Code: 133295**

Metonymy is referring to one thing in terms of another, closely related thing. This is similar to metaphor, but there is less distance between the description and the thing being described. An example of metonymy is referring to the news media as the "press," when of course the press is only the device by which newspapers are printed. Metonymy is a way of referring to something without having to repeat its name constantly. **Synecdoche**, on the other hand, is referring to a whole by one of its parts. An example of synecdoche would be calling a police officer a "badge." Synecdoche, like metonymy, is a handy way of referring without having to overuse certain words. It also allows the writer to emphasize aspects of the thing being described. For instance, referring to businessmen as "suits" suggests professionalism, conformity, and drabness.

> **Review Video: Metonymy and Synecdoche**
> Visit **mometrix.com/academy** and enter **Code: 900306**

Hyperbole is overstatement for effect. The following sentence is an example of hyperbole: *He jumped ten feet in the air when he heard the good news*. Obviously, no person has the ability to jump ten feet in the air. The author hyperbolizes not because he believes the statement will be taken literally, but because the exaggeration conveys the extremity of emotion. Consider how much less colorful the sentence would be if the author simply said, "He jumped when he heard the good news." Hyperbole can be dangerous if the author does not exaggerate enough. For instance, if the author wrote, "He jumped two feet in the air when he heard the good news," the reader might not be sure whether this is actually true or just hyperbole. Of course, in many situations this distinction will not really matter. However, an author should avoid confusing or vague hyperbole when he needs to maintain credibility or authority with readers.

Understatement is the opposite of hyperbole: that is, it is describing something as less than it is, for effect. As an example, consider a person who climbs Mount Everest and then describes the journey as "a little stroll." This is an almost extreme example of understatement. Like other types of figurative language, understatement has a range of uses. It may convey self-deprecation or modesty, as in the above example. Of course, some people might interpret understatement as false modesty, a deliberate attempt to call attention to the magnitude of what is being discussed. For example, a woman is complimented on her enormous diamond engagement ring and says, "Oh, this little thing?" Her understatement might be viewed as snobby or insensitive. Understatement can have various effects, but it always calls attention to itself.

> **Review Video: Hyperbole and Understatement**
> Visit **mometrix.com/academy** and enter **Code: 308470**

A **simile** is a figurative expression similar to a metaphor, though it requires the use of a distancing word like *like* or *as*. Some examples are "The sun was like an orange," "eager as a beaver," and "nimble as a mountain goat." Because a simile includes *like* or *as*, it creates a little space between

- 35 -

the description and the thing being described. If an author says that a house was "like a shoebox," the tone is slightly different than if the author said that the house *was* a shoebox. In a simile, the author indicates an awareness that the description is not the same thing as the thing being described. In a metaphor, there is no such distinction, even though one may safely assume that the author is aware of it. This is a subtle difference, but authors will alternately use metaphors and similes depending on their intended tone.

> ➤ **Review Video: <u>Simile</u>**
> *Visit **mometrix.com/academy** and enter Code:* **642949**

Another type of figurative language is **personification.** This is the description of the nonhuman as if it were human. Literally, the word means the process of making something into a person. There is a wide range of approaches to personification, from common expressions like "whispering wind" to full novels like *Animal Farm*, by George Orwell, in which the Bolshevik Revolution is reenacted by farmyard animals. The general intent of personification is to describe things in a manner that will be comprehensible to readers. When an author states that a tree "groans" in the wind, she of course does not mean that the tree is emitting a low, pained sound from its mouth. Instead, she means that the tree is making a noise similar to a human groan. Of course, this personification establishes a tone of sadness or suffering. A different tone would be established if the author said the tree was "swaying" or "dancing."

> ➤ **Review Video: <u>Personification</u>**
> *Visit **mometrix.com/academy** and enter Code:* **260066**

Irony is a statement that suggests its opposite. In other words, it is when an author or character says one thing but means another. For example, imagine a man walks in his front door, covered in mud and in tattered clothes. His wife asks him, "How was your day?" and he says "Great!" The man's comment is an example of irony. As in this example, irony often depends on information the reader obtains elsewhere. There is a fine distinction between irony and sarcasm. Irony is any statement in which the literal meaning is opposite from the intended meaning, while sarcasm is a statement of this type that is also insulting to the person at whom it is directed. A sarcastic statement suggests that the other person is stupid enough to believe an obviously false statement is true. Irony is a bit more subtle than sarcasm.

The more words a person is exposed to, the greater their vocabulary will become. By reading on a regular basis, a person can increase the number of ways they have seen a word in context. Based on experience, a person can recall how a word was used in the past and apply that knowledge to a new context. For example, a person may have seen the word *gull* used to mean a bird that is found near the seashore. However, a *gull* can also be a person who is easily tricked. If the word is used in context in reference to a character, the reader can recognize that the character is being called a bird that is not seen as extremely intelligent. Using what the reader knows about a word can be useful when making comparisons or figuring out the meaning of a new use of a word, as in figurative language, idioms, analogies, and multiple-meaning words.

> ➤ **Review Video: <u>Irony</u>**
> *Visit **mometrix.com/academy** and enter Code:* **374204**

Writing to Sources

Choosing Topics

Very often the choice of a subject may be assigned or determined by someone besides the writer. When the choice is left to the writer, it is sometimes wise to allow the topic itself to "select" the writer. That is to say those topics that interest, engage, puzzle, or stimulate someone may be good choices. Engaging the writer is the most important factor in choosing a topic. Engagement notes a strong interest and spirit of inquiry about the subject. It is a signal that the subject and author are interacting in some creative sense, which usually encourages good writing. Even with an assigned topic, a particular aspect of the subject may interest the writer more than others. The key to any writer's choice of topic is the ability of a subject to inspire the author to question, speculate, inquire and interact. From this natural interest and attraction, some of the most creative writing develops.

A common problem is limiting the scope of a writing assignment. Narrowing the scope is not always enough, because the new subject may itself be too broad. Focusing on an aspect of a topic often effectively results in a topic both interesting and manageable. For example narrowing a topic like the "Civil War" to the "Battle of Antietam" may still leave an unwieldy topic. To sharpen the focus, an aspect such as "The use of artillery by Confederates at the battle of Antietam" could be selected.

Understanding Assignments

Many writing assignments address specific audiences (physicians, attorneys, and teachers) and have specific goals. These writers know for whom and why they are writing. This can clarify the writing significantly. Other assignments, particularly in academic settings, may appear with no specific subject, audience, or apparent purpose. Assignments may come with some variables; a specified audience, subject, or approach and leave the rest up to the writer. Because of these variables, it is useful to consider the following questions:
1. What specifically is the assignment asking the writer to do?
2. What information or knowledge in necessary to fulfill the assignment?
3. Can the topic be broadened or limited to more effectively complete the project?
4. Are there specific parameters or other requirements for the project?
5. What is the purpose of the assignment?
6. Who is the intended audience for the work?
7. What is the length of the assignment? Does it limit or require a certain number of pages? If so, what are the parameters?
8. What is the deadline for the assignment? Sometimes preliminary materials are to be submitted before the main assignment. Considering these factors will give a writer information needed to set a schedule for the project.

Length and Document Design

Writers seldom have control over length and document design. Usually a academic assignment has a specified length, while journalists work within tight word count parameters. Document design often follows the purpose of a writing project. Specific formats are required for lab reports, research papers, and abstracts. The business world operates within fairly narrow format styles, the business letter, memo, and report allowing only a small departure from the standard format. There are some assignments that allow the writer to choose the specific format for the work. The increased flourishes provided by computers allow a great deal of creativity in designing an visually stimulating and functional document. Improving readability is always a worthwhile goal for any project, and this is becoming much easier with available software.

Deadlines

Deadlines are a critical element in any writing assignment. They help a writer budget their time to complete the assignment on schedule. For elaborate or complex writing projects, it is useful to create a working schedule that includes time for research, writing, revising, and editing. Breaking the process down into more workable parts with their own deadlines, helps keep a writer aware of the progress being made.

Purposes of Writing

What is the main purpose of the proposed piece? This may be very clear and focused, or ambiguous. A writer should be clear about the purpose of his writing, as this will determine the direction and elements of the work. Generally purposes may be divided into three groups:
1. To entertain.
2. To persuade or convince.
3. To educate or inform.

Some or all of these purposes may be the goal in a given writing assignment. It is helpful to try and identify the major purpose of a writing piece, as well as any secondary purposes involved. Purpose in writing must be linked closely to the writer's goals in undertaking the assignment. In academic settings, it is usually more accurate to think in terms of several goals. A student may wish to convince the audience in an entertaining and informative fashion. However one goal should be paramount. Expectations of the instructor play an important role in an academic assignment.

> ➤ **Review Video: <u>Purpose of the Writer</u>**
> *Visit* ***mometrix.com/academy*** *and enter* ***Code:*** **983664**

Recursive Nature

The process of writing is described as recursive; This means that the goals and parts of the writing process are often a seamless flow, constantly influencing each other without clear boundaries. The "steps' in the writing process occur organically, with planning, drafting and revising all taking place simultaneously, in no necessary or orderly fashion. The writer rarely pays attention to the recursive patterns. The process unfolds naturally, without attention or dependence on a predetermined sequence. The writing process is a series of recursive activities, which rarely occur in a linear fashion, rather moving back and forth between planning, drafting, revising, more planning, more drafting, polishing until the writing is complete. Forthcoming topics will cover many parts of the process individually, but they go on together as a seamless flow.

> ➤ **Review Video: <u>Recursive Writing Process</u>**
> *Visit* ***mometrix.com/academy*** *and enter* ***Code:*** **951611**

Considering an Audience

The careful consideration of the anticipated audience is a requisite for any project. Although much of this work is intuitive, some guidelines are helpful in the analysis of an audience:

1. Specifically identify your audience. Are they eclectic or share common characteristics?
2. Determine qualities of the audience such as age, education, sex, culture, and special interests.
3. Understand what the audience values; brevity, humor, originality, honesty are examples.
4. What is the audience's attitude toward the topic; skeptical, knowledgeable, pro or con?
5. Understand the writer's relationship to the audience; peer, authority, advocate, or antagonist?

Understanding the qualities of an audience allows the writer to form an organizational plan tailored to achieve the objectives of the writing with the audience in mind. It is essential to effective writing.

> ➤ **Review Video:** <u>Word-Choice and the Intended Audience</u>
> *Visit* **mometrix.com/academy** *and enter* **Code: 505088**

Level of Formality

In choosing a level of formality in writing, the subject and audience should be carefully considered. The subject may require a more dignified tone, or perhaps an informal style would be best. The relationship between writer and reader is important in choosing a level of formality. Is the audience one with which you can assume a close relationship, or should a more formal tone prevail?

Most student or business writing requires some degree of formality. Informal writing is appropriate for private letters, personal e-mails, and business correspondence between close associates. Vocabulary and language should be relatively simple.

It is important to be consistent in the level of formality in a piece of writing. Shifts in levels of formality can confuse readers and detract from the message of the writing.

Understanding the Topic

Easily overlooked is the basic question of ascertaining how knowledgeable the writer is about the subject. A careful evaluation should be made to determine what is known about the topic, and what information must be acquired to undertake the writing assignment. Most people have a good sense of how to go about researching a subject, using the obvious available resources: libraries, the internet, journals, research papers and other sources. There are however some specific strategies that can help a writer learn more about a subject, and just as importantly, what is not known and must be learned. These strategies or techniques not only are useful in researching a subject, they can also be used when problems come up during the actual writing phase of the assignment. These strategies include brainstorming, free writing, looping, and questioning.

<u>Brainstorming</u>
Brainstorming is a technique used frequently in business, industry, science, and engineering. It is accomplished by tossing out ideas, usually with several other people, in order to find a fresh approach or a creative way to approach a subject. This can be accomplished by an individual by simply free-associating about a topic. Sitting with paper and pen, every thought about the subject is

written down in a word or phrase. This is done without analytical thinking, just recording what arises in the mind about the topic. The list is then read over carefully several times. The writer looks for patterns, repetitions, clusters of ideas, or a recurring theme. Although brainstorming can be done individually, it works best when several people are involved. Three to five people is ideal. This allows an exchange of ideas, points of view, and often results in fresh ideas or approaches.

<u>Free Writing</u>
Free writing is a form of brainstorming in a structured way. The method involves exploring a topic by writing about it for a certain period of time without stopping. A writer sets a time limit, and begins writing in complete sentences everything that comes to mind about the topic. Writing continues without interruption until the set period expires. When time expires, read carefully everything that has been written down. Much of it may make little or no sense, but insights and observations may emerge that the free writer did not know existed in his mind. Writing has a unique quality about it of jogging loose ideas, and seeing a word or idea appear may trigger others. Freewrtiting usually results in a fuller expression of ideas than brainstorming, because thoughts and associations are written in a more comprehensive manner. Both techniques can be used to complement one another and can yield much different results.

<u>Looping</u>
Looping is a variation of freewriting that focuses a topic in short five-minute stages, or loops. Looping is done as follows:
1. With a subject in mind, spend five minutes freewriting without stopping. The results are the first loop.
2. Evaluate what has been written in the first loop. Locate the strongest or most recurring thought which should be summarized in a single sentence. This is the "center of gravity", and is the starting point of the next loop.
3. Using the summary sentence as a starting point, another five minute cycle of freewriting takes place. Evaluate the writing and locate the "center of gravity" for the second loop, and summarize it in a single sentence. This will be the start of the third loop.
4. Continue this process until a clear new direction to the subject emerges. Usually this will yield a starting point for a whole new approach to a topic.

Looping can be very helpful when a writer is blocked or unable to generate new ideas on a subject.

<u>Questioning</u>
Asking and answering questions provides a more structured approach to investigating a subject. Several types of questions may be used to illuminate an issue.
1. Questions to describe a topic. Questions such as "What is It?", "What caused it?", "What is it like or unlike?", "What is it a part of"? What do people say about it?" help explore a topic systematically.
2. Questions to explain a topic. Examples include" Who, how, and what is it?", "Where does it end and begin?" What is at issue?", and "How is it done?".
3. Questions to persuade include "What claims can be made about it?", "What evidence supports the claims?", "Can the claims be refuted?", and "What assumptions support the claims?"

Questioning can be a very effective device as it leads the writer through a process in a systematic manner in order to gain more information about a subject.

Thesis

A thesis states the main idea of the essay. A working or tentative thesis should be established early on in the writing process. This working thesis is subject to change and modification as writing progresses. It will serve to keep the writer focused as ideas develop.

The working thesis has two parts: a topic and a comment. The comment makes an important point about the topic. A working thesis should be interesting to an anticipated audience; it should be specific and limit the topic to a manageable scope. Theses three criteria are useful tools to measure the effectiveness of any working thesis. The writer applies these tools to ascertain:
1. Is the topic of sufficient interest to hold an audience?
2. Is the topic specific enough to generate interest?
3. Is the topic manageable? Too broad? Too narrow? Can it be adequately researched?

Creating an effective thesis is an art. The thesis should be a generalization rather than a fact, and should be neither too broad or narrow in scope. A thesis prepares readers for facts and details, so it may not be a fact itself. It is a generalization that requires further proof or supporting points. Any thesis too broad may be an unwieldy topic and must be narrowed. The thesis should have a sharp focus, and avoid vague, ambivalent language. The process of bringing the thesis into sharp focus may help in outlining major sections of the work. This process is known as blueprinting, and helps the writer control the shape and sequence of the paper. Blueprinting outlines major points and supporting arguments that are used in elaborating on the thesis. A completed blueprint often leads to a development of an accurate first draft of a work. Once the thesis and opening are complete, it is time to address the body of the work.

> ➤ **Review Video:** Thesis Statements
> *Visit mometrix.com/academy and enter* **Code: 326781**

Formal Outlines

A formal outline may be useful if the subject is complex, and includes many elements. here is a guide to preparing formal outlines:
1. Always put the thesis at the top so it may be referred to as often as necessary during the outlining.
2. Make subjects similar in generality as parallel as possible in the formal outline.
3. Use complete sentences rather than phrases or sentence fragments in the outline.
4. Use the conventional system of letters and numbers to designate levels of generality.
5. There should be at least two subdivisions for each category in the formal outline.
6. Limit the number of major sections in the outline. If there are too many major sections, combine some of them and supplement with additional sub-categories.
7. Remember the formal outline is still subject to change; remain flexible throughout the process.

Research

Research is a means of critical inquiry, investigations based on sources of knowledge. Research is the basis of scientific knowledge, of inventions, scholarly inquiry, and many personal and general decisions. Much of work consists of research - finding something out and reporting on it. We can list five basic precepts about research:

1. Everyone does research. To buy an car, go to a film, to investigate anything is research. We all have experience in doing research.
2. Good research draws a person into a "conversation" about a topic. Results are more knowledge about a subject, understanding different sides to issues, and be able to discuss intelligently nuances of the topic.
3. Research is always driven by a purpose. Reasons may vary from solving a problem to advocating a position, but research is almost always goal oriented.
4. Research is shaped by purpose, and in turn the fruits of research refine the research further.
5. Research is usually not a linear process; it is modified and changed by the results it yields.

Many writing assignments require research. Research is basically the process of gathering information for the writer's use. There are two broad categories of research:

1. Library research should be started after a research plan is outlined. Topics that require research should be listed, and catalogues, bibliographies, periodical indexes checked for references. Librarians are usually an excellent source of ideas and information on researching a topic.
2. Field research is based on observations, interviews, and questionnaires. This can be done by an individual or a team, depending on the scope of the field research.

The specific type and amount of research will vary widely with the topic and the writing assignment. A simple essay or story may require only a few hours of research, while a major project can consume weeks or months.

<u>Research Material</u>
- Primary sources are the raw material of research. This can include results of experiments, notes, and surveys or interviews done by the researcher. Other primary sources are books, letters, diaries, eyewitness accounts, and performances attended by the researcher.
- Secondary sources consist of oral and written accounts prepared by others. This includes reports, summaries, critical reviews, and other sources not developed by the researcher.

Most research writing uses both primary and secondary sources. Primary sources from first-hand accounts and secondary sources for background and supporting documentation. The research process calls for active reading and writing throughout. As research yields information, it often calls for more reading and research, and the cycle continues.

<u>Organizing Information</u>
Organizing information effectively is an important part of research. The data must be organized in a useful manner so that it can be effectively used. Three basic ways to organize information are:

1. Spatial organization - this is useful as it lets the user "see" the information, to fix it in space. This has benefits for those individuals who are visually adept at processing information.
2. Chronological organization is the most common presentation of information. This method places information in the sequence with which it occurs. Chronological organization is very useful in explaining a process that occurs in a step-by-step pattern.

3. Logical organization includes presenting material in a logical pattern that makes intuitive sense. Some patterns that are frequently used are illustrated, definition, compare/contrast, cause/effect, problem/solution, and division/classification. Each of these methods is discussed next.

Logical Organization

There are six major types of logical organization that are frequently used:
1. Illustrations may be used to support the thesis. Examples are the most common form of this organization.
2. Definitions say what something is or is not is another way of organization. What are the characteristics of the topic?
3. Dividing or classifying information into separate items according to their similarities is a common and effective organizing method.
4. Comparing, focusing on the similarities of things, and contrasting, highlighting the differences between things is an excellent tool to use with certain kinds of information.
5. Cause and effect is a simple tool to logically understand relationships between things. A phenomenon may be traced to its causes for organizing a subject logically.
6. Problem and solution is a simple and effective manner of logically organizing material. It is very commonly used and lucidly presents information.

Writing

An Initial Plan

After information gathering has been completed and the fruits of the research organized effectively, the writer now has a rough or initial plan for the work. A rough plan may be informal, consisting of a few elements such as "Introduction, Body, and Conclusions", or a more formal outline. The rough plan may include multiple organizational strategies within the over-all piece, or it may isolate one or two that can be used exclusively. At this stage the plan is just that, a rough plan subject to change as new ideas appear, and the organization takes a new approach. In these cases, the need for more research sometimes becomes apparent, or existing information should be considered in a new way. A more formal outline leads to an easier transition to a draft, but it can also limit the new possibilities that may arise as the plan unfolds. Until the outlines of the piece become clear, it is usually best to remain open to possible shifts in approaching the subject.

Supporting the Thesis

It is most important that the thesis of the paper be clearly expounded and adequately supported by additional points. The thesis sentence should contain a clear statement of the major theme and a comment about the thesis. The writer has an opportunity here to state what is significant or noteworthy of this particular treatment of the subject. Each sentence and paragraph in turn, should build on the thesis and support it.

Particular attention should be paid to insuring the organization properly uses the thesis and supporting points. It can be useful to outline the draft after writing, to insure that each paragraph leads smoothly to the next, and that the thesis is continually supported. The outline may highlight a weakness in flow or ideation that can be repaired. It will also spatially illustrate the flow of the argument, and provide a visual representation of the thesis and its supporting points. Often things become clearer when outlined than with a block of writing.

First Draft

Drafting is a mysterious art, and does not easily lend itself to rules. Generally, the more detailed the formal or informal outline, the easier is the transition to a first draft. The process of drafting is a learning one, and planning, organizing, and researching may be ongoing. Drafting is an evaluative process as well, and the whole project will be under scrutiny as the draft develops. The scope may be narrowed or widened, the approach may change, and different conclusions may emerge.

The process itself is shaped by the writer's preferences for atmosphere during the writing process. Time of day or night, physical location, ambient conditions, and any useful rituals can all play into the writer's comfort and productivity. The creation of an atmosphere conducive to the writer's best work is a subtle but important aspect of writing that is often overlooked. Although excellent writing has often been done in difficult situations, it is not the best prescription for success.

Evaluating the Draft

Once a draft is finished, an evaluation is in order. This can often mean reviewing the entire process with a critical eye. There is no formal checklist that insures a complete and effective evaluation, but there are some elements that can be considered:

1. It should be determined whether sufficient research was done to properly develop the assignment. Are there areas that call for additional information? If so, what type?
2. What are the major strengths of the draft? Are there any obvious weaknesses? How can these be fixed?
3. Who is the audience for this work and how well does the material appeal to them?
4. Does the material actually accomplish the goals of the assignment? If not, what needs to be done?

This is a stage for stepping back from the project and giving it an objective evaluation. Changes made now can improve the material significantly. Take time here to formulate a final approach to the subject.

Objective Criticism

Now is the time to obtain objective criticisms of the draft. It is helpful to provide readers with a list of questions to be answered about the draft. Some examples of effective questions are:

1. Does the introduction catch the reader's attention? How can it be improved?
2. Is the thesis clearly stated and supported by additional points?
3. What type of organizational plan is used? Is it appropriate for the subject?
4. Are paragraphs well developed and is there a smooth transition between them?
5. Are the sentences well written and convey the appropriate meaning?
6. Are words used effectively and colorfully in the text?
7. What is the tone of the writing? Is it appropriate to the audience and subject?
8. Is the conclusion satisfactory? Is there a sense of completion that the work is finished?
9. What are main strengths and weaknesses of the writing? Are there specific suggestions for improvement?

Title, Introduction, and Conclusion

1. A good title can identify the subject, describe it in a colorful manner, and give clues to the approach and sometimes conclusion of the writing. It usually defines the work in the mind of the reader.
2. A strong introduction follows the lead of the title; it draws the readers into the work, and clearly states the topic with a clarifying comment. A common style is to state the topic, and then provide additional details, finally leading to a statement of the thesis at the end. An

introduction can also begin with an arresting quote, question, or strong opinion, which grabs the reader's attention.

3. A good conclusion should leave readers satisfied and provide a sense of closure. Many conclusions restate the thesis and formulate general statements that grow out of it. Writers often find ways to conclude in a dramatic fashion, through a vivid image, quotation, or a warning. This in an effort to give the ending the "punch" to tie up any existing points.

An introduction announces the main point of the work. It will usually be a paragraph of 50 to 150 words, opening with a few sentences to engage the reader, and conclude with the essay's main point. The sentence stating the main point is called the thesis. If possible, the sentences leading to the thesis should attract the reader's attention with a provocative question, vivid image, description, paradoxical statement, quotation, anecdote, or a question. The thesis could also appear at the beginning of the introduction. There are some types of writing that do not lend themselves to stating a thesis in one sentence. Personal narratives and some types of business writing may be better served by conveying an overriding purpose of the text, which may or may not be stated directly. The important point is to impress the audience with the rationale for the writing.

The body of the essay should fulfill the promise of the introduction and thesis. If an informal outline has not been done, now is the time for a more formal one. Constructing the formal outline will create a "skeleton" of the paper. Using this skeleton, it is much easier to fill out the body of an essay. It is useful to block out paragraphs based on the outline, to insure they contain all the supporting points, and are in the appropriate sequence.

The conclusion of the essay should remind readers of the main point, without belaboring it. It may be relatively short, as the body of the text has already "made the case" for the thesis. A conclusion can summarize the main points, and offer advice or ask a question. Never introduce new ideas in a conclusion. Avoid vague and desultory endings, instead closing with a crisp, often positive, note. A dramatic or rhetorical flourish can end a piece colorfully.

Examining Paragraphs
Paragraphs are a key structural unit of prose utilized to break up long stretches of words into more manageable subsets, and to indicate a shift in topics or focus. Each paragraph may be examined by identifying the main point of the section, and insuring that every sentence supports or relates to the main theme. Paragraphs may be checked to make sure the organization used in each is appropriate, and that the number of sentences are adequate to develop the topic.

Examining Sentences
Sentences are the building blocks of the written word, and they can be varied by paying attention to sentence length, sentence structure, and sentence openings. These elements should be varied so that writing does not seem boring, repetitive, or choppy. A careful analysis of a piece of writing will expose these stylistic problems, and they can be corrected before the final draft is written. Varying sentence structure and length can make writing more inviting and appealing to a reader.

Examining Words
A writer's choice of words is a signature of their style. A careful analysis of the use of words can improve a piece of writing. Attention to the use of specific nouns rather than general ones can enliven language. Verbs should be active whenever possible to keep the writing stronger and energetic, and there should be an appropriate balance between numbers of nouns and verbs. Too many nouns can result in heavy, boring sentences.

Examining Tone

Tone may be defined as the writer's attitude toward the topic, and to the audience. This attitude is reflected in the language used in the writing. If the language is ambiguous, tone becomes very difficult to ascertain. The tone of a work should be appropriate to the topic and to the intended audience. Some writing should avoid slang and jargon, while it may be fine in a different piece. Tone can range from humorous, to serious, and all levels in between. It may be more or less formal depending on the purpose of the writing, and its intended audience. All these nuances in tone can flavor the entire writing and should be kept in mind as the work evolves.

Tone is distinguished from mood, which is the feeling the writing evokes. Tone and mood may often be similar, but can also be significantly different. Mood often depends on the manner in which words and language are employed by the writer. In a sense tone and mood are two sides of a coin which color and language enliven the total approach of a writer to his subject. Mood and tone add richness and texture to words, bringing them alive in a deliberate strategy by the writer.

Examining Point-of-View

Point-of-view is the perspective from which writing occurs. There are several possibilities:
1. First Person - Is written so that the "I" of the story is a participant or observer.
2. Second Person - Is a device to draw the reader in more closely. It is really a variation or refinement of the first person narrative.
3. Third Person - The most traditional form of third-person point-of-view is the "omniscient narrator", in which the narrative voice, (presumed to be the writer), is presumed to know everything about the characters, plot, and action. Most novels use this point-of-view.
4. A Multiple Point-Of-View - The narration is delivered from the perspective of several characters.

In modern writing, the "stream-of consciousness" technique developed fully by James Joyce where the interior monologue provides the narration through the thoughts, impressions, and fantasies of the narrator.

Voice

Writers should find an appropriate voice that is appropriate for the subject, appeals to the intended audience, and conforms to the conventions of the genre in which the writing is done. If there is doubt about the conventions of the genre, lab reports, informal essays, research papers, business memos, and so on - a writer may examine models of these works written by experts in the field. These models can serve as examples for form and style for a particular type of writing.

Voice can also include the writer's attitude toward the subject and audience. Care should be taken that the language and tone of the writing is considered in terms of the purpose of the writing and it intended audience.

Gauging the appropriate voice for a piece is part art, and part science. It can be a crucial element in the ultimate effectiveness of the writing.

> ➤ **Review Video:** Writing Process
> Visit *mometrix.com/academy* and enter *Code:* **438918**

Writing Conventions

Conventions in writing are traditional assumptions or practices used by authors of all types of text. Some basic conventions have survived through the centuries - for example the assumption that a first person narrator in a work is telling the truth - others such as having characters in melodramas speak in asides to the audience have become outmoded. Conventions are particularly important in specialized types of writing which demand specific formats and styles. This is true of scientific and research papers, as well as much of academic and business writing. This formality has relaxed somewhat in several areas but still holds true for many fields of technical writing. Conventions are particularly useful for writers working in various types of nonfiction writing, where guidelines help the writer conform to the rules expected for that field. Conventions are part of the unspoken contract between writer and audience, and should be respected.

Writing Preparation

Effective writing requires preparation. The planning process includes everything done prior to drafting. Depending on the project, this could take a few minutes or several months. Elements in planning, and include considering the purpose of the writing, exploring a topic, developing a working thesis, gathering necessary materials, and developing a plan for organizing the writing. The organizational plan may vary in length and components, from a detailed outline or a stack of research cards. The organizational plan is a guide to help draft a writing project, and may change as writing progresses, but having a guide to refer to can keep a project on track. Planning is usually an ongoing process throughout the writing, but it is essential to begin with a structure.

Editing

Time must always be allowed for thorough and careful editing in order to insure clean and error-free work. It is helpful to create a checklist of editing to use as the manuscript is proofed. Patterns of editing problems often become apparent and understanding these patterns can eliminate them. Examples of patterns of errors include misuse of commas, difficulty in shifting tenses, and spelling problems. Once these patterns are seen, it is much easier to avoid them in the original writing. A checklist should be prepared based on every piece of writing, and should be cumulative. In this manner. progress may be checked regularly and the quantity and type of errors should be reduced over time. It is often helpful to have peer proof a manuscript, to get a fresh set of eyes on the material. Editing should be treated as an opportunity to polish and perfect a written work, rather than a chore that must be done. A good editor usually turns into a better writer over time.

Proofreading

As a proofreader, the goal is always to eliminate all errors. This includes typographical errors as well as any inconsistencies in spelling and punctuation. Begin by reading the prose aloud, calling out all punctuation marks and insuring that all sentences are complete and no words are left out. It is helpful to read the material again, backwards, so the focus is on each individual word, and the tendency to skip ahead is avoided.

A computer is a blessing to writers who have trouble proofreading their work. Spelling and grammar check programs may be utilized to reduce errors significantly. However it is still important for a writer to do the manual proofing necessary to insure errors of pattern are not repeated. Computers are a wonderful tool for writers but they must be employed by the writer, rather than as the writer. Skillful use of computers should result in a finely polished manuscript free of errors.

> **Review Video:** <u>Revising and Editing</u>
> *Visit* ***mometrix.com/academy*** *and enter* ***Code:* 569931**

Evaluating Student Writing

The evaluation of student writing should be structured to include three basic goals:
1. To provide students a description of what they are doing when they respond.
2. To provide a pathway for potential improvement.
3. To help students learn to evaluate themselves.

To fulfill these goals it is necessary for the concept of evaluation be broadened beyond correcting or judging students. Any teacher response to a student's response should be considered part of the evaluation. In responding to student's responses, a teacher may use written or taped comments, dialogue with students, or conferencing between teachers and students to discuss classroom performance. Students may be asked to evaluate themselves and a teacher and student can review past progress and plan directions for potential improvement.

Teacher's Response:
There are seven basic components of teacher's responses to be considered:
1. Praise - To provide positive reinforcement for the student. Praise should be specific enough to bolster student's confidence.
2. Describing - Providing feedback on teacher's responses to student responses. This is best done in a conversational, non-judgmental mode.
3. Diagnosing - Determining the student's unique set of strengths, attitudes, needs, and abilities. This evaluation should take into consideration all elements of the student.
4. Judging - Evaluating the level, depth, insightfulness, completeness, and validity of a student's responses. This evaluation will depend on the criteria implied in the instructional approach.
5. Predicting - Predicting the potential improvement of student's responses based on specific criteria.
6. Record-keeping - The process of recording a student's reading interests, attitudes, and use of literary strategies, in order to chart student progress across time. Both qualitative and quantitative assessments may be used.
7. Recognition - Giving students recognition for growth and progress.

Assessments

Preparing for Literary Tests
Literary tests are measures of a student's individual performance. Literary assessments are measures of performance of a group of students without reference to individuals. Tests take into consideration what the teachers have taught the students, while assessments do not.

For either tests or assessments, the teacher needs a clear purpose on which to base their questions or activities. Students should be told of the purpose of the tests or assessments so they will know what to expect. Tests should be used sparingly as a one tool among many that can be used to evaluate students. Tests should encourage students on formulation of responses rather than rote answers. They should evaluate students on the basis of their responses rather than 'correct answers". Improvement over time may be noted and the student given praise for specific responses.

Standardized Achievement Tests

These multiple choice tests measure student's ability to understand text passages or apply literary concepts to texts. Although these tests are widely used, they have many limitations. They tend to be based on a simplistic model that ignores the complex nature of a reader's engagement with a text. These tests also do not measure student's articulation of responses. The purpose of these tests is to rank students in group norms, so that half the students are below the norm.

To accurately measure a student's abilities teachers should employ open ended written or oral response activities. In developing such tests, teachers must know what specific response patterns they wish to measure. The steps involved in measuring these response patterns must be clearly outlined. Teachers may wish to design questions that encourage personal expressions of responses. This would obviate the pitfall of testing primarily facts about literature rather than how students relate and use this information to engage texts.

Assessing Attitudes toward Literature

An important element in teaching literature is to understand the attitudes of students about reading and studying text. This may be done by group or individual interviews encouraging students to discuss their feelings about literature. Another way to measure attitudes is with a paper and pencil rating scale using six or eight point Liker scales. This type of assessment can be refined to explore preferences in form and genre.

Another type of assessment is done by using semantic scales to indicate students interest (or lack thereof) in reading in general and favored forms and genres.

Questionnaires can be developed to learn more about student's habits regarding literature. Do they use the library regularly, read books or periodicals, and what types of reading is done. Comparisons before and after instruction can indicate the effect of the instruction on habits and attitudes about literature.

Assessing Instructional Methods

Assessing instructional methods within a school, district, or state can help determine instructional goals and techniques relative to overall system goals. Results can indicate needed changes in the curriculum and can help an accreditation process measure the quality of an English or literature program.

An effective assessment usually includes interviews, questionnaires, and class-room observation. Trained observers rate the general type of instruction being provided, (lectures, modeling, small groups, and so on), the focus of instruction (novels, poetry, drama, and so on), the critical approach used, the response strategies used, and the response activities employed. Observers may also analyze the statements of goals and objectives in a curriculum, as well as the scope and sequence of the curriculum.

Interviews of both students and teachers are helpful in getting first hand accounts of instruction and results.

Classroom Based Research

Teacher's can conduct their own informal descriptive research to assess the effects of their teaching on student's responses. This allows teachers an opportunity to review and reflect on their instructional methods and results. This research can take many forms including:

- An analysis of student's perception of guided response- activities to determine which were most effective.
- An analysis of student's small and large group discussions.
- A teacher self analysis of their own taped, written, or conference feedback to students writing.
- Interviews with students about their responses and background experiences and attitudes.
- Evaluating student's responses to texts commonly used in their instruction.

These are only a few possibilities for effective classroom based research. Any research that provides insight into student needs and preferences can be a valuable tool.

Conducting Classroom Research:
1. Create a research question related to literature instruction or responses.
2. Summarize the theory and research related to the topic.
3. Describe the participants, setting, tasks, and methods of analysis.
4. Summarize the results of the research in a graph, table, or report.
5. Interpret or give reasons for the results.
6. Draw conclusions from the results that suggest ways to improve instruction and evaluation of students.

Teachers must always keep in mind the purposes driving the research. Evaluation itself is relatively easy, the challenge is using the evaluations to help both students and teachers to grow, and become better at what they are doing.

Reviewers

Many professional and business writers work with editors who provide advice and support throughout the writing process. In academic situations, the use of reviewers is increasing, either by instructors or perhaps at an academic writing center. Peer review sessions are sometimes scheduled for class, and afford an opportunity to hear what other students feel about a piece of writing. This gives a writer a chance to serve as a reviewer.

Perspective

Textual Perspective
A textual knowledge of literature implies readers are taking a perspective or stance on the text. They are examining ways in which separate parts of the text relate to its overall form or structure. Textual perspectives must be used as a part of overall learning, not as an isolated feature. Textual perspective alone excludes both the author's life and the emotional experiences and attitudes of the reader. It fails to account for the readers' prior knowledge in their engagement with the work.

A textual approach may include the ways in which the text shapes students' experience and emotional engagement. Based on previous reading, social acculturation, attitudes, and a host of other factors, students bring a wealth of information into any encounter with a text. Students may compare and contrast elements of their text with other works they have read or seen to form a more rounded engagement with a work.

Social Perspective

A rich resource for students' of literature is their own developing social knowledge. For adolescent students', social relationships are of primary importance. It is common for younger students' to impose their own social attitudes on a text, which is fertile ground for exploring how the understanding of texts is colored by social attitudes and experiences. Student's attitudes can help them reflect on the characters in a work, and can determine their relationship with the text itself.

Social perspectives can shed light on a number of important ways which can effect a reader's engagement with the text. A skillful teacher may probe these attitudes and experiences and make students' more aware of the impact of social attitudes to reading and studying a work of literature. This knowledge can become cumulative and promote more careful understanding of a literature over a period of time.

Cultural and Historical Context

The cultural knowledge and background of readers effects their response to texts. They can relate the works in a context of subcultures such as peer group, mass media, school, religion, and politics, social and historical communities. Engaging with the texts, readers can better understand how characters and authors are shaped by cultural influences. Cultural elements influence reader's reactions to events, including their responses to literature.

Cultural and historical context is important in understanding the roles of women and minorities in literature. Placing works of literature in their proper cultural setting can make a work more understandable and provoke reader interest in the milieu of the day. These factors can stimulate a reader's interest in how their own cultural background impacts the engagement with the text. Thus, the cultural aspects of literature become an opportunity for the reader to gain insight into their own attitudes.

> ➤ **Review Video: Historical Context**
> *Visit **mometrix.com/academy** and enter **Code: 169770***

Topical Perspective

In using a topical perspective, students apply their background in a variety of different fields, for instance sports, science, politics or cooking, to the literary work they are studying. Students may then engage the text in a holistic manner, bringing all their knowledge to bear on a work. It is useful to encourage students to determine how their own information pool relates to the work. There are an infinite number of fields or topics that relate to literature.

Students are most likely to integrate topics they are currently studying into their engagement with a text. These topics would include history, science, art, and music among others. Thinking about literature from these other topical point-of-view can help students ' understand that what they are learning in other courses enhances their experience of both literature and life.

Effects of Prior Knowledge

History

When students employ topical knowledge of history in their study of literature, they may do much more than remember date, events, and historical figures in relation to a text. They may well apply what they know about a historical period to better understand the attitudes and relationships in a work of literature. Students learn to think historically, considering different explanations for events, or cause and effect relationships in tracing a sequence of events. For example in reading Steinbeck's novels, students may draw on what they know about the historical period of the depression. Hemingway's "Farewell To Arms" may evoke a historical picture of Europe embroiled in World War I.

Literature offers an opportunity to apply historical knowledge in the context of a work. Students understand that both literary and historical accounts of an event or character may differ significantly, and that one may illuminate the other.

Scientific Knowledge
Students can apply their knowledge of science when reading literature. Their description of carefully observed phenomena can be used to describe a piece of writing. after reading essays by science writers, students' may be encouraged to transpose this knowledge into reading other texts. Understanding the scientific method gives readers' an opportunity to impose this process on events narrated in literature. The validity of events may be tested in the students' mind to assess the "reality" of the text.

There are many texts that take as their subject the role of the scientist in society. In reading "Frankenstein" or "Dr. Faustus", many issues can be raised about the responsibilities of scientists in conducting experiments.

The blending of science and literature is particularly compelling to some students' when they read science fiction or futuristic texts. An example would be "1984" which posits a authoritarian government controlling the lives of people.

Research Papers

Hypothesis
The result of a focusing process is a research question, a question or problem that can be solved by through research data. A hypothesis is a tentative answer to the research question that must be supported by the research. A research question must be manageable, specific, and interesting. Additionally, it must be argumentative, capable of being proved or disproved by research.

It is helpful to explore a topic with background reading and notes before formulating a research question and a hypothesis. Create a data base where all the knowledge of a topic is written down to be utilized in approaching the task of identifying the research question.   This background work will allow a narrowing to a specific question, and formulate a tentative answer, the hypothesis. The process of exploring a topic can include brainstorming, freewriting, and scanning your memory and experience for information.

> **Review Video:** Hypothesis
*Visit **mometrix.com/academy** and enter **Code:** 133239*

Observing Data
Collecting data in the field begins with direct observation, noting phenomena in a totally objective manner, and recording it. This requires a systematic approach to observation and recording information. Prior to beginning the observation process, certain steps must be accomplished:
1. Determine the purpose of the observation and review the research question and hypothesis to see that they relate to each other.
2. Set a limited time period for the observations.

3. Develop a system for recording information in a useful manner.
4. Obtain proper materials for taking notes.
5. Consider the use of cameras, video recorders, or audio tape recorders.
6. Use the journalistic technique of asking "who, what, where, when, and why" to garner information.

Research Interviews

After determining the exact purpose of the interview, check it against the research question and hypothesis. Set up the interview in advance, specifying the amount of time needed. Prepare a written list of questions for the interview, and try out questions on peers before the interview. Prepare a copy of your questions leaving room for notes. Insure that all the necessary equipment is on hand, and record the date, time, and subject of the interview.

The interview should be businesslike, and take only the allotted time. A flexible attitude will allow for questions or comments that have not been planned for, but may prove helpful to the process. Follow-up questions should be asked whenever appropriate. A follow-up thank you note is always appreciated and may pave the way for further interviews. Be mindful at all times of the research question and hypothesis under consideration.

Surveys

Surveys are usually in the form of questionnaires which have the advantage of speed and rapid compilation of data. Preparation of the questionnaire is of critical importance. Tie the questionnaire to the research question as closely as possible, and include questions which will bear on the hypothesis. Questions that can be answered "yes" or "no" can be easily tabulated. The following checklist may be helpful:
1. Determine the audience for the questionnaire and how best to reach them.
2. Draft questions that will provide short, specific answers.
3. Test the questions on friends or peers.
4. Remember to include a deadline for return of the questionnaire.
5. Format the questionnaire so that it is clear and easily completed.
6. Carefully proofread the questionnaire and insure that it is neatly reproduced.

Library Research

After reviewing personal resources for information, the library is the next stop. Use index cards or notepads for documentation. Create a system for reviewing data. It is helpful to create "key words" to trigger responses from sources. Some valuable guidelines for conducting library research include:
1. Consult the reference librarian for sources and ideas.
2. Select appropriate general and specific reference books for examination. Encyclopedias are a good place to start. There are numerous specialized encyclopedias to assist in research.
3. Survey biographical dictionaries and indexes for information.
4. Review almanacs, yearbooks, and statistical data.
5. Scan periodical indexes for articles on the research topic.
6. Determine if there are specialized indexes and abstracts that may be helpful.
7. Review the computer or card catalog for relevant references.

Drafting the Research Essay

Before beginning the research essay, revisit the purpose, audience, and scope of the essay. An explicit thesis statement should summarize major arguments and approaches to the subject. After determining the special format of the essay, a survey of the literature on the subject is helpful. If original or first-hand research is involved, a summary of the methods and conclusions should be prepared.

A clustering strategy assembles all pertinent information on a topic in one physical place. The preparation of an outline may be based on the clusters, or a first draft may be developed without an outline. Formal outlines use a format of "Thesis statement", "Main topic", and "Supporting ideas" to shape the information. Drafting the essay can vary considerably among researchers, but it is useful to use an outline or information clusters to get started. Drafts are usually done on a point-to-point basis.

Introduction

The introduction to a research essay is particularly important as it sets the context for the essay. It needs to draw the reader into the subject, and also provide necessary background to understand the subject. It is sometimes helpful to open with the research question, and explain how the question will be answered. The major points of the essay may be forecast or previewed to prepare readers for the coming arguments.

In a research essay it is a good idea to establish the writer's credibility by reviewing credentials and experience with the subject. Another useful opening involves quoting several sources that support the points of the essay, again to establish credibility. The tone should be appropriate to the audience and subject, maintaining a sense of careful authority while building the arguments. Jargon should be kept to a minimum, and language carefully chosen to reflect the appropriate tone.

Conclusion

The conclusion to a research essay helps readers' summarize what they have learned. Conclusions are not meant to convince, as this has been done in the body of the essay. It can be useful to leave the reader with a memorable phrase or example that supports the argument. Conclusions should be both memorable but logical restatements of the arguments in the body of the essay.

A specific-to-general pattern can be helpful, opening with the thesis statement and expanding to more general observations. A good idea is to restate the main points in the body of the essay, leading to the conclusion. An ending that evokes a vivid image or asks a provocative question makes the essay memorable. The same effect can be achieved by a call for action, or a warning. Conclusions may be tailored to the audience's background, both in terms of language, tone, and style.

> **Review Video:** <u>Drafting a Conclusion</u>
> *Visit **mometrix.com/academy** and enter **Code: 209408***

Reviewing the Draft

A quick checklist for reviewing a draft of a research essay includes:
1. Introduction - Is the reader's attention gained and held by the introduction?
2. Thesis - Does the essay fulfill the promise of the thesis? Is it strong enough?
3. Main Points - List the main points and rank them in order of importance.
4. Organization - What is the organizing principle of the essay? Does it work?
5. Supporting Information - Is the thesis adequately supported? Is the thesis convincing?
6. Source Material - Are there adequate sources and are they smoothly integrated into the essay?

7. Conclusion - Does the conclusion have sufficient power? Does it summarize the essay well?
8. Paragraphs, Sentences, and Words - Review all these for effectiveness in promoting the thesis.
9. Overall Review - Evaluate the essay's strengths and weaknesses. What revisions are needed?

Modern Language Association Style

The Modern Language Association style is widely used in literature and languages as well as other fields. The MLA style calls for noting brief references to sources in parentheses in the text of an essay, and adding an alphabetical list of sources, called "Works Cited", at the end. Specific recommendations of the MLA include:

1. Works Cited - Includes only works actually cited. List on a separate page with the author's name, title, and publication information, which must list the location of the publisher, the publishers' name, and the date of publication.
2. Parenthetical Citations - MLA style uses parenthetical citations following each quotation, reference, paraphrase, or summary to a source. Each citation is made up of the author's last name and page reference, keyed to a reference in "Works Cited".
3. Explanatory Notes - Explanatory notes are numbered consecutively, and identified by superscript numbers in the text. The full notes may appear as endnotes or as footnotes at the bottom of the page.

American Psychological Association Style

The American Psychological Association style is widely followed in the social sciences. The APA parenthetical citations within the text directs readers to a list of sources. In APA style this list is called "References". References are listed on a separate page, and each line includes the author's name, publication date, title, and publication information. Publication information includes the city where the publisher is located, and the publisher's name. Underline the titles of books and periodicals , but not articles.

APA parenthetical expressions citations include the author's last name, the date of publication, and the page number. APA style allows for content footnotes for information needed to be expanded or supplemented, marked in the text by superscript numbers in consecutive order. Footnotes are listed under a separate page, headed "Footnotes" after the last page of text. All entries should be double-spaced.

Revisions

Revising Sentences
Revising sentences is done to make writing more effective. Editing sentences is done to correct any errors. Revising sentences is usually best done on a computer, where it is possible to try several versions easily. Some writers prefer to print out a hard copy and work with this for revisions. Each works equally well and depends on the individual preference.

Spelling and grammar checks on software are a great aid to a writer but not a panacea. Many grammatical problems, such as faulty parallelism, mixed constructions, and misplaced modifiers can slip past the programs. Even if errors are caught, the writing still must be evaluated for effectiveness. A combination of software programs and writer awareness is necessary to insure an error free manuscript.

> **Review Video: <u>General Revision and Proofreading</u>**
> *Visit **mometrix.com/academy** and enter **Code: 385882***

<u>Global Revisions</u>
Global revisions address the larger elements of writing. They usually affect paragraphs or sections, and may involve condensing or merging sections of text to improve meaning and flow. Sometimes material may be rearranged to better present the arguments of the essay. It is usually better for the writer to get some distance from the work before starting a global revision. Reviewers and editors can be usefully employed to make suggestions for revision. If reviewers are utilized, it is helpful to emphasize the focus on the larger themes of the work, rather than the finer points. When undertaking a global review, the writer might wish to position himself as the audience, rather than the writer. This provides some additional objectivity, and can result in a more honest appraisal of the writing and revisions that should be made. Global revisions are the last major changes a writer will make in the text. seal to persuade, inform, or entertain them. Answering these questions as objectively as possible will allow for a useful global revision.

1. Purpose - Does the draft accomplish its purpose? Is the material and tone appropriate for the intended audience? Does it account for the audience's knowledge of the subject? Does it seek to persuade, inform, or entertain them?
2. Focus - Does the introduction and the conclusion focus on the main point? Are all supporting arguments focused on the thesis?
3. Organization and Paragraphing - Are there enough organizational cues to guide the reader? Are any paragraphs too long or too short?
4. Content - Is the supporting material persuasive? Are all ideas adequately developed? Is there any material that could be deleted?
5. Point -of-view - Is the draft free of distracting sifts in point-of-view? Is the point-of-view appropriate for the subject and intended audience?

Paragraphs

A paragraph should be unified around a main point. A good topic sentence summarizing the paragraphs main point. A topic sentence is more general than subsequent supporting sentences. Sometime the topic sentence will be used to close the paragraph if earlier sentences give a clear indication of the direction of the paragraph. Sticking to the main point means deleting or omitting unnecessary sentences that do not advance the main point.

The main point of a paragraph deserves adequate development, which usually means a substantial paragraph. A paragraph of two or three sentences often does not develop a point well enough, particularly if the point is a strong supporting argument of the thesis. An occasional short paragraph is fine, particularly it is used as a transitional device. A choppy appearance should be avoided.

<u>Methods of Development</u>:
1. Examples are a common method of development and may be effectively used when a reader may ask "For Example?" Examples are selected instances, not an inclusive catalog. They may be used to suggest the validity of topic sentences.
2. Illustrations are extended examples, sometimes presented in story form for interest. They usually require several sentences each, so they are used sparingly. Well selected illustrations can be a colorful and vivid way of developing a point.
3. Stories that command reader interest, developed in a story form, can be powerful methods of emphasizing key points in a essay. Stories and illustrations should be very specific and relate directly to a point or points being made in the text. They allow more colorful language and instill a sense of human interest in a subject. Used judiciously, illustrations and stories are an excellent device.
4. Analogies draw comparisons between items that appear to have nothing in common. Analogies are employed by writers to attempt to provoke fresh thoughts and changed feelings about a subject. They may be used to make the unfamiliar more familiar, to clarify an abstract point, or to argue a point. Although analogies are effective literary devices, they should be used thoughtfully in arguments. Two things may be alike in some respects but completely different in others.
5. Cause and effect is a excellent device and are best used when the cause and effect are generally accepted as true. As a matter of argument, cause and effect is usually too complex and subject to other interpretations to be used effectively. A valid way of using cause and effect is to state the effect in the topic sentence of a paragraph, and add the causes in the body of the paragraph. This adds logic and form to a paragraph, and usually makes it more effective.

<u>Types of Paragraphs</u>:
1. A paragraph of narration tells a story or part of a story. They are usually arranged in chronological order, but sometimes include flashbacks, taking the story back to an earlier time.
2. A descriptive paragraph paints a verbal portrait of a person, place, or thing, using specific details that appeal to one or more of our senses - sight, sound, smell, taste, and touch. It conveys a real sense of being present and observing phenomena.
3. A process paragraphs is related in time order, generally chronological. It usually describes a process or teaches readers how to perform the process.
4. Comparing two subjects draws attention to their similarities but can also indicate a consideration of differences. To contrast is to focus only on differences. Both comparisons and contrasts may be examined point-by-point, or in succeeding paragraphs.

<u>Organizing Information:</u>

1. A grouping of items into categories based on some consistent criteria is called classification. The principle of classification a writer chooses will depend on the purpose of the classification. Most items can be classified by a number of criteria, and the selection of the specific classification will depend on the writer's aims in using this device.
2. Division, on the other hand, takes one item and divides it into parts. Just as with classification, the division must be based on a valid and consistent principle. For example a body may be divided into various body systems easily, but not as easily divided into body functions, because the categories overlap
3. Definition classifies a concept or word in a general group, then distinguishes it from other members of the class. Usually simple definitions can be provided in a sentence or two, while more complex ones may need a paragraph or two to adequately define them.

> ➤ **Review Video: <u>Drafting Body Paragraphs</u>**
> *Visit **mometrix.com/academy** and enter **Code: 724590***

Coherence

A smooth flow of sentences and paragraphs without gaps, shifts, or bumps leads to paragraph coherence. Ties between old information and new, can be smoothed by several strategies.

1. Linking ideas clearly, from the topic sentence to the body of the paragraph is essential for a smooth transition. The topic sentence states the main point, and this should be followed by specific details, examples, and illustrations that support the topic sentence. The support may be direct or indirect. In indirect support the illustrations and examples may support a sentence that in turn supports the topic directly.
2. The repetition of key words adds coherence to a paragraph. To avoid dull language, variations of the key words may be used.
3. Parallel structures are often used within sentences to emphasize the similarity of ideas and connect sentences giving similar information.
4. Minimize shifting sentences from one verb tense to another. These shifts affect the smooth flows of words and can disrupt the coherence of the paragraph.

> ➤ **Review Video: <u>Methods to Obtain Coherence in Writing</u>**
> *Visit **mometrix.com/academy** and enter **Code: 592378***

Transitions

Transitions are bridges between what has been read and what is about to be read. Transitions smooth the reader's path between sentences, and inform readers of major connections to new ideas forthcoming in the text. Transitional phrases should be used with care, selecting the appropriate phrase for a transition. Tone is another important consideration in using transitional phrases, varying the tone for different audiences. For example in a scholarly essay, "in summary" would be preferable to the more informal "in short".

When working with transitional words and phrases, writers usually find a natural flow that indicates when a transition is needed. In reading a draft of the text, it should become apparent where the flow is uneven or rough. At this point, the writer can add transitional elements during the revision process. Revising can also afford an opportunity to delete transitional devices that seem heavy-handed or unnecessary.

> **Review Video: Transitions in Writing**
> *Visit* **mometrix.com/academy** *and enter* **Code: 233246**

Lengths of Paragraphs

The comfort level for readers is paragraphs of between 100 and 200 words. Shorter paragraphs cause too much starting and stopping, and give a "choppy" effect. Paragraphs that are too long often test the attention span of the reader. Two notable exceptions to this rule exist. In scientific or scholarly papers, longer paragraphs suggest seriousness and depth. In journalistic writing, constraints are placed on paragraph size by the narrow columns in a newspaper format.

The first and last paragraphs of a text will usually be the introduction and conclusion. These special purpose paragraphs are likely to be shorter than paragraphs in the body of the work. Paragraphs in the body of the essay follow the subject's outline; one paragraph per point in short essays, and a group of paragraphs per point in longer works. Some ideas require more development than others, so it is good for a writer to remain flexible. A too long paragraph may be divided, while shorter ones may be combined.

Paragraph breaks are used for many reasons, usually as devices to improve the flow or content of the text. Some examples for beginning new paragraphs include:
1. To mark off the introduction and concluding paragraphs.
2. To signal a shift to a new idea or topic.
3. To indicate an important shift in time or place.
4. To emphasize a point by repositioning a major sentence.
5. To highlight a comparison, contrast, or cause and effect relationship.
6. To signal a change in speakers, voice, or tense.

Argumentative Writing

Constructing a reasonable argument, the goal is not to "win" or have the last word, but rather to reveal current understanding of the question, and propose a solution to the perceived problem. The purpose of argument in a free society or a research field is to reach the best conclusion possible at the time.

Conventions of arguments vary from culture to culture. In America arguments tend to be direct rather than subtle, carefully organized rather than discursive, spoken plainly rather than poetically. Evidence presented is usually specific and factual, while appeals to intuition or communal wisdom are rare.

Argumentative writing takes a stand on a debatable issue , and seeks to explore all sides of the issue and reach the best possible solution. Argumentative writing should not be combative, at it's strongest it is assertive.

A prelude to argumentative writing is an examination of the issue's social and intellectual contexts.

Introduction

The introduction of an essay arguing an issue should end with a thesis sentence that states a position on the issue. A good strategy is to establish credibility with readers by showing both expert knowledge and fair-mindedness. Building common ground with undecided or neutral readers is helpful.

The thesis should be supported by strong arguments that support the stated position. The main lines of argument should have a cumulative effect of convincing readers that the thesis has merit. The sum of the main lines of argument will outline the overall argumentative essay. The outline will clearly illustrate the central thesis, and subordinate claims that support it.

Evidence must be provided that support both the thesis and supporting arguments. Evidence based on reading should be documented, to show the sources. Readers must know how to check sources for accuracy and validity.

Supporting Evidence

Most arguments must be supported by facts and statistics. Facts are something that is known with certainty, and have been objectively verified. Statistics may be used in selective ways to for partisan purposes. It is good to check statistics by reading authors writing on both sides of an issue. This will give a more accurate idea of how valid are the statistics cited.

Examples and illustrations add an emotional component to arguments, reaching readers in ways that facts and figures cannot. They are most effective when used in combination with objective information that can be verified. Expert opinion can contribute to a position on a question. The source should be an authority whose credentials are beyond dispute. Sometimes it is necessary to provide the credentials of the expert. Expert testimony can be quoted directly, or may be summarized by the writer. Sources must be well documented to insure their validity.

Counter Arguments

In addition to arguing a position, it is a good practice to review opposing arguments and attempt to counter them. This process can take place anywhere in the essay, but is perhaps best placed after the thesis is stated. Objections can be countered on a point-by-point analysis, or in a summary paragraph. Pointing out flaws in counter arguments is important, as is showing the counter arguments to have less weight than the supported thesis.

Building common ground with neutral or opposed readers can make a strong case. Sharing values with undecided readers can allow people to switch positions without giving up what they feel is important. People who may oppose a position need to feel they can change their minds without compromising their intelligence or their integrity. This appeal to open-mindedness can be a powerful tool in arguing a position without antagonizing opposing views.

> ➢ **Review Video: <u>Opposing Arguments and Supporting Evidence</u>**
> *Visit **mometrix.com/academy** and enter **Code: 355002***

Fallacious Arguments

A number of unreasonable argumentative tactics are known as logical fallacies. Most fallacies are misguided uses of legitimate argumentative arguments.

Generalizing is drawing a conclusion from an array of facts using inductive reasoning. These conclusions are a probability, not a certainty. The fallacy known as a "hasty generalization" is a conclusion based on insufficient or unrepresentative evidence. Stereotyping is a hasty generalization about a group. This is common because of the human tendency to perceive selectively. Observations are made through a filter of preconceptions, prejudices, and attitudes.

Analogies point out similarities between disparate things. When an analogy is unreasonable, it is called a "false analogy". This usually consists of assuming if two things are alike in one respect, they must be alike in others. This, of course, may or may not be true. Each comparison must be independently verified to make the argument valid.

Post Hoc Fallacy

Tracing cause and effect can be a complicated matter. Because of the complexity involved, writers often over-simplify it. A common error is to assume that because one event follows another, the first is the cause of the second. This common fallacy is known as "post hoc", from the Latin meaning "after this, therefore because of this".

A post hoc fallacy could run like this: "Since Abner Jones returned to the Giants lineup, the team has much better morale". The fact that Jones returned to the lineup may or may not have had an effect on team morale. The writer must show there is a cause and effect relationship between Jones' return and team morale. It is not enough to note that one event followed another. It must be proved beyond a reasonable doubt that morale was improved by the return of Jones to the lineup. The two may be true but do not necessarily follow a cause and effect pattern.

Assumptions

When considering problems and solutions, the full range of possible options should be mentioned before recommending one solution above others. It is unfair to state there are only two alternatives, when in fact there are more options. Writers who set up a choice between their preferred option and a clearly inferior one are committing the "either...or" fallacy. All reasonable alternatives should be included in the possible solutions.

Assumptions are claims that are taken to be true without proof. If a claim is controversial, proof should be provided to verify the assumption. When a claim is made that few would agree with, the writer is guilty of a "non sequitur" (Latin for "does not follow") fallacy. Thus any assumption that is subject to debate cannot be accepted without supporting evidence is suspect.

Syllogism

Deductive reasoning is constructed in a three-step method called a syllogism. The three steps are the major premise, the minor premise, and the conclusion. The major premise is a generalization, and the minor premise is a specific case. The conclusion is deduced from applying the generalization to the specific case. Deductive arguments fail if either the major or minor premise is not true, or if the conclusion does not logically follow from the premises. This means a deductive argument must stand on valid, verifiable premises, and the conclusion is a logical result of the premises.

"Straw man" Fallacy

The "straw man" fallacy consists of an oversimplification or distortion of opposing views. This fallacy is one of the most obvious and easily uncovered since it relies on gross distortions. The name comes from a side setting up a position so weak (the straw man) that is easily refuted.

Composition

Composition refers to a range of activities which include the achievement of literacy, transmission of culture, preparation for writing skills in the workplace, and writing as a mode of personal expression and identity. Composition has evolved into an interdisciplinary study and an eclectic practice. Writing is always a process, performing a critical role in education.

Composition studies, like its companion, rhetoric, is a practical and theoretical study Originally it was limited to teaching and correction of student's grammar. Composition has come of age as a writing process, a complex network of interweaving social, political, and individual components.

The field now includes collaborative writing, two or more students writing together, each assuming specific responsibilities with a heavy emphasis on joint revisions. Continued innovations and experimentation are an ongoing part of composition studies.

Literary Devices

Allusions
An allusion is a reference within a text to some person, place, or event outside the text. Allusions that refer to events more or less contemporary with the text are called topical allusions. Those referring to specific persons are called personal allusions. An example of personal allusion is William Butler Yeat's reference to "golden thighed Pythagoras" in his poem " Among School Children".

Allusions may be used to summarize an important idea or point out a contrast between contemporary life and a heroic past. An example of this would be James Joyce's classical parallels in "Ulysses" in which heroic deeds in the "Odyssey" are implicitly compared to the banal aspects of everyday life in Dublin.

Allusions may also be used to summarize an important idea such as the concluding line from "King Kong", "It was beauty killed the beast".

> ➤ **Review Video: <u>Allusion</u>**
> *Visit **mometrix.com/academy** and enter **Code: 294065***

Jargon
Jargon is a specialized language used among members of a trade, profession, or group. Jargon should be avoided and used only when the audience will be familiar with the language. Jargon includes exaggerated language usually designed to impress rather than inform. Sentences filled with jargon are both wordy and difficult to understand. Jargon is commonly used in such institutions as the military, politics, sports, and art.

Clichés
Clichés are sentences and phrases that have been overused to the point of triviality. They have no creativity or originality and add very little to modern writing. Writers should avoid clichés whenever possible. When editing writing, the best solution for clichés is to delete them. If this does not seem easily accomplished, a cliché can be modified so that it is not dully predictable and trite. This often means adding phrases or sentences to change the cliché.

Slang

Slang is an informal and sometimes private language that connotes the solidarity and exclusivity of a group such as teenagers, sports fans, ethnic groups, or rock musicians. Slang has a certain vitality, but it is not always widely understood and should be avoided in most writing. An exception could be when the audience is a specialized group who understand the jargon and slang commonly used by the members.

Sexist Language

Sexist language is language that stereotypes or demeans women or men, usually women. Such language is derived from stereotypical thinking, traditional pronoun use, and from words used to refer indefinitely to both sexes. Writers should avoid referring to a profession as being basically male or female, and using different conventions when referring to men and women. Pronouns "he,him,and his"should be avoided by using a pair of pronouns or revising the sentence to obviate the sexist language.

Pretentious Language

In an attempt to sound elegant, profound, poetic, or impressive, some writers embroider their thoughts with flowery phrases, inflated language, and generally pretentious wordage. Pretentious language is often so ornate and wordy that it obscures the true meaning of the writing.

Euphemisms

Euphemisms are pleasant sounding words that replace language that seems overly harsh or ugly. Euphemisms are wordy and indirect, clouding meaning through "pretty" words. However euphemisms are sometimes uses as conventions, when speaking about subjects such as death, bodily functions and sex.

Doublespeak

The term "doublespeak" was coined by George Orwell in his futuristic novel "1984". It applies to any evasive or deceptive language, particularly favored by politicians. Doublespeak is evident in advertising, journalism, and in political polemics. it should be avoided by serious writers.

Figures of Speech

A figure of speech is an expression that uses words imaginatively rather than literally to make abstract ideas concrete. Figures of speech compare unlike things to reveal surprising similarities. The pitfalls of using figures of speech is the failure of writers to think through the images they evoke. The result can be a mixed metaphor, a combination of two or more images that do not make sense together.

In a simile the writer makes an explicit comparison, usually by introducing it with "like" or "as". An example would be " white as a sheet" or "my love is like a red, red, rose". Effective use of similes can add color and vivid imagery to language. Used carefully and sparingly, they provide a writer with an effective device to enhance meaning and style.

Figures of speech are particularly effective when used with discretion and selectively. Examples of figures of speech can be found in all genres of writing.

> ➤ **Review Video:** Figure of Speech
> *Visit **mometrix.com/academy** and enter **Code: 111295***

Allegories

Allegories are a type of narrative in which the story reflects at least one other meaning. Traditional allegory often employs personification, the use of human characters to represent abstract ideas. Early examples of the use of allegory were the medieval mystery plays in which abstractions such as Good, Evil, Penance, and Death appeared as characters.

Another type of allegory uses a surface story to refer to historical or political events. Jonathan Swift was a master at using allegory in this manner, particularly in his "Tale of a Tub" (1704), a satirical allegory of the reformation.

Allegory has been largely replaced by symbolism by modern writers. Although they are sometimes confused, symbolism bears a natural relationship to the events in a story, while in allegory the surface story is only an excuse for the secondary and more important meaning. Allegory has had a revival in postmodern writing, and is seen in much contemporary literature.

Ambiguity

In writing historically, ambiguity is generally viewed as an error or flaw. The word now means a literary technique in which a word or phrase conveys two or more different meanings. William Empson defines ambiguity as " any verbal nuance, however slight, which gives room for alternative reactions to the same piece of language." Empons chief purpose in defining ambiguity was to note how this device affects the interpretation of poetry. Empson identified seven types of ambiguity including the traditional meaning. These seven types of ambiguity each provided a different view of possible interpretation of text in writing. Empsons's "Seven Types of Ambiguity" was the first detailed analysis of the phenomena of multiple meanings, sometimes called plurisignation. Ambiguity can be a useful device for some types of writing but does lend itself to informative or persuasive text.

Phonetics

Phonetics seeks to provide a descriptive terminology for the sounds of spoken language. This includes the physiology for the production of speech sounds, the classification of speech sounds including vowels and consonants, the dynamic features of speech production, and the study of instrumental phonetics, the investigation of human speech by laboratory techniques. The dynamic aspects of phonetics include voice quality, stress, rhythm, and speech melody.

Instrumental phonetics underlines both the complexity of speech production, and the subtlety of the human brain in interpreting a constantly changing flow of acoustic data as recognizable speech-sounds. The correlation between acoustic quality, auditory perception, and articulatory position is a complex and not yet fully understood process. It represents a fertile area of research for phoneticians, psychologists, and perhaps philosophers.

General phonetics classifies the speech sounds of all languages. Any one language uses only possibilities of the selections available. Sounds and how they are used in a language is the phonology of a language. Dynamic features of phonology include speech melody, stress, rhythmic organization, length and syllabicity. The central unit of phonology is the phoneme, the smallest distinct sound in a given language. Two words are composed of different phonemes only if they differ phonetically in ways that are found to make a difference in meaning. Phonemic transcription of a word or phrase is its representation as a sequence or other combinations of phonemes.

Phonology

Phonology is a controversial and enigmatic part of linguistics. It is widely studied and defined but there is no agreement on the definition of a phoneme or phonology theory. There may be as many theories as there are phonologies in linguistics.

Linguistics

Linguistics is the branch of knowledge that deals with language. Grammar, an integral part of linguistics, in its widest sense, includes the study of the structure of words and syntactic constructions, and that of sound systems. Linguistics is concerned with the lexical and grammatical categories of individual languages, and the differences between languages and the historical relations between families of languages. Each lexical entry informs us about the linguistic properties of the word. It will indicate a word's phonological, grammatical, and somatic properties.

1. Grammar may be said to generate a set of phrases and sentences, so linguistics is also the study of generative grammar. Grammar must also contain a phonological component, since this determines the phonetic form of words in speech.
2. Phonology, the study of sound systems and processes affecting the way words are pronounced, is another aspect of linguistics.

Psycholinguistics

Psycholinguistics is concerned with how linguistic competence is employed in the production and comprehension of speech.

1. The first step in language comprehension is to use the phonological processor to identify sounds.
2. Then the lexical processor identifies the component words.
3. Finally the syntactic processor provides a syntactic representation of the sentence.
4. The last step is for the semantic processor to compute a meaning representation for the sentence, on the basis of syntactical and lexical information supplied by previous steps in the process.

The relevant meaning of the words serves as the end-product of the process, and once this has been computed the sentence is understood. All stages of the psycholinguistic process take place in real time, so that measurements of each specific part of the process may be compared to the level of complexity of the grammar itself. Such is the experimental study of psycholinguistics applied.

Developmental Linguistics

Neurolinguistics is concerned with the physical representations of linguistic processes in the brain. The most effective way to study this is to observe the effects on language capacity in brain-injured individuals. The frontal lobe of the brain appears to be the area responsible for controlling the production of speech. As research has become more refined over the years, it is evident that language functions are located in different parts of the brain. As improved diagnostic and sophisticated imaging techniques are developed, it is anticipated that the mysteries of language capacity and competence corresponding to specific parts of the brain will become clearer. For now, our knowledge in this field is imperfect, and the process of mapping the brain for linguistic capacity and performance is limited. Neurolinguistics is closely tied to neurology and neuro-physiology.

Sociolinguistics

Sociolinguistics is the study of the relationship between language and the structure of society. It takes into account the social backgrounds of both the speaker and the addressee, the relationship between the speaker and the addressee, and the context and manner of the interaction. Because the emphasis in sociolinguistics is on language use, the analysis of language in this field is typically based on taped recordings of everyday interactions. The sociolinguists seek to discover universal properties of languages, attempting to analyze questions such as "do all languages change in the same ways"? Answers are sought to the larger questions about universals in society in which language plays a major role. The multifaceted nature of language and its broad impact on many areas of society make this field an exciting and cutting edge part of linguistics.

Meaning

Meaning is traditionally something said to be expressed by a sentence. Modern theories in linguistics often elaborate on this. The four major theories are:
1. The meaning of a sentence is different depending on the context of the utterance.
2. Sentence meanings are part of the language system and form a level of semantic representation independent of other levels.
3. Representations are derivable from the level of syntax, given a lexicon which specifies the meaning of words and a set of semantic rules.
4. The meaning of utterances follows from separate principles that are in the domain of context or pragmatics.

Other theories assert that neither words or sentences can be assigned meanings independently of situations in which they are uttered. These theories all seek to establish a standard understanding of meaning so that linguists can refine and extend their research.

Etymology

Etymology is the study of the historical relation between a word and earlier form or forms from which it has developed. Etymology can be loosely defined as the study of the origins of words. This study may occur on different levels of linguistic approach. Word meanings and their historical antecedents are often a complicated and controversial source of study. Tracing the meaning of words often includes understanding the social, political, and cultural time that the definition existed. The evolution of words from earlier forms suggests a cross-fertilization of social contexts and common usage that is a fascinating field of study.

An etymological fallacy is that the notion that a true meaning of a word can be derived from it etymology. Modern linguistic theory provides a substantial body of knowledge that compares and evaluates etymology and provides numerous avenues for new research.

Lexicology

Lexicon is the aspect of a language that is centered on individual words or similar units. Its scope varies widely from one theory to another. In some systems, lexicon is a simple component of generative grammar. In others it is the basis for all grammatical patterns. some view a lexicon as an unstructured list, while others see it as an elaborate network of entries governed by lexical rules and shared features. Lexicon in linguistics is to be distinguished as a theory from a dictionary or part of a practical description.

Lexicology is the branch of linguistics concerned with the semantic structure of the lexicon. Lexical diffusion is the gradual spread of a phonetic or other change across the vocabulary of a language or across a speech community? The term may also refer to the diffusion of individual lexical units within a lexicon.

Lexical decomposition is the analysis of word meanings into smaller units.

Grammar

Grammar may be practically defined as the study of how words are put together or the study of sentences. There are multiple approaches to grammar in modern linguistics. Any systematic account of the structure of a language and the patterns it describes is grammar. Modern definitions of grammar state grammar is the knowledge of a language developed in the minds of the speakers.

A grammar in the broadest sense is a set of rules internalized by members of a speech community, and an account, by a linguist, of such a grammar. This internalized grammar is what is commonly called a language. Grammar is often restricted to units that have meaning. The expanded scope of grammar includes morphology and syntax, and a lexicon. Grammatical meaning is described as part of the syntax and morphology of a language as distinct from its lexicon.

The ability to learn language is determined by a biologically determined innate language facility. This widely accepted theory is known as the innateness hypothesis. The knowledge of adult grammar appears to go far beyond anything supplied by the child's linguistic experience, implying an innate ability to learn language. A language facility must incorporate a set of Universal Grammar principles which enable a child to form and interpret sentences in any natural language. Children have the ability to acquire any natural language so it follows that the contents of the innate language facility must not be specific to any one human language. Developmental linguistics is concerned with examining children's grammar and the conditions under which they emerge. The language faculty is species-specific and the ability to develop a grammar of a language is unique to human beings. The study of non-human communication forms a different field of study.

Structuralized Grammar

Structuralize grammar tends to be formal in nature as it is concerned with grammatical and phonological considerations, rather than semantics. The chief goal is to uncover the structure of a language. There are valid criticisms of the structural approach to grammar. problems exist in the available descriptive frameworks to manage, difficulties with definitions, and inconsistency and contradiction between theory and practice. These concerns have not invalidated the study of structural grammar, but have been utilized by linguists to perfect the analysis.

Transformational Grammar

Transformational grammar is any grammar in which different syntactic structures are related by transformations. The main role of transformations was to relate the sentences of a language as a whole to a small set of kernel sentences. A base component of a grammar generated a deep structure for each sentence. these structures were an input to a transformational component, which was an ordered structure of transformational rules. Its output was a set of surface structures, which combined with the deep structures, formed its syntactic description. Further rules supplied its semantic representation and phonetic representation.

Transformational grammar was invented and promulgated by Noam Chomsky, a revolutionary figure in linguistics. Much of Chomsky's work has been directed to the development of a universal grammar, conceived as an account of what is inherited by the individual. Chomsky remains the dominant figure of the 20th century in linguistics.

Sentences

The largest structural unit normally recognized by grammar is the sentence. Any attempt to accurately define the sentence is in error. Any such definition will not bear up under Linguistic Analysis. In every language, there are a limited number of favorite sentence-types to which most others can be related. They vary from language to language. Certain utterances, while not immediately conforming to favorite sentence types, can be expanded in their context to become one sentence of a particular type. These can be called referable sentences. Other utterances that do not conform to favorite sentence types may reveal obsolete sentence types; these are proverbial sayings and are called gnomic or fossilized sentences. A very small number of utterances not conforming to the favorite sentence-types are found in prescribed social situations, such as "Hello" or "Bye".

Sentence Patterns
Sentence patterns fall into five common modes with some exceptions. They are:
1. Subject / linking verb / subject complement
2. Subject / transitive verb / direct object
3. Subject / transitive verb / indirect object / direct object
4. Subject / transitive verb / direct object / object complement
5. Subject / intransitive verb

Common exceptions to these patterns are questions and commands, sentences with delayed subjects, and passive transformations. Writers sometimes use the passive voice when the active voice would be more appropriate.

Sentences Classification
Sentences are classified in two ways:
1. according to their structure
2. according to their purpose

Writers use declarative sentences to make statements, imperative sentences to issue requests or commands, interrogative sentences to ask questions, and exclamatory sentences to make exclamations.

Depending on the number and types of clauses they contain, sentences may be classified as simple, compound, complex, or compound-complex.
Clauses come in two varieties: independent and subordinate.
1. An independent clause is a full sentence pattern that does not function within another sentence pattern; it contains a subject and modifiers plus a verb and any objects, complements, and modifiers of that verb. It either stands alone or could stand alone.
2. A subordinate clause is a full sentence pattern that functions within a sentence as an adjective, an adverb, or a noun but that cannot stand alone as a complete sentence.

Sentence Structures
The four major types of sentence structure are:
1. Simple sentences - Simple sentences have one independent clause with no subordinate clauses. a simple sentence may contain compound elements,- a compound subject, verb, or object for example, but does not contain more than one full sentence pattern.

2. Compound sentences - Compound sentences are composed of two or more independent clauses with no subordinate clauses. The independent clauses are usually joined with a comma and a coordinating conjunction, or with a semicolon.
3. Complex sentences - A complex sentence is composed of one independent clause with one or more dependent clauses.
4. Compound-complex sentences - A compound-complex sentence contains at least two independent clauses and at least one subordinate clause. sometimes they contain two full sentence patters that can stand alone. When each independent clause contains a subordinate clause, this makes the sentence both compound and complex.

> **Review Video:** Sentence Structure
*Visit **mometrix.com/academy** and enter **Code: 958982***

Chomsky's Sentence Structure
Deep structure is a representation of the syntax of a sentence distinguished by various criteria from its surface structure. Initially defined by Noam Chomsky as the part of the syntactic description of a of a sentence that determines its semantic interpretation by the base component of a generative grammar.

Surface sentence structure is a representation of the syntax of a sentence seen as deriving by one ore more transformations, from a an underlying deep structure. Such a sentence is in the order in which the corresponding phonetic forms are spoken. Surface structure was later broadened by Chomsky to include semantic structure. Chomsky's later minimalist program no longer takes this for granted. Minimalist theory assumes no more than a minimum of types of statements and levels of representation.

The technical analysis outlined by Chomsky over three decades forms an integral part of transformational grammar.

Language Investigation

The investigation of a language by classification is the goal of the modern linguist. When the observer has determined the phonemic structure of a language, and has classified all its constructions, both morphological and syntactic, the resulting description will be an accurate and usable grammar of the language, accounting in the simplest way for all the utterances of the speech community.

Language Families

A language family is a group of languages that have been developed from a single ancestor. An example would be Indo-European, of which English is one of many members. Language families are identified whenever a common origin can be accepted as certain. When a family origin in speculative or uncertain, it may be called a projected family, a proposed family, or a probable family.

Some linguists have tried to apply a biological method of classification of language families, following the genus, order, species model. They have classed languages as beginning with "superficies", "macro families", "stocks", "super stocks", or "phyla" at the top. Below those will be "subfamilies", "branches", and "groups". This attempt has proved faulty as the classifications imply more than is known about family origins. It has been difficult and largely unaccepted to class language families in these descending modes of importance.

Language Descriptions

The levels of language descriptions represent a distinct phase in the description of a language at which specific types of elements and the relations between them are studied or investigated.
1. At the level of phonology, one studies the sound structure of a language, words or larger units that are specific to that level.
2. At the level of syntax, sentences are represented as the configuration of words or morphemes standing in specific construction in relationship to one another.

Levels of language are an important part of structural linguistics, whether they focus on formal analyses or representation. Some give an order of procedures which govern the formal structural analysis of language. Others propose a hierarchy of greater or lesser degrees of abstraction, ranging from phonetics as the highest and semantics as the lowest. In many of these levels are defined by the different components of an integrated structural grammar.

Morphology

Morphology is the grammatical structure of words and their categories. The morphological process includes any of the formal processes or operations by which the forms of words are derived from stems or roots. Types of morphological processes include affix, any element in the structure of a word other than a root; reduplication, where all or part of a form is duplicated; subtraction, where part of a form is deleted; supple ton, where one part of the morphological process replaces another; compound, where two parts of the morphological process are joined; and modification, where one part of a form is modified.

Forms of morphological classification distinguished isolating, in which each grammatical classification is represented by a single word, agglutinating, where words are easily divided into separate sections, and inflectional, concerned with inflections in languages.

Functions of Language

1. Language is a means of social control making human society possible. The communication of thoughts is but a small part of this.
2. Language acts as an index to various things about the speaker - age, sex, physical and mental wellbeing, and personality characteristics.
3. Language acts to limit classes within a society, either by accent, dialect, choice of words and grammatical features.
4. Language brings human beings into relationship with the external world. It mediates between man and his environment.
5. Language is the material of artistic creation, including not only literary works but poetic and oral traditions.

Any list of languages functions is arbitrary. There are dozens of other possible classifications of language functions in the literature of linguistics. The classification given above includes the basic elements of language and their societal effect.

Semantics

Semantics studies the meaning of utterances and why particular utterances have the meanings they do. Semantics originally covered grammar, the account of meaningful forms, and the lexicon or body of words contained in a language. When the study of forms was separated from that of meanings, the field of generative grammar became associated with semantics. Currently, the scope of semantics will cover word meanings or lexical semantics, and the meaning of utterances studied in pragmatics, the meaning of language in everyday life.

Some narrow definitions of semantics understand the term to mean the study of problems encounted in formal semantics, excluding lexical meaning completely. This last definition is an extreme one, and is included to illustrate the broad vistas that are opened when we discuss semantics. What can be asserted is that semantics in its broadest and most common usage is the field of study in linguistics that deals with meaning in all its forms.

Spoken and Written Language

The relationship of spoken language and written form has been the subject of differences of attitudes among linguists. The spoken form is historically prior, both for the language community and the individual. It is also more complicated. For these reasons, emphasis is placed on the sound systems of languages which has led some linguists to describe the spoken form as language, and the written form as written language. Both are equal examples of language. The relationship is not a straightforward case of deriving the written from the spoken form. When a written form evolves, it tends to take on a life of its own and acquires usages different from the spoken. Linguists are concerned with the analysis and development of language as a whole, both written and spoken. Much of the controversy in linguistic theory is concerned with both forms of languages. Linguistics is in a sense a search for the universals in language, which includes both spoken and written forms.

Parts of Speech

Nouns
Nouns are the name of a person, place, or thing, and are usually signaled by an article (a, an, the). Nouns sometimes function as adjectives modifying other nouns. Nouns used in this manner are called noun/adjectives. Nouns are classified for a number of purposes: capitalization, word choice, count/no count nouns, and collective nouns are examples.

Pronouns
Pronouns is a word used in place of a noun. Usually the pronoun substitutes for the specific noun, called the antecedent. Although most pronouns function as substitutes for nouns, some can function as adjectives modifying nouns. pronouns may be classed as personal, possessive, intensive, relative, interrogative, demonstrative, indefinite, and reciprocal. pronouns can cause a number of problems for writers including pronoun-antecedent agreement, distinguishing between who and whom, and differentiating pronouns such as I and me.

> ➤ **Review Video: Nouns and Pronouns**
> *Visit **mometrix.com/academy** and enter **Code: 312073***

Problems with Pronouns
Pronouns are words that substitute for nouns: he, it, them, her, me, and so on. Four frequently encountered problems with pronouns include:

1. Pronoun - antecedent agreement - The antecedent of a pronoun is the word the pronoun refers to. A pronoun and its antecedent agree when they are both singular or plural.
2. Pronoun reference - A pronoun should refer clearly to its antecedent. A pronoun's reference will be unclear if it id ambiguous, implied, vague, or indefinite.
3. Personal pronouns - Some pronouns change their case form according to their grammatical structure in a sentence. Pronouns functioning as subjects appear in the subjective case, those functioning as objects appear in the objective case, and those functioning as possessives appear in the possessive case.
4. Who or whom - Who, a subjective-case pronoun, can only be used subjects and subject complements. Whom, an objective case pronoun, can only be used for objects. The words who and whom appear primarily in subordinate clauses or in questions.

Verbs

The verb of a sentence usually expresses action or being. It is composed of a main verb and sometimes supporting verbs. These helping verbs are forms of have, do, and be, and nine modals. The modals are "can, could, may, might, shall, should, will, would, and ought". Some verbs are followed by words that look like prepositions, but are so closely associated with the verb to be part of its meaning. These words are known as particles, and examples include "call off", "look up", and "drop off".

The main verb of a sentence is always one that would change form from base form to past tense, past participle, present participle and, -s forms. When both the past-tense and past-participle forms of a verb end in "ed", the verb is regular. In all other cases the verb is irregular. The verb "be" is highly irregular, having eight forms instead of the usual five.

1. Linking verbs link the subject to a subject complement, a word or word group that completes the meaning of the subject by renaming or describing it.
2. A transitive verb takes a direct object, a word or word group that names a receiver of the action. The direct object of a transitive verb is sometimes preceded by an indirect object. Transitive verbs usually appear in the active voice, with a subject doing the action and a direct object receiving the action. The direct object of a transitive verb is sometimes followed by an object complement, a word or word group that completes the direct object's meaning by renaming or describing it.
3. Intransitive verbs take no objects or complements. Their pattern is subject verb.

A dictionary will disclose whether a verb is transitive or intransitive. Some verbs have both transitive and intransitive functions.

➢ **Review Video:** <u>**Subjects and Verbs**</u>
Visit ***mometrix.com/academy*** *and enter* ***Code:*** **987207**

Verb Phrases

A verbal phrase is a verb form that does not function as the verb of a clause. There are three major types of verbal phrases:
1. Participial phrases - These always function as adjectives. Their verbals are always present participles, always ending in "ing", or past participles frequently ending in "-d,-ed,-n.-en,or -t". Participial phrases frequently appear immediately following the noun or pronoun they modify.

2. Gerund phrases - Gerund phrases are built around present participles and they always function as nouns. : usually as subjects subject complements, direct objects, or objects of a preposition.
3. Infinitive phrases are usually structured around "to" plus the base form of the verb. they can function as nouns, as adjectives, or as adverbs. When functioning as a noun, an infinitive phrase may appear in almost any noun slot in a sentence, usually as a subject, subject complement, or direct object. Infinitive phrases functioning as adjectives usually appear immediately following the noun or pronoun they modify. adverbial phrases usually qualify the meaning of the verb.

Problems with Verbs

The verb is the heart of the sentence. Verbs have several potential problems including:
1. Irregular verbs - Verbs that do not follow usual grammatical rules.
2. Tense - Tenses indicate the time of an action in relation to the time of speaking or writing about the action.
3. Mood - There are three moods in English: the indicative, used for facts, opinions, and questions; the imperative, used for orders or advice, and the subjunctive, used for wishes. The subjective mood is the most likely to cause problems. The subjective mood is used for wishes, and in "if"clauses expressing conditions contrary to facts. The subjective in such cases is the past tense form of the verb; in the case of "be", it is always "were", even if the subject is singular. The subjective mood is also used in "that' clauses following verbs such as "ask, insist, recommend, and request. The subjunctive in such cases is the base or dictionary form of the verb.

Adjectives

An adjective is a word use to modify or describe a noun or pronoun. An adjective usually answers one of these question: "Which one?, What kind of?, and How many?" Adjectives usually precede the words they modify, although they sometimes follow linking verbs, in which case they describe the subject. Most adjectives have three forms: the positive, the comparative, and the superlative. The comparative should be used to compare two things, the superlative to compare three or more things.

Articles

Articles, sometimes classed as adjectives, are used to mark nouns. There are only three: the definite article "the" and the indefinite articles "a" and "an."

Adverbs

An adverb is a word used to modify or qualify a verb, adjective, or another adverb. It usually answers one of these questions: "When?, where?, how?, and why?" Adverbs modifying adjectives or other adverbs usually intensify or limit the intensity of words they modify. The negators "not" and "never" are classified as adverbs. Writers sometimes misuse adverbs, and multilingual speakers have trouble placing them correctly. Most adverbs also have three forms: the positive, the comparative, and the superlative. The comparative should be used to compare two things, the superlative to compare three or more things.

> **Review Video: Adjectives and Adverbs**
*Visit **mometrix.com/academy** and enter **Code: 520888***

Prepositions

A preposition is a word placed before a noun or pronoun to form a phrase modifying another word in the sentence. The prepositional phrase usually functions as an adjective or adverb. There are a limited number of prepositions in English, perhaps around 80. Some prepositions are more than one word long. "Along with", "listen to", and "next to" are some examples.

> ➤ **Review Video: What is a Preposition?**
> *Visit **mometrix.com/academy** and enter **Code: 946763***

Conjunctions

Conjunctions join words, phrases, or clauses, and they indicate the relationship between the elements that are joined. There are coordinating conjunctions that connect grammatically equal element, correlative conjunctions that connect pairs, subordinating conjunctions that introduces a subordinate clause, and conjunctive adverbs which may be used with a semicolon to connect independent clauses. The most common conjunctive adverbs include "then, thus, and however". Using adverbs correctly helps avoid sentence fragments and run-on sentences.

> ➤ **Review Video: Conjunctions**
> *Visit **mometrix.com/academy** and enter **Code: 904603***

Subjects

The subject of a sentence names who or what the sentence is about. The complete subject is composed of the simple subject and all of its modifiers.

To find the complete subject, ask "Who" or "What", and insert the verb to complete the question. The answer is the complete subject. To find the simple subject, strip away all the modifiers in the complete subject.

In imperative sentences, the verb's subject is understood but not actually present in the sentence. Although the subject ordinarily comes before the verb, sentences that begin with "There are" or "There was", the subject follows the verb.

The ability to recognize the subject of a sentence helps in editing a variety of problems such as sentence fragments and subject-verb agreement, as well as the choice of pronouns.

> ➤ **Review Video: Subjects**
> *Visit **mometrix.com/academy** and enter **Code: 444771***

Subordinate Word Groups

Subordinate word groups cannot stand alone. They function only within sentences, as adjectives, adverbs, or nouns.
1. Prepositional phrases begins with a preposition and ends with a noun or noun equivalent called its object. Prepositional phrases function as adjectives or adverbs.
2. Subordinate clauses are patterned like sentences, having subject, verbs, and objects or complements. They function within sentences as adverbs, adjectives, or nouns.
3. Adjective clauses modify nouns or pronouns and begin with a relative pronoun or relative adverb.

4. Adverb clauses modify verbs, adjectives, and other adverbs.
5. Noun clauses function as subjects, objects, or complements. In both adjective and noun clauses words may appear out of their normal order. The parts of a noun clause may also appear in their normal order.

Appositive and Absolute Phrases

Strictly speaking, appositive phrases are not subordinate word groups. Appositive phrases function somewhat as adjectives do, to describe nouns or pronouns. Instead of modifying nouns or pronouns however, appositive phrases rename them. In form they are nouns or nouns equivalents. Appositives are said to be in " in apposition" to the nouns or pronouns they rename. For example, in the sentence "Terriers, hunters at heart, have been dandled up to look like lap dogs", "hunters at heart" is apposition to the noun "terriers".

An absolute phrase modifies a whole clause or sentence, not just one word, and it may appear nearly anywhere in the sentence. It consists of a noun or noun equivalent usually followed by a participial phrase. Both appositive and absolute phrases can cause confusion in their usage in grammatical structures. They are particularly difficult for a person whose first language is not English.

Common Problems with Sentences

Subject-Verb Agreement
In the present tense, verbs agree with their subjects in number, (singular or plural), and in person, (first ,second, or third). The present tense ending -s is used on a verb if its subject is third person singular; otherwise the verb takes no ending. The verb "be" varies from this pattern, and alone among verbs it has special forms in both the present and past tense.

Problems with subject-verb agreement tend to arise in certain contexts:
1. Words between subject and verbs.
2. Subjects joined by "and".
3. Subjects joined by "or" or "nor".
4. Indefinite pronouns such as "someone".
5. Collective nouns.
6. Subject after verb.
7. Who, which, and that.
8. Plural form, singular meaning.
9. Titles, company names, and words mentioned as words.

> ➤ **Review Video: Subject Verb Agreement**
> *Visit mometrix.com/academy and enter Code: 479190*

Sentence Fragments
As a rule a part of a sentence should not be treated as a complete sentence. A sentence must be composed of at least one full independent clause. An independent clause has a subject, a verb, and can stand alone as a sentence. Some fragments are clauses that contain a subject and a verb, but begin with a subordinating word. Other fragments lack a subject, verb, or both.

A sentence fragment can be repaired by combining the fragment with a nearby sentence, punctuating the new sentence correctly, or turn the fragment into a sentence by adding the missing elements. Some sentence fragments are used by writers for emphasis. Although sentence fragments are sometimes acceptable, readers and writers do not always agree on when they are appropriate. A conservative approach is to write in complete sentences only unless a special circumstance dictates otherwise.

Run-on Sentences

Run-on sentences are independent clauses that have not been joined correctly. An independent clause is a word group that does or could stand alone in a sentence. When two or more independent clauses appear in one sentence, they must be joined in one of these ways:

1. Revision with a comma and a coordinating conjunction.
2. Revision with a semicolon, a colon, or a dash. Used when independent clauses are closely related and their relationship is clear without a coordinating conjunction.
3. Revision by separating sentences. This approach may be used when both independent clauses are long,
4. or if one is a question and one is not. Separate sentences may be the best option in this case.
5. Revision by restructuring the sentence. For sentence variety, consider restructuring the sentence, perhaps by turning one of the independent clauses into a subordinate phrase or clause.

Usually one of these choices will be an obvious solution to the run-on sentence. The fourth technique above is often the most effective solution, but requires the most revision.

> ➤ **Review Video: Fragments and Run-On Sentences**
> *Visit mometrix.com/academy and enter Code:* **541989**

Double Negatives

Standard English allows two negatives only if a positive meaning is intended. "The team was not displeased with their performance" is an example. Double negatives used to emphasize negation are nonstandard.

Negative modifiers such as "never, no, and not" should not be paired with other negative modifiers or negative words such as " none, nobody, nothing, or neither". The modifiers "hardly, barely, and scarcely" are also considered negatives in standard English, so they should not be used with other negatives such as "not, no one, or never".

> ➤ **Review Video: Double Negatives**
> *Visit mometrix.com/academy and enter Code:* **920016**

Double Superlatives

Do not use double superlatives or comparatives. When "er" or "est" has been added to an adjective or adverb, avoid using "more" or "most". Avoid expressions such as "more perfect", and "very round". Either something is or is not. It is not logical to suggest that absolute concepts come in degrees. Use the comparative to compare two things, and the superlative to compare three or more things.

Punctuation

<u>Commas</u>
The comma was invented to help readers. Without it, sentence parts can run together, making meanings unclear. Various rules for comma use include:
1. Use a comma between a coordinating conjunction joining independent clauses.
2. Use a comma after an introductory clause or phrase.
3. Use a comma between items in a series.
4. Use a comma between coordinate adjectives not joined with "and". Do not use a comma between cumulative adjectives.
5. Use commas to set off nonrestrictive elements. Do not use commas to set off restrictive elements.
6. Use commas to set off transitional and parenthetical expressions, absolute phrases, and elements expressing contrast.
7. Use commas to set off nouns of direct address, the words yes and no, interrogative tags, and interjections.
8. Use commas with dates, addresses, titles, and numbers.

Some situations where commas are unnecessary include:
1. Do not use a comma between compound elements that are not independent clauses.
2. Do not use a comma after a phrase that begins with an inverted sentence.
3. Do not use a comma between the first or after the last item in a series or before the word "although".
4. Do not use a comma between cumulative adjectives, between an adjective and a noun, or between an adverb and an adjective.
5. Do not use commas to set off restrictive or mildly parenthetical elements or to set off an indirect quotation.
6. Do not use a comma to set off a concluding adverb clause that is essential to the meaning of the sentence or after the word "although".
7. Do not use a comma to separate a verb from its subject or object. Do not use a comma after a coordinating conjunction or before a parenthesis.
8. Do not use a comma with a question mark or an exclamation point.
9. Use commas to prevent confusion.
10. Use commas to set off direct quotations.

> ➤ **Review Video:** <u>**Commas**</u>
*Visit **mometrix.com/academy** and enter **Code:** 770334*

<u>Semicolons</u>
The semicolon is used to connect major sentence elements of equal grammatical rank. Some rules regarding semicolons include:
1. Use a semicolon between closely related independent clauses not joined with a coordinating conjunction.
2. Use a semicolon between independent clauses linked with a transitional expression.
3. Use a semicolon between items in a series containing internal punctuation.
4. Avoid using a semicolon between a subordinate clause and the rest of the sentence.
5. Avoid using a semicolon between an appositive word and the word it refers to.

6. Avoid using a semicolon to introduce a list.
7. Avoid using a semicolon between independent clauses joined by "and, but, or, nor, for, so, or yet".

➤ **Review Video: Semi-Colon Usage**
*Visit **mometrix.com/academy** and enter **Code: 370605***

Colons

The colon is used primarily to call attention to the words that follow it. In addition the colon has some other conventional uses:
1. Use a colon after an independent clause to direct attention to a list, an appositive, or a quotation.
2. Use a colon between independent clauses if the second summarizes or explains the first.
3. Use a colon after the salutation in a formal letter, to indicate hours and minutes, to show proportions between a title and subtitle, and between city and publisher in bibliographic entries.

A colon must be preceded by a full independent clause. Avoid using colons in the following situations:
1. Avoid using a colon between a verb and its object or complement.
2. Avoid using a colon between a preposition and its object.
3. Avoid using a colon after "such as, including, or for example"

➤ **Review Video: Colons**
*Visit **mometrix.com/academy** and enter **Code: 868673***

Apostrophes

An apostrophe is used to indicate that a noun is possessive. Possessive nouns usually indicate ownership, as in Bill's coat or the dog's biscuit. Sometimes ownership is only loosely implied, as in the dog's coat or the forest's trees. If it is unclear whether a noun is possessive, turning into phrase may clarify it.

If the noun is plural and ends in-s, add only an apostrophe. To show joint possession, use -'s with the last noun only. To show individual possession, make all nouns possessive.

An apostrophe is often optional in plural numbers, letters, abbreviations, and words mentioned as words.

Common errors in using apostrophes include:
1. Do not use an apostrophe with nouns that are not possessive.
2. Do not use an apostrophe in the possessive pronouns "its, whose, his, hers, ours, yours, and theirs".

➤ **Review Video: Apostrophes**
*Visit **mometrix.com/academy** and enter **Code: 213068***

Quotation Marks

Use quotation marks to enclose direct quotations of a person's words, spoken or written. Do not use quotation marks around indirect quotations. An indirect quotation reports someone's ideas without using that person's exact words.

Set off long quotations of prose or poetry by indenting. Use single quotation marks to enclose a quotation within a quotation. Quotation marks should be used around the titles of short works: newspaper and magazine articles, poems, short stories, songs, episodes of television and radio programs, and subdivisions of books or web sites.

Quotation marks may be used to set off words used as words. Punctuation is used with quotation marks according to convention. Periods and commas are placed inside quotation marks, while colons and semicolons are placed outside quotation marks. Question marks and exclamation points are placed inside quotation marks.

Do not use quotation marks around the title of your own essay.

Dashes
When typing, use two hyphens to form a dash. Do not put spaces before or after the dash. Dashes are used for the following purposes:
1. To set off parenthetical material that deserves emphasis.
2. To set off appositives that contain commas.
3. To prepare for a list, a restatement, an amplification, or a dramatic shift in tone or thought.

Unless there is a specific reason for using the dash, omit it. It can give text a choppy effect.

> **Review Video:** Dashes
*Visit **mometrix.com/academy** and enter **Code:* 351706**

Parentheses
Parentheses are used to enclose supplemental material, minor digressions, and afterthoughts. They are also used to enclose letters or numbers labeling them items in a series. Parentheses should be used sparingly, as they break up text in a distracting manner when overused.

> **Review Video:** Parentheses
*Visit **mometrix.com/academy** and enter **Code:* 947743**

Brackets
Brackets are used to enclose any words or phrases that have been inserted into an otherwise word-for-word quotation.

> **Review Video:** Brackets
*Visit **mometrix.com/academy** and enter **Code:* 727546**

Ellipsis Marks
The ellipsis mark consists of three spaced periods (...), and is used to indicate when certain words have been deleted from an otherwise word-for-word quotation. If a full sentence or more is deleted in the middle of quoted passage, a person should be inserted before the ellipsis dots. The ellipsis mark should not be used at the beginning of a quotation. It should also not be used at the end of a quotation unless some words have been deleted from the end of the final sentence.

> **Review Video:** Ellipsis
*Visit **mometrix.com/academy** and enter **Code:* 402626**

<u>Slashes</u>

The slash, (/), may be used to separate two or three lines of poetry that have been run into a text. If there are more than three lines of poetry they should be handled as an indented quotation. The slash may occasionally be used to separate paired terms such as passed/failed or either/or. In this case, apace is not placed before or after the slash. The slash should be used sparingly, only when it is clearly appropriate.

> **Review Video:** <u>Slashes</u>
Visit **mometrix.com/academy** *and enter* **Code: 881954**

<u>End Punctuations</u>
1. Use a period to end all sentences except direct questions or genuine exclamations. Periods should be used in abbreviations according to convention. Problems can arise when there is a choice between a period and a question mark or exclamation point. If a sentence reports a question rather than asking it directly, it should end with a period, not a question mark.
2. Question marks should be used following a direct question. If a polite request is written in the form of a question, it may be followed by a period. Questions in a series may be followed by question marks even when they are not in complete sentences.
3. Exclamation marks are used after a word group or sentence that expresses exceptional feeling or deserves special emphasis. Exclamation marks should not be overused, being reserved for appropriate exclamatory interjections.

Essays

Essays are generally defined to describe a prose composition, relatively brief (rarely exceeding 25 pages), dealing with a specific topic. Originally, essays tended to be informal in tone and exploratory and tentative in approach and conclusions. In more modern writing, essays have divided into the formal and informal. The formal essays have dominated the professional and scientific fields, while the informal style is written primarily to entertain or give opinions. Writers should be mindful of the style of essay their subject lends itself to, and conform to the conventions of that style.

Some types of essays, particularly scientific and academic writing, have style manuals to guide the format and conventions of the writing. The Modern Language Association and the American Psychological Association have two of the most widely followed style manuals. They are widely available for writers' reference.

Practice Test #1

Practice Questions

Questions 1 to9 pertain to the following scenario:

The Story of an Hour
by Kate Chopin (1894)

1   Knowing that Mrs. Mallard was afflicted with a heart trouble, great care was taken to break to her as gently as possible the news of her husband's death.

2   It was her sister Josephine who told her, in broken sentences; veiled hints that revealed in half concealing. Her husband's friend Richards was there, too, near her. It was he who had been in the newspaper office when intelligence of the railroad disaster was received, with Brently Mallard's name leading the list of "killed." He had only taken the time to assure himself of its truth by a second telegram, and had hastened to forestall any less careful, less tender friend in bearing the sad message.

3   She did not hear the story as many women have heard the same, with a paralyzed inability to accept its significance. She wept at once, with sudden, wild abandonment, in her sister's arms. When the storm of grief had spent itself she went away to her room alone. She would have no one follow her.

4   There stood, facing the open window, a comfortable, roomy armchair. Into this she sank, pressed down by a physical exhaustion that haunted her body and seemed to reach into her soul.

5   She could see in the open square before her house the tops of trees that were all aquiver with the new spring life. The delicious breath of rain was in the air. In the street below a peddler was crying his wares. The notes of a distant song which some one was singing reached her faintly, and countless sparrows were twittering in the eaves.

6   There were patches of blue sky showing here and there through the clouds that had met and piled one above the other in the west facing her window.

7   She sat with her head thrown back upon the cushion of the chair, quite motionless, except when a sob came up into her throat and shook her, as a child who has cried itself to sleep continues to sob in its dreams.

8   She was young, with a fair, calm face, whose lines bespoke repression and even a certain strength. But now there was a dull stare in her eyes, whose gaze was fixed away off yonder on one of those patches of blue sky. It was not a glance of reflection, but rather indicated a suspension of intelligent thought.

9   There was something coming to her and she was waiting for it, fearfully. What was it? She did not know; it was too subtle and elusive to name. But she felt it,

creeping out of the sky, reaching toward her through the sounds, the scents, the color that filled the air.

10   Now her bosom rose and fell tumultuously. She was beginning to recognize this thing that was approaching to possess her, and she was striving to beat it back with her will - as powerless as her two white slender hands would have been.

11   When she abandoned herself a little whispered word escaped her slightly parted lips. She said it over and over under her breath: "free, free, free!" The vacant stare and the look of terror that had followed it went from her eyes. They stayed keen and bright. Her pulses beat fast, and the coursing blood warmed and relaxed every inch of her body.

12   She did not stop to ask if it were or were not a monstrous joy that held her. A clear and exalted perception enabled her to dismiss the suggestion as trivial.

13   She knew that she would weep again when she saw the kind, tender hands folded in death; the face that had never looked save with love upon her, fixed and gray and dead. But she saw beyond that bitter moment a long procession of years to come that would belong to her absolutely. And she opened and spread her arms out to them in welcome.

14   There would be no one to live for during those coming years; she would live for herself. There would be no powerful will bending hers in that blind persistence with which men and women believe they have a right to impose a private will upon a fellow-creature. A kind intention or a cruel intention made the act seem no less a crime as she looked upon it in that brief moment of illumination.

15   And yet she had loved him - sometimes. Often she had not. What did it matter! What could love, the unsolved mystery, count for in face of this possession of self-assertion which she suddenly recognized as the strongest impulse of her being!

16   "Free! Body and soul free!" she kept whispering.

17   Josephine was kneeling before the closed door with her lips to the keyhole, imploring for admission. "Louise, open the door! I beg, open the door - you will make yourself ill. What are you doing Louise? For heaven's sake open the door."

18   "Go away. I am not making myself ill." No; she was drinking in a very elixir of life through that open window.

19   Her fancy was running riot along those days ahead of her. Spring days, and summer days, and all sorts of days that would be her own. She breathed a quick prayer that life might be long. It was only yesterday she had thought with a shudder that life might be long.

20   She arose at length and opened the door to her sister's importunities. There was a feverish triumph in her eyes, and she carried herself unwittingly like a

goddess of Victory. She clasped her sister's waist, and together they descended the stairs. Richards stood waiting for them at the bottom.

21   Some one was opening the front door with a latchkey. It was Brently Mallard who entered, a little travel-stained, composedly carrying his grip-sack and umbrella. He had been far from the scene of accident, and did not even know there had been one. He stood amazed at Josephine's piercing cry; at Richards' quick motion to screen him from the view of his wife.

22   But Richards was too late.

23   When the doctors came they said she had died of heart disease - of joy that kills.

1. Why does the first sentence/paragraph say great care was taken to break the news as gently as possible to Mrs. Mallard?
    a. Because the news would be a big shock to anyone
    b. Because she was known to have a heart condition
    c. Because she was known for her emotional fragility
    d. Because everybody always protected her from life

2. In paragraph 2, what is the most accurate meaning of "veiled hints that revealed in half concealing"?
    a. Josephine concealed the full truth from her sister.
    b. Josephine revealed the truth, but concealed half.
    c. Josephine revealed the truth by half concealing it.
    d. Josephine concealed the truth by half revealing it.

3. What can you infer from the text about Richards?
    a. Richards felt protective toward Louise Mallard.
    b. Richards was Brently's friend, but not Louise's.
    c. Richards jumped to a conclusion about Brently.
    d. Richards knew of the accident via being there.

4. Based on textual evidence, what can you conclude about the main character as a person?
    a. She always hid her feelings from everyone around her.
    b. She had to reflect on news before having any reaction.
    c. She reacted very emotionally, but did not contemplate.
    d. She was passionate, self-controlled, and introspective.

5. Which of the following best describes a central theme in this story?
    a. How individual selfhood can supersede any relationship
    b. How guilt over not loving someone can cause a downfall
    c. How loving someone too much can end with heartbreak
    d. How loss can completely change someone's personality

6. How do the descriptive details of springtime in paragraph 5 function thematically in the story?
   a. They serve as a contrast of new life versus the death of the husband.
   b. They serve as a comparison reflecting the new life Louise envisioned.
   c. They serve to draw readers into the scene, but without any meaning.
   d. They serve to accomplish both (a) and (b) together in different ways.

7. Which choice comes closest to characterizing the irony of the story's final sentence/paragraph?
   a. That her joy over seeing her husband was still alive killed her
   b. That his being alive was a stronger shock than his having died
   c. That her heart condition made intense emotions fatal for her
   d. That her life was cut short just when learning it was not over

8. In paragraph 5, the word choice in "a peddler was crying his wares" echoes which of these?
   a. The "delicious breath of rain" that could be felt in the air
   b. The "notes of a distant song" that someone was singing
   c. The account that the main character had been weeping
   d. That "countless sparrows were twittering in the eaves"

9. Based on the text, which choice do you think is closest to the author's point of view toward marriage in the 19th century?
   a. It was more than worth the sacrifices it required.
   b. It ultimately would never allow equal partnership.
   c. It only imposed one's will on another without love.
   d. It met the necessity of living for another individual.

Questions 10 to 20 pertain to the following scenario:

An Empty Desk is an Opportunity Missed

1   When students miss class, not only do they lose out on important instructional time, but they also miss opportunities to build critical connections with other students and adults. While students are identified as truant when they miss multiple unexcused days of school in a row, students who miss many non-sequential days (excused or unexcused) can fly under the radar. When these absences add up to more or a month or more of school, students are considered "chronically absent."

2   At a national level, an estimate 7.5 million students are considered chronically absent each year. In some states, this translates to 1 in 5 students that do not regularly attend.

3   While missing one or two days of school each month may seem like a non-issue, time away can quickly accumulate and negatively impact mathematics and reading achievement during that school year as well as in the years that follow. For example, chronic absence in kindergarten has a negative impact on academic performance and socio-emotional skills, critical building blocks to success.

4   "Students cannot learn or develop or demonstrate how brilliant they are if they are not in school on time every day," said David Johns, executive Director of the White House Initiative on Educational Excellence for African Americans. "It is

essential that all caring and concerned adults help ensure our students show up, feel safe and are engaged in the spaces they need to move through daily."

5   African American youth are more likely to miss school as they face more barriers to attendance, such as logistical challenges (think unreliable transportation), school suspension/expulsion or residential instability (consider homelessness or frequent moves). Fortunately, there is an old proverb that guides us to the solution: it takes a village to ensure that all children, especially African American children are present in order to learn and develop on a consistent basis.

6   To increase attendance and reduce the impact of chronic absence we must identify students who are or may be at risk of chronic absence and design an intervention that best meets their need.

7   A new report from Attendance Works and Healthy Schools Campaign, _Mapping the Early Attendance Gaps_, found that chronic absence is a problem in every state, with kindergartners missing nearly as much school as teenagers. The study also found that excused absences contribute to many of these missed days. For example, students miss 14 million days a year to asthma, a condition that afflicts African American students at higher rates than other students. Dental problems lead to another 2 million missed days each year.

8   "Too often, absences aren't seen as a problem as long as they're excused," said Hedy Chang, director of Attendance Works. "Or schools and families only worry when a child misses several days in a row and fail to recognize the cumulative impact of missing a day every couple weeks. In fact, research shows all absences matter for student success."

9   "As a school leader we constantly had to remind parents that high school was not the time to be hands off with their scholars." said Khalilah Harris, deputy Director of the White House Initiative on Educational Excellence for African Americans. "It was critical for us to use tools like advisory and restorative circles to ensure every student felt safe and had at least one, if not more, adult who knew them well enough to notice and intervene when something was wrong and to celebrate when something was really right."

10   Reaching the 7.5 million students who aren't in their seats is possible and change begins with each of us. Tell your schools to collect data and identify students who need our support. Reach out and form a relationship that can make a lasting difference. Once you have made that connection, reach out to another caring and concerned adult to do the same. An empty desk is an opportunity missed, but the opportunities in a filled classroom with adults monitoring and championing students behind the scenes are limitless.

--Lauren Mims, Fellow, White House Initiative on Educational Excellence, HOMEROOM – official US Department of Education (ED) blog, 10/07/2015

10. To what does the title of this piece refer?
   a. The empty desk refers to low school enrollments.
   b. The empty desk refers to chronic school absence.
   c. The empty desk refers to deficient school funding.
   d. They empty desk refers to a shortage of teachers.

11. In the first paragraph, which of the following phrases has a figurative meaning?
   a. "Identified as truant"
   b. "Non-sequential days"
   c. "Fly under the radar"
   d. "'Chronically absent'"

12. According to the text, how is chronic school absence defined?
   a. A month or more of discrete unexcused/excused absences
   b. A month or more consecutive unexcused/excused days out
   c. A month or more of consecutive unexcused school absence
   d. A month or more of discrete absence days that are excused

13. The text identifies c. 7.5 million chronically absent students annually nationwide, and equates this number with what proportion of students on a US state level?
   a. About 30 percent of students in some states
   b. About 33 percent of students in all the states
   c. About 25 percent of students in most states
   d. About 20 percent of students in some states

14. Of the following, which type of evidence does this text NOT cite to support some of its points?
   a. A scholarly publication only available in print
   b. A published research report available online
   c. A relevant non-profit organization's website
   d. Quotations from authorities on the subject

15. A major theme reiterated throughout this piece involves which of the following?
   a. The need for improving African-American student health
   b. The need for solving residential and transportation issues
   c. The need for meaningful student connections with adults
   d. The need for addressing truancy caused by discrimination

16. The author cites two health issues as examples of excused absences, one of which is disproportionately represented among African-American students. Which is accurate about these?
   a. Asthma accounts for twice as many annual excused absences as dental problems.
   b. Asthma accounts for seven times the annual excused absences as dental excuses.
   c. Asthma accounts for one-seventh the annual excused absences as dental excuses.
   d. Asthma accounts for about an equal number of excused absences as dental issues.

17. Attendance barriers for African-American students are identified in this text. Which of them could *most* be prevented by school systems?
   a. Unreliable transportation
   b. Homelessness and moves
   c. Asthma and dental issues
   d. Suspension and expulsion

18. The final paragraph of this blog is written *primarily* for which purpose?
   a. To provide a summary of the main points in preceding text
   b. To convey a call to action for adults to contribute to change
   c. To draw a logical conclusion based on a sequence of points
   d. To raise concerns leaving readers with persisting questions

19. Which of the following best characterizes the author's attitude or point of view?
   a. The author believes the issue can be addressed.
   b. The author believes the issue cannot be solved.
   c. The author believes the issue is not that serious.
   d. The author believes the issue is from prejudice.

20. In the concluding sentence, the author repeats the title of the piece. Why does she do this?
   a. She repeats it as a device to make the piece appear to be more cohesive.
   b. She repeats it to reinforce the negative main idea of missed opportunity.
   c. She repeats it as a conclusion to the piece by summarizing the title's idea.
   d. She repeats it to add a contrasting, positive solution, like a counter-claim.

Questions 21 to 31 pertain to the following scenario:

1	HAMLET: To be, or not to be--that is the question:
2	Whether 'tis nobler in the mind to suffer
3	The slings and arrows of outrageous fortune
4	Or to take arms against a sea of troubles
5	And by opposing end them. To die, to sleep--
6	No more--and by a sleep to say we end
7	The heartache, and the thousand natural shocks
8	That flesh is heir to. 'Tis a consummation
9	Devoutly to be wished. To die, to sleep--
10	To sleep--perchance to dream: ay, there's the rub,
11	For in that sleep of death what dreams may come
12	When we have shuffled off this mortal coil,
13	Must give us pause. There's the respect
14	That makes calamity of so long life.
15	For who would bear the whips and scorns of time,
16	Th' oppressor's wrong, the proud man's contumely
17	The pangs of despised love, the law's delay,
18	The insolence of office, and the spurns
19	That patient merit of th' unworthy takes,
20	When he himself might his quietus make
21	With a bare bodkin? Who would fardels bear,
22	To grunt and sweat under a weary life,
23	But that the dread of something after death,
24	The undiscovered country, from whose bourn
25	No traveller returns, puzzles the will,
26	And makes us rather bear those ills we have
27	Than fly to others that we know not of?
28	Thus conscience does make cowards of us all,
29	And thus the native hue of resolution
30	Is sicklied o'er with the pale cast of thought,

31   And enterprise of great pith and moment
32   With this regard their currents turn awry
33   And lose the name of action. -- Soft you now,
34   The fair Ophelia! -- Nymph, in thy orisons
35   Be all my sins remembered.
                --*Hamlet* by William Shakespeare (1603)

21. Hamlet's main conflict, expressed at the outset of this soliloquy, is which of the following?
    a. Whether to stay awake or to go to sleep
    b. Whether to take action or remain passive
    c. Whether to stay alive or to commit suicide
    d. Whether to suffer or fight to end troubles

22. Of the following expressions Shakespeare uses here, which one is NOT a metaphor?
    a. "The slings and arrows" (3)
    b. "To take arms against" (4)
    c. "A sea of troubles" (4)
    d. "Natural shocks" (7)

23. When Hamlet says, (10) "To die, to sleep--...ay, there's the rub," what does he mean is the "rub"?
    a. Death is like sleep, except we will never awaken.
    b. Death is like sleep, so we might still awake again.
    c. Death is like sleep, so we could have bad dreams.
    d. Death is like sleep, so it is equally familiar.

24. Which of the following words used in this passage originated from references specific to Shakespeare's time?
    a. "Rub" (10)
    b. "Coil" (12)
    c. "Whips" (15)
    d. (a) and (b)

25. Placing this speech in the context of the play, when Hamlet said, (28) "Thus conscience does make cowards of us all," which of these did he mean?
    a. Fear of the unknown prevented his committing either suicide or murder.
    b. Both (a) and (c) were considerations, but (d) was not another meaning.
    c. Knowing suicide and murder were sins prevented his committing either.
    d. The demand to avenge his father outweighed the sin of killing another.

26. As he is reflecting about his situation in particular and life and death in general, which of the following does Hamlet most seem to conclude about such deliberations?
    a. Thinking about things will inform any action he takes.
    b. Thinking about things will motivate his coming action.
    c. Thinking about things will prevent his taking an action.
    d. Thinking about things will alter those actions he takes.

27. Shakespeare appropriates the Latin term *quietus* ([20] "When he himself might his quietus make") from which profession and original meaning?
    a. Medical, meaning the ending of all signs of life
    b. Religious, meaning to make a final peace in life
    c. Legal, meaning a definitive end to an argument
    d. Scientific, meaning a logical problem resolution

28. From the context, what is the best meaning of "a bare bodkin" (21)?
    a. A sharp object
    b. A naked body
    c. A flimsy shirt
    d. A bared soul

29. In Hamlet's last lines here, "-- Soft you now, the fair Ophelia!" refers to which of the following?
    a. Hamlet is calling upon Ophelia to come and see him.
    b. Hamlet is recognizing that Ophelia has just entered.
    c. Hamlet is rhetorically addressing an absent Ophelia.
    d. Hamlet addresses Ophelia, who was there all along.

30. "The undiscovered country from whose bourn/No traveler returns" (24-25) refers to what?
    a. Death
    b. Sleeping
    c. Dreaming
    d. Post-death

31. Which of the following is the most accurate meaning of (34-35) "...in thy orisons/Be all my sins remembered" (spoken to Ophelia)?
    a. Please remember me in your prayers.
    b. Your prayers remember all of my sins.
    c. Your prayers are only about all my sins.
    d. Please recall all my sins when you pray.

Questions 32 to40 pertain to the following scenario:

The Tell-Tale Heart
by Edgar A. Poe (1843)

1   TRUE! — nervous — very, very dreadfully nervous I had been, and am; but why *will* you say that I am mad? The disease had sharpened my senses — not destroyed — not dulled them. Above all was the sense of hearing acute. I heard all things in the heaven and in the earth. I heard many things in hell. How, then, am I mad? Harken! and observe how healthily — how calmly I can tell you the whole story.

2   It is impossible to say how first the idea entered my brain; but, once conceived, it haunted me day and night. Object there was none. Passion there was none. I loved the old man. He had never wronged me. He had never given me insult. For his gold I had no desire. I think it was his eye! — yes, it was this! He had the eye of a vulture — a pale blue eye, with a film over it. Whenever it fell upon me, my blood ran cold; and so, by degrees — very gradually — I made up my mind to take the life of the old man, and thus rid myself of the eye forever.

3   Now this is the point. You fancy me mad. Madmen know nothing. But you should have seen *me*. You should have seen how wisely I proceeded — with what caution — with what foresight — with what dissimulation I went to work! I was never kinder to the old man than during the whole week before I killed him...

[In the elided portion, the narrator describes in detail how he prepared to murder the old man.]

4   And have I not told you that what you mistake for madness is but over-acuteness of the sense?--now, I say, there came to my ears a low, dull, quick sound, such as a watch makes when enveloped in cotton. I knew that sound well, too. It was the beating of the old man's heart. It increased my fury, as the beating of a drum stimulates the soldier into courage.

[In the elided portions, he describes how the sound of the heartbeat became faster and louder until he was anxious a neighbor would hear it, and how he murdered the old man.]

5   . . . I placed my hand upon the heart and held it there many minutes. There was no pulsation. He was stone dead. His eye would trouble me no more.

6   If still you think me mad, you will think so no longer when I describe the wise precautions I took for the concealment of the body. The night waned, and I worked hastily, but in silence. First of all I dismembered the corpse. I cut off the head and the arms and the legs.

7   I then took up three planks from the flooring of the chamber, and deposited all between the scantlings. I then replaced the boards so cleverly, so cunningly, that no human eye--not even his--could have detected any thing wrong. There was nothing to wash out--no stain of any kind--no blood-spot whatever. I had been too wary for that. A tub had caught all--ha! ha!

8   When I had made an end of these labors, it was four o'clock--still dark as midnight. As the bell sounded the hour, there came a knocking at the street door. I went down to open it with a light heart,--for what had I now to fear? There entered three men, who introduced themselves, with perfect suavity, as officers of the police. A shriek had been heard by a neighbour during the night; suspicion of foul play had been aroused; information had been lodged at the police office, and they (the officers) had been deputed to search the premises.

9   I smiled,--for what had I to fear? I bade the gentlemen welcome. The shriek, I said, was my own in a dream. The old man, I mentioned, was absent in the country. I took my visitors all over the house. I bade them search—search well. I led them, at length, to his chamber. I showed them his treasures, secure, undisturbed. In the enthusiasm of my confidence, I brought chairs into the room, and desired them here to rest from their fatigues, while I myself, in the wild audacity of my perfect triumph, placed my own seat upon the very spot beneath which reposed the corpse of the victim.

10   The officers were satisfied. My manner had convinced them. I was singularly at ease. They sat, and while I answered cheerily, they chatted of familiar things. But, ere long, I felt myself getting pale and wished them gone. My head ached, and I fancied a ringing in my ears: but still they sat and still chatted. The ringing became more distinct:--It continued and became more distinct: I talked more freely to get rid of the feeling: but it continued and gained definiteness--until, at length, I found that the noise was not within my ears.

11   No doubt I now grew very pale;—but I talked more fluently, and with a heightened voice. Yet the sound increased—and what could I do? It was a low, dull, quick sound—much such a sound as a watch makes when enveloped in cotton. I gasped for breath—and yet the officers heard it not. I talked more quickly—more vehemently; but the noise steadily increased. I arose and argued about trifles, in a high key and with violent gesticulations; but the noise steadily increased. Why would they not be gone? I paced the floor to and fro with heavy strides, as if excited to fury by the observations of the men--but the noise steadily increased. Oh God! what could I do? I foamed—I raved—I swore! I swung the chair upon which I had been sitting, and grated it upon the boards, but the noise arose over all and continually increased. It grew louder—louder—! And still the men chatted pleasantly, and smiled. Was it possible they heard not? Almighty God!—no, no! They heard!—they suspected!—they knew!—they were making a mockery of my horror!—this I thought, and this I think. But anything was better than this agony! Anything was more tolerable than this derision! I could bear those hypocritical smiles no longer! I felt that I must scream or die! and now—again!—hark! louder! louder! louder! louder!

12   "Villains!" I shrieked, "dissemble no more! I admit the deed!--tear up the planks! here, here!--It is the beating of his hideous heart!"

32. What is the person of the narrative voice in this story?
    a. First person
    b. Third person
    c. Second person
    d. Omniscient narrator

33. What best describes the relationship among the first three paragraphs on the subject of insanity?
    a. The narrator insists he is not mad in the first and third paragraphs but shows he is in the second.
    b. The narrator questions if he is mad in the first paragraph, showing he is not in the following two.
    c. The narrator protests he is not mad in the first and third paragraphs, developing it in the second.
    d. The narrator denies madness in the first paragraph, develops it in the second, and repeats in the third.

34. According to the narrator, what was his motivation for wanting to kill the old man?
    a. He secretly hated the old man
    b. To get rid of the old man's eye
    c. The old man had wronged him
    d. He wanted the old man's gold

35. In paragraph 4, the narrator says of the old man's heartbeat, "It increased my fury, as the beating of a drum stimulates the soldier into courage." What best describes the author's use of literary devices?
    a. This sentence only employs a simile.
    b. This sentence uses only verbal irony.
    c. This sentence uses a simile and irony.
    d. This sentence uses neither simile nor irony.

36. What is/are a motif(s) in this story, i.e., they recur throughout and help to develop the main idea and/or theme?
    a. The old man's eye
    b. The old man's heart
    c. The narrator's madness
    d. (a) and (b) rather than (c)

37. Which of the following statements by the narrator does Poe include as evidence that the character has delusions of grandeur (i.e., unrealistic beliefs of his own superiority)?
    a. "They knew!–they were making a mockery of my horror!" (Paragraph 11)
    b. "Very, very dreadfully nervous I had been and am" (p1)
    c. "It fell upon me, my blood ran cold" (p2)
    d. "A tub had caught all—ha! ha!" (p7)

38. What can you best infer about the sound of the "Tell-Tale Heart" heard in paragraph 11?
    a. The victim had been buried alive and his heart was still beating.
    b. There was no sound; the guilty murderer simply imagined one.
    c. The guilty man mistook his own heartbeat for that of the victim.
    d. It was some other sound, as he said, "not within my ears." (Paragraph 10)

39. Which device does Poe use in paragraph 11 that builds dramatic tension most notably?
    a. Repetition
    b. Alliteration
    c. Circumlocution
    d. Characterization

40. Of the following excerpts from the passage, which one indicates through word choice that, despite his delusions of sanity and having committed the perfect crime, in his retelling the narrator retrospectively admits he had been unrealistic?

    a. "How wisely I proceeded—with what caution—with what foresight—with what dissimulation..." (Paragraph 3)

    b. "I myself, in the wild audacity of my perfect triumph, placed my own seat" (above the corpse) (paragraph 9)

    c. "With a light heart,—for what had I now to fear? ...I smiled,—for what had I to fear?" (Paragraph 8-9)

    d. "Hearken! and observe how healthily—how calmly I can tell you the whole story." (Paragraph 1)

Constructed Response

Read the passages and examine the graphic below, and then answer the essay questions that follow.

PASSAGE A

Thank you for contacting me to express your concerns over the proposed elimination of the EPA's Clean Power Plan, which seeks to reduce carbon pollution by power plants and address the risks of climate change. I welcome feedback from my constituents and I appreciate your interest in this issue. I am pleased to tell you that I am a staunch advocate for addressing climate change and that I would oppose any measure that sought to eliminate the Environmental Protection Agency's Clean Power Plan.

President Barack Obama proposed the Clean Power Plan in June 2014 as a part of his Climate Change Action Plan. The Clean Power Plan sets standards for carbon pollution from power plants and could result in a 30 percent reduction in carbon pollution from the power sector by 2030. Climate change has the potential to cause a tremendous amount of potentially catastrophic consequences for people around the world. Scientists agree that human action, such as carbon pollution by power plants, is the cause for a majority of the current warming. While the situation is an increasing cause for concern, most scientists also agree that it is not too late to take action to stop this serious threat to our planet. Climate change is a cause for national concern, requiring national solutions, and as your Congressman, I will support legislation that seeks to stop the causes and to moderate the effects of climate change.

I am honored to be your representative in Congress and I hope that my office can be a useful resource for you now and in the future. For more information, please visit my office online at www.HankJohnson.house.gov and do not hesitate to contact me if you have any future questions or concerns.

Sincerely,

Henry C. "Hank" Johnson, Jr.
Member of Congress

PASSAGE B

Thank you for contacting me regarding the Environmental Protection Agency's (EPA) Clean Power regulations. I appreciate hearing from you and am grateful for the opportunity to respond.

The Clean Power regulations were introduced by the EPA on August 3, 2015. Under these regulations, existing power plants will be required to reduce their emissions 32 percent by 2030 and must submit a plan outlining their strategy for doing so by 2016. States also have the option to engage in a regional "cap and trade" system where emission credits can be traded in order to ease states' transition to new emission standards.

The authority to impose federal carbon mandates lies with Congress, not the EPA. These regulations will ultimately result in what could be called an "energy tax" that will be felt in the form of higher electricity bills for consumers. I share your concerns with overreaching rules and regulations promulgated by unelected officials at the EPA and have been actively fighting them in the Senate. Coal-fired power plants provide 36 percent of Georgia's electricity and support nearly 8,800 Georgia jobs. When these Clean Power regulations were originally proposed in 2014, I wrote a letter to the EPA expressing my concern over the detrimental impact the rule would have on electricity providers, consumers and the U.S. economy as a whole.

On May 13, 2015, I cosponsored S.1324, the *Affordable Reliable Electricity Now Act of 2015*. This bill would allow states to opt out of the Clean Power regulations. The implementation of these regulations would also be halted until states that have filed lawsuits against the EPA have completed their proceedings, and the federal government would be prohibited from withholding highway funding from states that fail to submit an implementation strategy. I will keep your thoughts and concerns in mind if the *Affordable Reliable Electricity Now Act* is brought to the Senate floor for consideration.

Thank you again for contacting me. Please visit my webpage at http://isakson.senate.gov/ for more information on the issues important to you and to sign up for my e-newsletter.

Sincerely,
Johnny Isakson
United States Senator

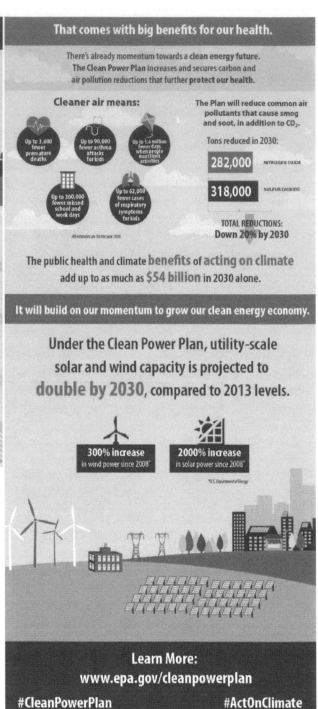

1. In an essay of approximately 100-200 words, identify which passage argues more effectively. Identify which specific claims each writer makes. Identify what evidence each provides to support his claims, and evaluate whether that evidence is sufficient, relevant, and valid. Support this evaluation using examples from each of the passages. Write your essay for an adult, educated audience in your own words (except for quotations). Your final draft should adhere to standard American English writing conventions.

2. In an approximately 100- to 200-word essay, explain how the information given in the preceding graphic supports or refutes the statements of the writer in Passage A. Support your explanation by giving examples from both the graphic and the passage, including specific, relevant statistics. Write for an adult, educated audience, using your own words (except for quotations). Ensure that your final draft adheres to all standard American English writing conventions.

3. In an essay approximately 400-600 words long, write a well-developed argument evaluating the pros and cons of the Clean Power Plan. This must include: (1) a claim that shows knowledge and comprehension of this subject; (2) valid and logical reasoning that builds upon the arguments in both passages; (3) support for your claim using enough pertinent evidence from all three sources provided; and (4) an anticipation of, and response to, at least one counterclaim. Write in your own words (except for quotations) for an adult, educated audience while consistently using precise, clear language in an appropriate tone and style. Make sure your final draft follows all the writing conventions for standard American English.

Answers and Explanations

1. B: The first sentence/paragraph explicitly states that Mrs. Mallard had "a heart trouble," so people around her did not want to exacerbate it—not just because such news would shock anybody (a). Neither the first sentence nor the rest of the story states that she was emotionally fragile (c) or that everybody always protected her from life (d).

2. C: By "revealed in half concealing," the author means that the way(s) in which Josephine halfway hid the truth of her message served to reveal it rather than to hide it. Hence she did not actually conceal the full truth (a) because her "veiled hints" revealed it, and she did not conceal half of it (b). Choice (d) is the reverse of the actual meaning.

3. A: In paragraph 2, Chopin describes Richards as not only there but "near her" and having hurried to prevent "any less careful, less tender friend" from breaking grievous news. In paragraph 21, she describes Richards's "quick motion to screen him from the view of his wife" to protect her from shock. Though Chopin introduces Richards as "her husband's friend" in paragraph 2, the examples above implies he cared about her (b). Paragraph 2 indicates Richards verified the report "by a second telegram" (c), and knew of the accident by being in the newspaper office (d).

4. D: She did not always hide her feelings from everyone (a): she "wept... in her sister's arms" (paragraph 3). She wept "at once" and reflected thereafter, not vice versa (b); after her initial "storm of grief" she spent time alone contemplating (c). Her initial reaction demonstrated her passionate nature; the descriptions of her subsequent behavior show her self-control (along with the "repression and even a certain strength" her face showed [paragraph 8]); and the many paragraphs describing her thoughts, feelings, and insights illustrate her introspective nature (d).

5. A: Louise's gradual realization that her individual freedom and identity superseded her relationship with and "sometimes" love for her husband culminates in the insight (paragraph 15) that love could not compete with "this possession of self-assertion which she suddenly recognized as the strongest impulse of her being!" Guilt (b) and loving too much (c) are not themes in this story. Loss did not change Louise's personality (d), but rather revealed to her a fundamental aspect of it.

6. D: Upon news of an apparent death, the springtime details both contrast with the idea of death (a) and reflect the new life that Louise was envisioning (b) upon being freed from the constraints of marriage, even a loving one. Descriptive details do serve to draw readers into the scene, but in this case they also carry meaning (c).

7. B: Part of the ending's irony in equating heart disease with the appositive "joy that kills" is that, based on preceding text, Louise's heart failure was not from joy (a), but the shock of finding her husband still alive (b). The irony lies not in Louise's heart condition (c), but in her psychological responses to her husband's "dying" and being alive. She died not because life was not over (d), but because freedom was: she had dreaded long married life "only yesterday" (paragraph 19), but upon feeling free, prayed "that life might be long."

8. C: Although the other choices are all sensory details included in the description of springtime outside, the author's choice of the word "crying" rather than calling, shouting, singing, etc. reflects the description in paragraph 3 of the main character's having "wept at once" on hearing the news.

9. B: Chopin portrays the main character's sacrifices of will, physical and spiritual freedom, etc. in a light that made marriage NOT worth giving up those things (a). As reflected in the story, the author's point of view toward marriage seems to be that the two members could not be equal partners (b), as one inevitably imposes his or her will upon the other, even when they love each other (c). Living for one's spouse (d) was a common 19th-century ideal (or myth), but one that Chopin challenged in her point of view.

10. B: The "empty desk" in the title of this piece refers to chronic school absence. It does not refer to low school enrollments (a)—students are enrolled but many are chronically absent. Many schools today struggle with inadequate funding (c), but this piece and its title do not refer to underfunding. There is also a shortage of qualified teachers (d), but the title and text here do not refer to this problem.

11. C: To "fly under the radar" in the literal sense refers to aircraft flying at altitudes too low for radar waves to identify their presence. It is commonly used in the figurative sense to refer to any activity that goes undetected by usual monitoring methods. The other three choices are used to have only literal but no figurative meanings. Additionally, "chronically absent" (d) refers to both a literal meaning and a specific terminology used by the Department of Education, school district officials, school administrators, and educators regarding school attendance.

12. A: Paragraph 1 defines "chronically absent" as missing "non-sequential," i.e., discrete (separate) days, NOT consecutive days (b), (c) of school, which absences are excused AND/OR unexcused—not just unexcused (c) or excused (d) absences—that add up to a month or more in total days missed. The author's point is that whereas multiple *consecutive* absence days are identified as truancy, multiple *non-sequential* absence days often go undetected.

13. D: The text equates this number to one in five students in *some* states, i.e., about 20 percent. About 30 percent (a) or 33 percent (b) would each equate to approximately one in three students; 25 percent (c) would equate to about one in four students. The total cannot be equated to the same proportion in all states (b) or even most (c) because each US state's total population, and hence total school enrollment, varies too much among states for the same proportion to apply to all or most of them.

14. A: This text does NOT cite a print-only scholarly publication. It does, however, cite a published research study report available online (b), including a link to it in paragraph 7; a link to a non-profit organization's website on school attendance (c) in paragraph 8; and quotations from authorities on the subject (d) in paragraphs 4, 8, and 9.

15. C: The importance to school attendance of meaningful connections with adults is discussed specifically in paragraphs 1, 4, 9, and 10. Two health issues are examples with greater impacts on African-American students (paragraph 7), but improving their health is not a major theme throughout (a). Residential and transportation issues are examples of greater barriers to African-American attendance (p5), but only to reinforce the major point that all adults must act ("it takes a village"), not reiterated throughout as a theme (b). The focus is on chronic absence, not truancy; discrimination is not discussed (d).

16. B: In paragraph 7, the author cites a research report that asthma accounts for 14 million excused absences and dental problems account for 2 million excused absences annually; hence asthma accounts for seven times as many annual excused absences as dental problems. The author also points out that asthma affects African-American students at higher rates than other students.

17. D: Schools often provide transportation (a), but not always to all areas. Furthermore, special-needs transportation costs more, funding may be insufficient, and arranging transport for homeless students presents additional challenges. Homelessness makes it harder for students to attend school; school systems have difficulty tracking students whose families move often (b). Schools may connect families with charities like Habitat for Humanity, government housing, free health clinics, and low-cost healthcare. Unfortunately, they cannot solve housing, transportation, or health problems (c) as readily as they can eliminate and/or reduce suspensions and expulsions (d), e.g., through school-wide prevention and early intervention programs providing academic and behavioral supports.

18. B: In the last paragraph, the author does NOT summarize the text's main points (a), but rather calls on adult readers to take actions that will change chronic school absence (b). The author does not use the final paragraph to draw a logical conclusion based on a sequence of points (c), but rather explicitly defines adult actions that can address this identified problem of chronic school absence. This does not leave readers with questions (d) as much as answers by identifying actions to take.

19. A: Although she cites plenty of evidence that the issue discussed is a problem, the author also identifies important protective factors (e.g., connections with adults) throughout, and ends with a call to action naming three things adults can do to address it. Hence she does not express a belief that the issue cannot be solved (b). The supporting evidence she cites establishes her belief that the issue IS serious, even more than many adults recognize (c), e.g., with chronic and excused absences. While she emphasizes additional attendance difficulties for African-American students, she never attributes these to prejudice (d).

20. D: In the sense that the title's negative statement is akin to a type of claim, the author's repetition of it in the last sentence enables her to add a positive counter-claim to it (a missed opportunity vs. limitless opportunities), strengthening this positive statement through contrast. This repetition is not simply a device to simulate cohesion (a) because it also ties the title into the conclusion. It does not reinforce the negative idea (b), but counters it with a positive one. It does not merely summarize the title (c), but adds to and modifies it.

21. C: Hamlet's main conflict is whether to stay alive or commit suicide. He only mentions sleep (a) as a metaphor for death. Action ("to take arms against a sea of troubles") vs. passivity ("to suffer/The slings and arrows of outrageous fortune") (b) is really another form of the same conflict—whether to suffer life's troubles by staying alive or end them by ending one's life—and as such is secondary to it. While lines 3-5 seem to describe choice (d), the structure suggests this is parallel to the main conflict ("to sleep... we end/The heartache....").

22. D: Shakespeare refers to "The slings and arrows" (a) "of outrageous fortune," so these cannot be literal or physical weapons, but a metaphor for injurious life events. Likewise, he refers to taking arms (b) not literally, as in fighting with physical weapons, but figuratively, as in "opposing" troubles. Similarly, in "a sea of troubles" (c), the "sea" is not a literal body of water but a metaphor meaning a great many. However, "the thousand natural shocks/That flesh is heir to" (d) is not a figurative metaphor, but a more literal description of injuries and/or problems inherent to human life.

23. C: The "rub" (i.e., the problem and/or distraction) is that if death is like sleep, it could be possible to have bad dreams in that sleep of death: "To die, to sleep--/To sleep—perchance to

dream: ay, there's the rub,/For in that sleep of death what dreams may come/...Must give us pause." He does not mean that the "rub" is that the sleep of death is permanent (a) or temporary (b). He especially does not mean it is as familiar as sleep (d): he emphasizes fear of the unknown ("the dread of something after death").

24. D: The "rub" refers to the Elizabethan game of bowls: an obstacle on the lawn that diverts the bowl's course is called a "rub." Shakespeare applied it here meaning the possibility of dreams in the sleep of death was an obstacle that could divert our thinking and "give us pause." In the "mortal coil" (b) we shuffle off, Shakespeare referred to the Elizabethan meaning of "coil" as a lot of ado and bustle. "Whips" (c) meant the same thing then as now, literally and figuratively.

25. B: Hamlet meant his conscience interfered with killing himself, from both fear of the unknown following death (a) and knowing suicide was a sin (c); and also interfered with killing Claudius from knowing murder was also a sin (c). Although in Shakespeare's time, convention would demand he avenge his father by killing Claudius, who murdered Hamlet's father, his conscience told him murder was a sin, so the demand for revenge did not outweigh the sin (d) but rather conflicted with it, adding to Hamlet's prolonged indecision.

26. C: Hamlet concludes that thinking about things as much as he has been will only prevent his taking any action: "And thus the native hue of resolution/Is sicklied o'er with the pale cast of thought,/And enterprise of great pith and moment/With this regard their currents turn awry/And lose the name of action." In other words, thinking too much weakens his resolve to act, diverting the "currents" of his "enterprise" (motivation or impetus) to act until action is lost. He does not conclude that thinking informs his actions (a), motivates him to act (b), or changes his actions (d).

27. C: The Latin term *quietus* is from the legal profession, meaning a definitive end to an argument. Shakespeare uses it here as a metaphor to represent ending one's own life. It is not a medical term for death (a), a religious term for making peace in life (b) before dying, or a scientific term meaning a logical resolution to a problem (d).

28. A: Dictionary definitions for *bodkin* include a small knife, a needle-like sewing instrument, a type of hairpin, and an awl—in other words, an exposed blade or sharp object whereby one might easily end one's life more easily than enduring it. This meaning is the only correct choice and the only one that makes sense in context. This word does not mean a naked body (b), a flimsy shirt (c), or a bared soul (d), neither in any dictionary nor in this text.

29.B: Hamlet is acknowledging the entrance of Ophelia into the scene. He is not calling for her to come see him (a), as he continues speaking to her in the same line: "—Nymph, in thy orisons/Be all my sins remembered." He is not addressing her rhetorically (c): A soliloquy is spoken by the character alone, and this line signals its end as he announces and greets Ophelia. Since this speech (like all dramatic soliloquies) is spoken alone, Ophelia was obviously not there all along (d).

30. D: This "undiscovered country" refers to "something after death" (23), reinforced through context by Hamlet's repeated descriptions of fear of the unknown, countering potential relief from life's ills in a "consummation/Devoutly to be wished. To die" (8-9). This feared unknown is included in the description cited: "And makes us rather bear those ills we have/Than fly to others that we know not of?" (26-27). This eliminates death itself (a), sleep (b), and dreams (c) as meanings.

31. A: Hamlet is asking Ophelia to remember him in her prayers. He is not telling her that her prayers recall all of his sins (b), that she only prays about all his sins (c), or asking her to remember

all his sins when she prays (d). Notice that the syntactic reversals/rearrangement in these lines are typical throughout Shakespeare's works as ways of getting audience attention, emphasizing meaning, etc.

32. A: This story is narrated in the first person, in the main character's voice, not the author's. In the third person (b) most common in fiction, the narrator describes the characters and story using *he, she, it, they,* etc. but does not use *I, me, my,* etc. like first person. In the second person (c), the least common, the author addresses the reader directly by *you, your, yours* or "you understood." The omniscient narrator (d) knows all characters' histories, inner thoughts, feelings, and motivations, typically also describing characters in the third person.

33. C: The narrator insists that the audience's saying he is mad is untrue in the first paragraph, but demonstrates that he is in the second paragraph by describing his irrational obsession with the old man's eye and his even crazier eventual decision to eradicate it through murder. In the third paragraph he reiterates his denial of insanity. (He additionally repeats his refutation of any belief that he is mad in paragraphs 4 and 6.)

34. B: In paragraph 2, the narrator first concedes the lack of a reasonable motive: "Object there was none. Passion there was none." He continues, "I loved the old man" (a). "He had never wronged me" (c). "For his gold I had no desire" (d). "I think it was his eye! yes, it was this!...I made up my mind to take the life of the old man, and thus rid myself of the eye forever" (b).

35. C: Poe uses two literary devices in this sentence: (1) a simile (a), i.e., an explicitly stated comparison using *like* or *as* (he uses *as*); and (2) verbal irony (b) by comparing a negative and murderous impulse ("fury") escalated by the maddening sound of a heartbeat to a positive and heroic impulse (a soldier's courage) stimulated by the sound of the drumbeat. Therefore, choice (d) is incorrect.

36. D: Motifs are images, objects, or sounds (as in this case, or figures and/or actions in other cases) with symbolic significance that recur throughout the work and contribute to developing the theme. In this story, the old man's eye (a) and the old man's beating heart (b) are both motifs. The narrator's madness (c) is not a motif but rather a main theme of the story.

37. D: Choice (a) provides evidence the character also had paranoid delusions of persecution about the police, who suspected nothing; projecting his own knowledge of his deed onto them (also calling them "villains" who "dissemble" [paragraph 12]), he imagined they knew. His guilt created their "mockery," "derision," "hypocritical smiles," and his own "agony." Choice (b) provides evidence the character also suffered guilt-induced anxiety, choice (c) provides evidence of the character's irrational obsession over the old man's eye with the cataract (common during Poe's time). Choice (d) is evidence of the character's gloating over his "perfect" execution of the crime.

38. C: Though Poe does not state it explicitly, readers can infer the steadily increasing sound the narrator believed was the old man's heart was actually his own heart, beating louder as his guilt and horror grew. This is not a tale of the supernatural wherein the dead man's heart could still beat (a), but a psychological horror story. The sound was not imaginary (b); the killer mistook its source. The heartbeat began as ringing in his ears (paragraph 10), increasing until he imagined it outside his body though it was not (d), then recognized it as a heartbeat.

39. A: Poe's repetition, especially of the word "louder," plus other repetitions (e.g., "I talked," "I gasped," "I arose," "I paced," "I foamed—I raved—I swore! I swung..."; "They heard!—they

suspected!—they knew!—they were making a mockery...”; “anything was better than,” “Anything was more tolerable than...” etc.), build tension to an unbearable level in the penultimate paragraph. Alliteration (b) repeats sounds across words (e.g., little old lady). Circumlocution (c) indirectly writes or talks around the meaning using unnecessarily complex sentences. Poe uses characterization (d) throughout to describe the narrator, not specifically to build tension in paragraph 11.

40. B: Choice (a) indicates the extent of the narrator’s delusion in believing that his planning, caution, foresight, and deceit in murder were evidence of sanity. Choice (c) indicates his delusion of security in having gotten away with the act. Choice (d) indicates his delusion that his ability to recount the story “healthily” and “calmly” proves his sanity. However, choice (c) indicates through the word choice of “wild audacity” (i.e., crazy boldness) that retrospectively, even while still insisting he is not mad, he realizes his belief in his “perfect triumph” was unrealistic.

Practice Test #2

Practice Questions

Questions 1 to10 pertain to the following scenario:

1   In addition to helping you feel and look better, reaching a healthier body weight is good for your overall health and wellbeing. If you are overweight or obsess, you have a greater risk of developing many diseases including type 2 diabetes, heart disease, and some types of cancer.

2   The secret to success is making changes and sticking with them.
- First - Find out What you eat and drink. This is a key step in managing your weight.
- Next - Find out What to eat and drink. Get a personalized Daily Food Plan - just for you - to help guide your food choices.
- Then - Make better choices. Everyone is different. Compare what you eat and drink to what you should eat and drink. The ideas and tips in this section can help you make better choices, which can have a lasting impact on your body weight over time.

3   Did you know that:
- The #1 source of calories in the American diet is desserts - like cakes and cookies?
- Americans get more calories from sugary drinks than any other beverage choice?

4   Identifying what you are eating and drinking *now* will help you see where you can make better choices in the *future.*

5   If you want to make changes to improve the way you eat and your body weight, the first step is to identify what you do now. This includes becoming more aware of:
- What and how much you eat and drink
- How physically active you are
- Your body weight

6   People who are most successful at losing weight and keeping it off track their intake regularly. Tracking physical activity and body weight can also help you reach your weight goals.

7   Get started identifying what you eat and drink

Write down <u>what</u> and <u>how much</u> you eat and drink. Find a way that works for you. Use a journal, log your intake on your calendar, keep track on your phone, or use an online tool like the SuperTracker.

Start by identifying what you've already eaten today. Be sure to include how much as well as what you ate. Don't forget to include drinks, sauces, spreads, and sides. It all counts.

In addition, write down the physical activities you do, and how long you spend doing each one. Log each activity that you do for at least 10 minutes at a time. Every bit adds up. Use the SuperTracker, a journal, or mark a calendar.

Once you've identified what you are doing now, keep it up! Tracking what and how much you eat and drink, your body weight, and your physical activity can help you manage your body weight over the long term.

8   Stumbling blocks

Concerned about identifying what you eat and drink? Below are some common "stumbling blocks" and ideas to help you overcome these barriers. Note: If you are on a mobile device, you may need to turn your phone 90 degrees to see the full chart.

"I'm interested in using an online tool, but I don't have internet access every day."	If you don't have regular access to a computer, you can begin by simply writing down what, when, and how much you eat in a journal. Just writing down what you eat and drink helps you become more aware. When you are able to access a computer, you can enter several days of intake into the SuperTracker at once.
"It takes a lot of time to track my intake."	The fact is that tracking works. Find a way that you can track your intake that works for you – whether it be writing what and how much you eat and drink in a journal, your day planner, or your calendar. With the SuperTracker, you can develop lists of your favorite foods that can help you enter your intake more quickly.
"By the time I get to a computer, I've forgotten what I ate."	For tracking to work, it needs to be complete. If necessary, carry a food journal or log your intake on your smart phone. Logging what you eat immediately will help your tracking to be more accurate.
"I can identify what I ate, but have no idea of how to figure out how much I ate".	Measure out foods you regularly eat (such as a bowl of cereal) once or twice, to get a sense of how big your typical portion is. Also measure out what 1/2 or 1 cup portion size looks like to help you estimate how much you eat. Check the serving size information on the Nutrition Facts label of packaged foods. It describes what the "standard" serving size is, and how many are in the package. Use the food galleries for each of the 5 food groups -- fruits, vegetables, grains, dairy, and protein foods -- to see what sample portion sizes look like, and compare them to how much you ate.

- See more at: http://www.choosemyplate.gov/learn-what-you
-United States Department of Agriculture (USDA) website (choosemyplate.gov, 2015)

1. According to the text, what is the *first* thing you should do for weight management?
    a. First you should get information about what to consume.
    b. First you should start improving your nutritional choices.
    c. First you should determine your current dietary content.
    d. First you should exercise more rather than changing diet.

2. Obesity is associated with higher risks of which health problems, according to the textual evidence?
    a. Type 1 diabetes
    b. Cardiovascular
    c. All cancer types
    d. Joint problems

3. The text identifies which of the following as the leading calorie source in the diet of Americans?
    a. Beverages that are sweetened using sugars
    b. Meats that have high saturated fat content
    c. Breads that are produced with refined flour
    d. Cakes, cookies, and other kinds of desserts

4. What does the text say is necessary to improving diet and weight?
    a. Awareness of one's current diet, activity, and weight
    b. Awareness of one's diet is the only requirement
    c. Awareness of one's physical activity is unneeded
    d. Awareness of one's current weight is immaterial

5. According to the text, which of these is associated with the greatest weight loss and maintenance success?
    a. Tracking physical activity regularly
    b. Tracking dietary intake regularly
    c. Tracking body weight regularly
    d. Tracking nothing too regularly

6. Which of the following can you infer about the solutions offered to the first stumbling block cited?
    a. Continuous Internet access is required to track diet.
    b. This site does not offer its own online tracking tool.
    c. Simply writing down dietary intake is also effective.
    d. Online tools only allow entering one day at a time.

7. How does the chart of stumbling blocks address the issue of time management in tracking intake?
    a. It maintains the time is worth it, no matter how long it takes.
    b. It maintains that if it takes too long, one is not doing it right.
    c. It maintains that writing down intake is the fastest method.
    d. It maintains using the online tool can enable faster tracking.

8. What can you logically conclude from the text about portion sizes?
    a. The only way to determine portion size is measurement.
    b. Food packages list numbers of servings, not serving size.
    c. You should compare your usual serving to standard sizes.
    d. The text's website does not offer images of portion size.

9. Which of the following is *most* representative of a main idea in this text?
    a. "If you are overweight or obese, you have a greater risk of developing many diseases including type 2 diabetes, heart disease, and some types of cancer."
    b. "Identifying what you are eating and drinking *now* will help you see where you can make better choices in the *future*."
    c. "In addition to helping you feel and look better, reaching a healthier body weight is good for your overall health and wellbeing."
    d. "Be sure to include how much as well as what you ate. Don't forget to include drinks, sauces, spreads, and sides. It all counts."

10. What would be the most appropriate title for this text?
    a. How to Know What You Eat and Drink
    b. How to Lower Your Risks for Diseases
    c. Why You Should Become More Active
    d. Why Americans Need to Lose Weight

Questions 11 to 20 pertain to the following scenario:

Global Mental Health Day: Spotlight on Suicide Prevention

October 9, 2015

By: Kevin Griffis, *HHS Assistant Secretary for Public Affairs*

1   The middle can be a difficult place. In a family with seven children – six boys and a girl – my brother Todd was right in the center - number four.

2   There was plenty of love in our house, but it could also be a competitive, rough-and-tumble place. Sensitivity might help you get the girl, but when you have five brothers, it can also be a little bit like those nature videos where the sickly wildebeest is trying to look inconspicuous as the pride of lions scopes out the watering hole for lunch.

3   Todd was average height, average build, sometimes carrying a few extra pounds. He had blond hair that slowly turned darker as he grew up, and as a teenager, he often wore it longer than his mom and dad would have liked. It was one of the perks of being the fourth child: parents who could discern which fights were worth picking.

4   Todd's feelings bruised more easily than the rest of ours. But as he matured, despite pressure he must have felt to play the same sports and pursue the same interests, he showed courage in forging his own way. He discovered his own

pursuits, his own style, his own music, no matter the needling from his brothers. To me, the eldest, he seemed normal, maybe not the top student among us, but plenty smart, and maybe not the best athlete, but plenty active.

5   One night, 16 years ago last May, after his shift ended at the restaurant where he worked, he walked into the parking lot, just off a busy five-lane highway. He opened his car and got out a shotgun – his own shotgun, the barrel of which he had sawed off. Then he shot himself. The police came to my parents' house in the early morning hours. Words cannot adequately capture the sadness that followed.

6   No one knew Todd was hurting. The only warning sign came the day of his death when we learned that he hadn't been attending the college class he was supposed to be taking his senior year of high school.

7   The lonely note he left made clear his feelings of isolation, but he didn't ask for help, and his family didn't see a child who needed it. In truth, I don't think of any of us thought something like that could happen.

8   After Todd's death, I learned the unfortunate truth of just how unremarkable our experience was. It plays out every day in communities across the U.S.

9   Since Todd's suicide, Congress passed the Mental Health Parity and Addiction Equity Act of 2008, preventing group health plans from offering weaker mental health or substance abuse benefits than medical or surgical benefits. The Affordable Care Act then expanded that protection to individual plans – a change that went into effect in January of this year. More work needs to be done to ensure people get the care they deserve, but taken together, these two measures represent a sea change in how our country deals with mental illness.

10   Still, there are more than 41,000 suicide deaths every year in the U.S., and 800,000 worldwide. Despite all the work that's been done to curb suicides – on prevention, outreach and awareness – the rates haven't changed much over the last three decades.

11   We're doing something about that. Today, as part of Global Mental Health Day, the Obama Administration is bringing together doctors and data scientists, tool developers and advocates for an all-day meeting at the White House to talk about new ways to approach this problem.

12   DJ Patil and Jo Handelsman, from the White House Office of Science and Technology Policy, explained in a recent blog: "Deciphering why loved ones commit suicide is a complex topic without easy answers, yet data and data analysis tools may help shed new light on patterns and subtleties never before detected." With more data collection and better analysis, we can come at this problem with creative, evidence-driven solutions. We could create innovative suicide prevention strategies that could begin to finally stem the tide and offer hope to individuals and families.

13   Patil and Handelsman have asked for the data scientists, analysts, tech entrepreneurs, and other innovators to reach out and share their ideas and resources for suicide prevention. They can be submitted here.

14   "It is up to us," they wrote, "to find new ways to reach out to those in need and make it easier for them to seek help when they need it."

15   As a country, we've made progress putting mental health treatment on par with medical and surgical benefits. Now, we look forward to some of our best and most innovative minds applying new thinking to suicide prevention. We look towards a tomorrow where more Americans get the help they deserve and fewer families experience the pain and grief of suicide.

--US Department of Health and Human Services (HHS) blog (October 9, 2015)

11. What is the author's attitude about being his brother's being the middle child in a large family?
    a. He thought it gave disadvantages.
    b. He thought it offered advantages.
    c. He thought it posed both of these.
    d. He thought it did neither of these.

12. The simile in paragraph 2 does which of the following?
    a. It compares the parents with a pride of lions.
    b. It compares Todd with the sickly wildebeest.
    c. It compares the whole family with the lions.
    d. It compares the author with the wildebeest.

13. This text includes a photograph. What do you infer are the content and purpose of this picture?
    a. It shows what Todd looked like to make it easier for readers to perceive him as a real person.
    b. It shows what the author looks like so readers can relate to him as a person and his message.
    c. It shows what a person who had mental illness looked like so readers can identify it in others.
    d. It shows what a typical employee of the HHS looks like so readers will have a reference point.

14. What salient quality that Todd developed as he grew up does the author identify in paragraph 4?
    a. He was the best student among his siblings.
    b. He was the most independent individual.
    c. He was the most athletic among his siblings.
    d. He was the least sensitive one in the family.

15. Based on the textual evidence, when did the author's brother commit suicide?
    a. In May of 1999
    b. In April of 2000
    c. It is not known
    d. In June of 2014

16. What is true about Todd and the family, according to the author?
    a. The family knew Todd was suffering but not how to help him.
    b. There were no warning signs at all that he could be suffering.
    c. There was only one warning sign, but it came too late to help.
    d. The family knew he was missing his college class but not why.

17. The author cites two pieces of landmark legislation relative to mental health benefits. Which of the following excerpts illustrates his point of view that these laws have had profound influences?
    a. "More work needs to be done to ensure people get the care they deserve."
    b. "There are more than 41,000 suicide deaths every year in the U.S., and 800,000 worldwide."
    c. "These two measures represent a sea change in how our country deals with mental illness."
    d. "Despite all the work that's been done to curb suicides... the rates haven't changed much."

18. Where in the piece does the author's tone shift most to a more overtly positive one?
    a. Paragraph 11
    b. Paragraph 10
    c. Paragraph 13
    d. Paragraph 12

19. Which of the following accurately represents the main idea expressed in the concluding paragraph?
    a. The future will involve equal reforms to insure mental health treatments and prevent suicides.
    b. Now that mental health is insured like other treatment, suicide prevention is the future focus.
    c. For the future, our best minds need to concentrate on new thinking to prevent mental illness.
    d. The most important task of the future for innovative minds is to discover mental illness causes.

20. How can the concluding paragraph best be characterized in its tone and attitude?
    a. Pessimistic
    b. Optimistic
    c. Pragmatic
    d. Sarcastic

Questions 21 to30 pertain to the following scenario:

A Modest Proposal for preventing the children of poor people in Ireland, from being a burden on their parents or country, and for making them beneficial to the publick.

by Dr. Jonathan Swift. 1729

[Swift describes the sad plight of poor Irish parents with too many children they cannot afford to support. He announces he proposes a way to make these children contributors to parents and society instead of drains on them, while preventing voluntary abortions and infanticides. He calculates the numbers of such children, observing they cannot earn livings or be sold.]

1   I shall now therefore humbly propose my own thoughts, which I hope will not be liable to the least objection.

2   I have been assured by a very knowing American of my acquaintance in London, that a young healthy child well nursed, is, at a year old, a most delicious nourishing and wholesome food, whether stewed, roasted, baked, or boiled; and I make no doubt that it will equally serve in a fricasie, or a ragoust.

3   I do therefore humbly offer it to publick consideration, that of the hundred and twenty thousand children, already computed, twenty thousand may be reserved for breed, whereof only one fourth part to be males; which is more than we allow to sheep, black cattle, or swine, and my reason is, that these children are seldom the fruits of marriage, a circumstance not much regarded by our savages, therefore, one male will be sufficient to serve four females. That the remaining hundred thousand may, at a year old, be offered in sale to the persons of quality and fortune, through the kingdom, always advising the mother to let them suck plentifully in the last month, so as to render them plump, and fat for a good table. A child will make two dishes at an entertainment for friends, and when the family dines alone, the fore or hind quarter will make a reasonable dish, and seasoned with a little pepper or salt, will be very good boiled on the fourth day, especially in winter.

4   I grant this food will be somewhat dear, and therefore very proper for landlords, who, as they have already devoured most of the parents, seem to have the best title to the children.

5   I have already computed the charge of nursing a beggar's child (in which list I reckon all cottagers, labourers, and four-fifths of the farmers) to be about two shillings per annum, rags included; and I believe no gentleman would repine to give ten shillings for the carcass of a good fat child, which, as I have said, will make four dishes of excellent nutritive meat, when he hath only some particular friend, or his own family to dine with him. Thus the squire will learn to be a good landlord, and grow popular among his tenants, the mother will have eight shillings neat profit, and be fit for work till she produces another child.

6   Those who are more thrifty (as I must confess the times require) may flay the carcass; the skin of which, artificially dressed, will make admirable gloves for ladies, and summer boots for fine gentlemen.

7   For first, as I have already observed, it would greatly lessen the number of Papists, with whom we are yearly over-run, being the principal breeders of the nation, as well as our most dangerous enemies, and who stay at home on purpose with a design to deliver the kingdom to the Pretender, hoping to take their advantage by the absence of so many good Protestants, who have chosen rather to leave their country, than stay at home and pay tithes against their conscience to an episcopal curate.

8   Secondly, The poorer tenants will have something valuable of their own, which by law may be made liable to a distress, and help to pay their landlord's rent, their corn and cattle being already seized, and money a thing unknown.

9   Thirdly, Whereas the maintenance of an hundred thousand children, from two years old, and upwards, cannot be computed, at less than ten shillings a piece per annum, the nation's stock will be thereby increased fifty thousand pounds per annum, besides the profit of a new dish, introduced to the tables of all gentlemen of fortune in the kingdom, who have any refinement in taste. And the money will circulate among ourselves, the goods being entirely of our own growth and manufacture.

10   Fourthly, The constant breeders, besides the gain of eight shillings sterling per annum by the sale of their children, will be rid of the charge of maintaining them after the first year.

11   Fifthly, This food would likewise bring great custom to taverns, where the vintners will certainly be so prudent as to procure the best receipts for dressing it to perfection; and consequently have their houses frequented by all the fine gentlemen, who justly value themselves upon their knowledge in good eating; and a skilful cook, who understands how to oblige his guests, will contrive to make it as expensive as they please.

12   Sixthly, This would be a great inducement to marriage, which all wise nations have either encouraged by rewards, or enforced by laws and penalties. It would increase the care and tenderness of mothers towards their children, when they were sure of a settlement for life to the poor babes, provided in some sort by the publick, to their annual profit instead of expense. We should soon see an honest emulation among the married women, which of them could bring the fattest child to the market. Men would become as fond of their wives, during the time of their pregnancy, as they are now of their mares in foal, their cows in calf, or sow when they are ready to farrow; nor offer to beat or kick them (as is too frequent a practice) for fear of a miscarriage.

13   Many other advantages might be enumerated. For instance,...But this, and many others, I omit, being studious of brevity.

[Swift anticipates an objection of reducing population, saying this is intended in the design, specifically for Ireland only; and challenges other solutions like higher luxes, import bans, merchant fairness, etc. as unrealistic and/or impracticable. He reiterates the value of his proposal as new, real, cheap, easy, within Ireland's power, and not "disobliging England." He challenges critics to offer better solutions, considering the current impossibility of supporting the population; and to ask parents, who would prefer his solution over their current plight.]

14   I profess, in the sincerity of my heart, that I have not the least personal interest in endeavouring to promote this necessary work, having no other motive than the publick good of my country, by advancing our trade, providing for infants, relieving the poor, and giving some pleasure to the rich. I have no children, by which I can propose to get a single penny; the youngest being nine years old, and my wife past child-bearing.

21. The text from which this passage is taken exemplifies what genre of writing?
    a. Description
    b. Exposition
    c. Narrative
    d. Satire

22. Why do you think Swift attributes the knowledge he has received (paragraph 2) to an American?
    a. Because attributing it to America was acceptable in the UK
    b. Because attributing it to a British person was overly insulting
    c. Because attributing it to the Irish would reveal the real truth
    d. Because attributing it to a foreigner would give it credibility

23. Swift's title describes his proposal as "modest," and early on (paragraph 3 here) describes his "humbly" offering it for public consideration. Why does he use these descriptors?
    a. To increase the chances that his audience accept it
    b. To increase the appearance of its being a serious idea
    c. To increase public perception of his genius via humility
    d. To increase the contrast of its brilliance with modesty

24. In enumerating evidence supporting his claim and proposal, Swift cites six benefits as rationales. In which one does he identify the elimination of a problem in addition to the gain of an advantage(s)?
    a. In the fourth benefit
    b. In the third benefit
    c. In the second benefit
    d. In the fifth benefit

25. In Swift's time, political essays, tracts, and pamphlets were highly popular. How can the text of this passage best be described relative to this fact and to Swift's point of view?
    a. He wrote it as a perfect example of the political essay's method and style.
    b. He wrote this as an exact parody of the political essay's method and style.
    c. He wrote this to show how ineffective all such political literature had been.
    d. He wrote this as a demonstration of both (b) and (c) rather than one of (a).

26. How does Swift make his points in this essay?
    a. Logically, by proving his point via accumulating evidence
    b. Neutrally, by citing facts and figures and being objective
    c. Positively, by proposing a radical yet more effective plan
    d. Negatively, by proposing morally unacceptable practices

27. Why would Swift have taken positions and proposed actions so startling?
    a. To break through the apathy of his reading audience
    b. To increase attention and readership, and thus fame
    c. To raise publishing revenues to acquire more money
    d. To entertain his audience to forget reality for a while

28. Swift writes, "I grant this food will be somewhat dear, and therefore very proper for landlords, who, as they have already devoured most of the parents, seem to have the best title to the children" (paragraph 4). What is the best interpretation of this sentence?
    a. Irish landlords were already eating poor Irish parents.
    b. British oppression was tantamount to eating the Irish.
    c. Irish treatment of its peasants compounded Britain's.
    d. Irish parents owe debts, hence children, to landlords.

29. The persona of the proposer that Swift has created concludes by supporting his lack of potential personal gain from the proposal. What reason does he give?
   a. His own moral standards are higher than others'.
   b. He cannot be tempted without saleable children.
   c. He is too scientifically objective to consider gains.
   d. He is among many unwilling to sell their children.

30. Based on the text, what do the poor Irish population and the upper-class Irish author (or the persona of the social reformer he adopts) have in common?
   a. They both follow the same religion.
   b. They both want relief from children.
   c. They both have economic priorities.
   d. They both have nothing in common.

Questions 31 to40 pertain to the following scenario:

Openly Licensed Educational Resources: Providing Equitable Access to Education for All Learners

1   *Cross-posted from the <u>White House blog</u>.*

2   Summary: The Federal government is supporting the use of open educational resources to provide equitable access to quality education.

3   *Everyone has the right to education...Education shall be directed to the full development of the human personality and to the strengthening of respect for human rights and fundamental freedoms. It shall promote understanding, tolerance and friendship among all nations, racial or religious groups, and shall further the activities of the United Nations for the maintenance of peace. —<u>Article 26 of the United Nations Declaration of Human Rights</u>*

4   Access to quality education is an essential component of addressing many of our biggest global and societal challenges. Last year, the United Nations surveyed youth around the world about their priorities—what opportunities they want to be offered. More than improvements in electricity and infrastructure, healthcare, and better jobs, what young people asked for was a good education. It's no surprise that young people value education. World Bank economists estimate that for every year of study, individual income increases by 10-15 percent. These increases don't just affect individuals; they often generate a "ripple effect" of benefits to families and entire communities. Openly licensed learning resources, also known as open educational resources (OER), can increase access to high-quality education opportunities and reduce the cost of education around the world.

5   On September 28, the White House Office of Science and Technology Policy, U.S. Department of Education, and U.S. Department of State co-hosted an International Open Education Workshop, bringing together 40 civil society and foreign government participants from eight countries to examine existing open education efforts and identify opportunities for future collaboration between government and civil society. This workshop is one of several open education commitments made as part of the second U.S. Open Government Partnership National Action Plan.

6   At the workshop, participants shared examples of ways that openly licensed educational materials are being used to solve local education challenges around the world. For example, one participant shared open-source tools that enable offline access to openly licensed educational videos — technology that has supported education for Syrian refugees, inmates in U.S. correctional facilities, and over 2 million other learners from around the world. Open licenses grant anyone the rights to revise, remix, and redistribute these educational materials, so investments in content or tools made by one organization or government can be leveraged by other institutions and used in new ways.

7   Another participant, drawing on her recent experience serving as a Foreign Service Officer in the Balkans, noted the potential for openly licensed educational materials to honor local knowledge and information needs. In particular, she described how an open-source model could empower educators to collaborate on and adapt textbooks across local and international borders, retaining fundamental content while tailoring certain features, like names in math word problems, to reflect students' ethnic diversity and culture. Empowering local communities to adapt, translate, and create collections of learning materials that meet their information, learning, or language needs helps side-step assumptions and honor learners' lived experiences.

8   Open education advances key national priorities, including supporting shared economic prosperity, strengthening civil society, and investing in human development. Over the next year, the U.S. Government will continue efforts to expand and accelerate the use and availability of openly licensed educational materials worldwide. In addition, we will begin to model the transition to openly licensed educational materials at scale in U.S. K-12 schools. We look forward to engaging with the national and global community to identify opportunities for open licensing to accelerate educational equity for all learners regardless of their financial situations or geographic locations.
Richard Culatta is Director of the Office of Educational Technology at the U.S. Department of Education.

Sunshine Ison is Director of the ECA Collaboratory at the U.S. Department of State.

Nancy Weiss is Senior Advisor to the Chief Technology Officer at the White House Office of Science and Technology Policy.

31. What does the line of text directly below the title mean?
    a. This article is reproduced in another government blog.
    b. This article is reproduced from another federal article.
    c. This article is cross-referenced, separately, to another.
    d. This article is cross-referenced within a different blog.

32. What is the source of the quotation opening this article?
    a. A US federal government agency
    b. A private education company
    c. The United States Constitution
    d. An international agreement

33. What did the UN find from surveying global youth regarding what opportunities were most important to them?
    a. A good education was equal in importance with better jobs.
    b. A good education took priority over all other improvements.
    c. A good education took second priority, behind healthcare.
    d. A good education was after infrastructure and before electricity.

34. What does this piece identify about the relationship between education and earnings?
    a. Individuals earn 10-15 percent more per additional year of education.
    b. Individuals are hired 10-15 percent more often per year of education.
    c. Individuals are promoted 10-15 percent more often due to education.
    d. Individuals earning higher wages have 10-15 percent more education.

35. From this blog, what might you logically infer about open-source or openly licensed educational materials?
    a. They can be used by educators, as long as they do not alter them.
    b. They are free of charge for use by educators and publicly funded.
    c. They can not only be used, but also altered and shared by anyone.
    d. They can be inferred as (b), (c) is explicit, and (a) is explicitly incorrect.

36. The title and summary (paragraph 2) of this piece are most directly related to which of the following main ideas included in the text?
    a. Lowering the costs of education the world over
    b. The "ripple effect" to families and communities
    c. Enabling more equal access to quality education
    d. The high value young people have for education

37. How does this piece move from its opening paragraph (4) to the following one (5)?
    a. It creates a transition by referring to the end of the first paragraph with the second.
    b. It directly continues the same train of thought from the first paragraph to the next.
    c. It introduces a new but related topic with date, co-hosts, participants, and purpose.
    d. It makes no transition at all, just abruptly changing the subject to an alternate topic.

38. Which of these is an accurate conclusion based on the textual evidence?
    a. Open licenses benefit only learners and educators who have Internet access.
    b. Open licenses enable one government's investment to benefit other groups.
    c. Open licenses enable one government's investment to be stolen by others'.
    d. Open licenses benefit over 2 million learners, but not prisoners or refugees.

39. According to the authors, which of the following are components of open education initiatives?
    a. Collaboration among governments but not members of civil society
    b. Collaboration among educators, only within their local communities
    c. Collaboration of educators for learning materials reflecting diversity
    d. Collaboration by both parts of (a) and by educators, as limited to (b)

40. How does the concluding paragraph (8) function relative to the rest of this text?
    a. It summarizes each main point that was made in each of the preceding paragraphs.
    b. It introduces some new material to encourage readers to research the topic more.
    c. It communicates a conclusion the authors reach via the preceding logical sequence.
    d. It summarizes some key points in the first sentence and then forecasts the future.

Constructed Response

Read the passages and examine the graphic below, and then answer the essay questions that follow.

PASSAGE A

Thank you for contacting me regarding the Land and Water Conservation Fund (LWCF). I always appreciate the opportunity to hear from my fellow Georgians.

The LWCF was created by Congress in 1965 to set aside federal funds to protect our natural resources, as well as to provide matching grants to state and local governments for conservation projects. As the Chairman of the Subcommittee on Conservation, Forestry, and Natural Resources, I understand the importance of conservation and the role it plays in preserving wildlife habitat, as well as providing outdoor recreational opportunities that spur economies. Currently, the LWCF is authorized through September 30, 2015, and Congress has appropriated varying amounts each year since the inception of the program. I believe we need to ensure that Congress retains the ability to exercise oversight when reauthorizing this program.

When the Senate turns its attention to funding the agencies, programs, and projects that make up our federal government, please know that the management of our country's financial resources are of great importance to me. Years of mismanagement and overspending were what drew me to run for the Senate in the first place. That said, I will prioritize spending that provides a good return on taxpayer investment. Those programs should be encouraged and adequately funded.

Thank you for taking the time to contact me. Your thoughts are important, and I will keep them in mind should the Senate consider legislation regarding the LWCF.

Kindest regards,

David Perdue
United States Senator

PASSAGE B

Thank you for contacting me to express your support for the Land and Water Conservation Fund (LWCF). I welcome feedback from my constituents and I appreciate your interest in this issue. You will be pleased to know that I share your support for this very important program.

As you know, the Land and Water Conservation Fund was established to assist in preserving, developing, and assuring to all citizens of the United States quality and quantity of outdoor recreation resources. The Land and Water Conservation Fund Coalition is an informal partnership of national, state, and local conservation and recreation organizations working together to support full and dedicated funding for LWCF. The program provides matching grants to states and through states to local governments, for the acquisition and development of public outdoor recreation sites and facilities. Grant funds are also available, to states only, for fulfilling the statewide comprehensive outdoor recreation planning requirements of the program.

The President's FY1 6 budget request allocates $900 million for LWCF, with $400 million in discretionary funding and $500 million in permanent funding. I applaud President Obama for his investment in the Land and Water Conservation Fund, which protects our land, water and quality of life. The President has proposed key investments that protect landscapes including Montana's Crown of the Continent, Tennessee's Cumberland Mountains, and Oregon's Hells Canyon National Recreation Area.

You may be interested to know that I joined my colleagues in requesting appropriations funding for LWCF during the 114th Congress. I am glad we can agree on this issue and I am proud to be your Representative in Congress. I will keep your thoughts in mind as the FY1 6 budget continues its way through the legislative process.

I am eager to hear from you and I look forward to working with you in the future. For more information, please visit my office online at www.HankJohnson.House.gov , where you may sign up to receive my e-newsletter. Thank you again for contacting me.

Sincerely,

Henry C. "Hank" Johnson, Jr.
Member of Congress

Figure 1. LWCF Appropriations, FY1965-FY2014

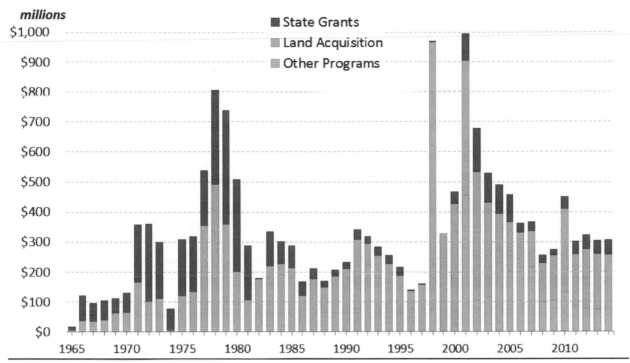

Key to preserving America's recreation lands

1. Write an essay approximately 100-200 words long explaining which of the two passages argues more effectively. Identify which claims each writer makes in each passage. Evaluate what evidence each uses to support his claims, including if there is insufficient evidence and why you think more evidence is not provided. Evaluate how relevant and valid the existing evidence is. Provide examples from each passage in support of your assessment. Write for an adult, educated audience, using your own words (except for quotations). Ensure that your final draft adheres to all standard American English writing conventions.

2. In about 100-200 words, write an essay explaining how the information shown in the graphic above relates to what is written in the second passage above. Give examples from both of these sources to support your claims. Write for an intended audience of adult, well-educated readers. Use your own words (other than in quotations). Adhere to all standard conventions for American English writing in your final draft.

3. Compose an approximately 400- to 600-word essay that discusses and evaluates advantages and disadvantages of the Land and Water Conservation Fund (LWCF). Include the following: (1) Argue for a claim that shows knowledge and understanding of this subject. (2) Support your argument using logical reasoning that connects with and builds upon the claims or arguments in the sources above. (3) Cite enough pertinent evidence from all three sources above to support your claim. (4) Identify at least one counterclaim that you can anticipate, and propose a response to it.

Answers and Explanations

1. C: Section 2 identifies determining the content of your current diet as the first step to take. Getting information about what you should consume (a) is identified as the second step. Improving your nutritional choices (b) is identified as the third step. This text does confirm the importance of physical activity to weight management, but does not identify exercising more as the first step in weight management (d).

2. B: In section 1, the text states that obesity raises the risk of developing type 2 diabetes, not type 1 (a); cardiovascular (b), i.e., heart (and blood vessel) disease; and some types of cancer, not all (c). Obesity can also raise the risk of joint problems (d), but the text does NOT identify these as an example of the "many diseases" for which obesity raises the risk.

3. D: Section 3 of the text identifies desserts like cakes and cookies as the leading calorie source in American diets. Sugar-sweetened beverages (a) are identified as the leading source of calories *from drinks* in the American diet, not of all calories consumed. Neither fatty meats (b) nor breads made with refined flour (c) are identified as the primary source of calories in the American diet.

4. A: In Section 5, the text states that, in order to improve your diet and weight, you must first increase your awareness of your current diet, physical activity, and body weight so you can compare these to recommended levels and change them as needed. Therefore, diet awareness is not the only requirement (b); you need to maintain awareness of both your current amounts of physical activity (c) and weight (d).

5. B: As the text emphasizes through boldface in section 6, the people succeeding most at weight loss and maintenance regularly track their dietary intake. In a regular (non-bold) font, the text says tracking physical activity (a) and body weight (c) also helps in weight management, but these are not associated with the MOST success as tracking diet is. The text never says not to track anything too regularly (d).

6. C: The chart of stumbling blocks presented in this text states that continuous Internet access is NOT required to track one's diet (a). Solutions to the first two stumbling blocks include links to the website's own online tracking tool (b). The solutions to the first stumbling block include that simply writing down one's dietary intake is also effective (c) to raise awareness; and that the linked online tool enables entering several days at a time, not one (d).

7. D: In the second row, the chart maintains that tracking does work, but does NOT say the time is worth it regardless of how long it takes (a) or that taking too long means you are not doing it right (b). It offers writing intake down as one method, but does NOT identify this as the fastest method (c). It points out the importance of finding a method that works for you. It does explain that the online tool provides for making favorite foods lists, which can then enable entering items faster (d).

8. C: The fourth row of the stumbling blocks chart advises not only measuring portion sizes (a), but also reading nutritional information on food packaging, which lists both number of servings per package AND standard serving size (b); measuring both your own typical serving sizes and standard portion sizes like a half-cup or full cup to estimate how much you eat; and using pictures on the text's website (www.choosemyplate.gov) of sample portion sizes (d). You can logically conclude that in doing all these, you should also compare your customary serving sizes to standard serving sizes (c).

9. C: This choice is most representative of a main idea as it is a generalized statement encompassing all related topics in the text. Choices (a), (b), and (d) are all examples of supporting evidence or supporting details that are provided as ways of reinforcing the main idea, e.g., by substantiating it with facts, supplying rationales, giving examples, or offering more specific directions.

10. A: This is most appropriate choice for the text content. In fact, the *actual* title is "Learn What You Currently Eat and Drink"; choice (a) closely paraphrases the real title, identifying the topic. Choice (b) refers to one fact given as a rationale and supporting evidence for attaining healthy body weight, not the overall subject. This source (the USDA website, www.choosemyplate.gov) has another page about physical activity and mentions it on this page, but it is not the main topic here (c). Choice (d) refers to supporting evidence for weight management, not this text's more specific topic (a).

11. C: In paragraph 1, Griffis opens by describing Todd's position as one that "can be a difficult place" (a). In paragraph 3, he describes his parents' being able to pick their battles as "one of the perks of being the fourth child." (b) Therefore, he saw both (c) advantages and disadvantages to being the middle child, and (d) is incorrect.

12. B: The author uses a simile ("a little bit *like*") to compare his sensitive brother Todd—not himself (d)—to a "sickly wildebeest... trying to look inconspicuous" and Todd's five brothers—neither the parents (a) nor the entire family (c)—to a pride of lions. This comparison makes the point that being sensitive, though it "might help you get the girl," makes a boy vulnerable to attack when he has five "competitive, rough-and-tumble" brothers.

13. A: Although the photo has no caption or identifying information, readers can infer it is a picture of the author's late brother Todd because he is the subject of the author's description as a personal example illustrating the importance of suicide prevention and Global Mental Health Day. It is not a photo of the author (b). An individual with mental illness does not look a certain identifiable way (c)—one of the author's points is how easily and often it goes undetected. It is not a photo of a typical HHS employee (d).

14. B: In this paragraph, the author describes Todd's "courage in forging his own way" as he discovered interests, activities, and a style all his own in spite of "pressure" and "needling" from his brothers. To emphasize how normal Todd seemed, he adds that Todd was "maybe not the top student among us" (a), "and maybe not the best athlete" (c), but "plenty smart" and "plenty active." He begins this paragraph, "Todd's feelings bruised more easily than the rest of ours." Hence Todd was not the least sensitive, but the most sensitive (d).

15. A: In paragraph 5, the author identifies the date as "16 years ago last May," and the blog's publication date is given as October 2015, so it was in May 1999 (a), not April 2000 (b). June of 2014 (d) is 16 *months* before the publication date, not 16 years. Therefore, choice (c) is incorrect.

16. C: The author writes in paragraph 6, "*No one knew* Todd was hurting (a). The *only warning sign* (b) *came the day of his death* (c) when *we learned that he hadn't been attending the college class* he was supposed to be taking his senior year of high school." (d)

17. C: Excerpt (a) illustrates that, even with the passage of these laws improving mental health insurance benefits, more effort is required to get MH services to people in need—not how influential the laws have been. Excerpt (b) illustrates that high annual suicide rates continue

despite the laws—not their influence. Excerpt (c) illustrates the influence of these laws by identifying them as representing a "sea change" in American approaches to mental illness. Excerpt (d) illustrates that, regardless of the laws and other efforts, suicide rates have not declined significantly.

18. A: After citing high and relatively unchanging suicide rates over 30 years, which creates a negative tone in paragraph 10 (b), the author begins paragraph 11, "We're doing something about that." This shift to a more positive tone accompanies the introduction of the title topic, Global Mental Health Day, and associated initiatives. Paragraph 12 (d) provides supporting evidence for paragraph 11 by quoting federal policy experts and explaining how to address the problem, rather than shifting the tone. Paragraph 13 (c) relays the experts' call for contributions, including a link.

19. B: In the concluding paragraph, the author first summarizes the progress made through the laws giving mental health the same insurance coverage as other healthcare treatments, and then the importance of new thinking in future suicide prevention efforts. He does not call for equal reforms to both (a), as the first has already been legislated. He stresses the need to prevent suicide through identifying and treating mental illness, not to prevent mental illness (c) or discover its causes (d).

20. B: The author's tone and attitude can best be described as obviously optimistic. His word choices indicate this: "We've made progress... Now, we *look forward* to... suicide prevention. We *look towards a tomorrow* where more Americans get the help they deserve and fewer families experience the pain and grief of suicide." There is nothing pessimistic (a) in this paragraph. It is not as pragmatic (c), i.e., practical, as it is positive. Its hopeful tone is genuine, not sarcastic (d).

21. D: Descriptive (a) text uses many sensory details to paint a vivid picture of a moment, scene, setting, character, event, etc. to enable readers to feel they are experiencing it firsthand. Expository (b) text provides facts, directions, and/or other information objectively to educate, illustrate for, guide, and otherwise inform readers. Narrative (c) text tells readers a story. This is satire (d), which indirectly lampoons societal foibles using irony.

22. A: In 1729, Americans were British colonials. Many UK citizens regarded them as inferior or barbaric, and for those who did not, their foreignness over a century after British settlement made them a safer target to insult by suggesting familiarity with cannibalism. Swift would not fear to insult the British (b), whose political and commercial control of and injustices against Ireland he hated. He would not attribute it to his own people, which was not the truth (c). Attributing this knowledge to a foreigner distances it from UK citizens more than lending it credibility (d).

23. B: Swift never meant for his reading audience to accept (a) an idea so patently absurd; he pretended to offer a "solution" no civilized people would consider to satirize human societal behaviors. Hence he couched this offer in "modest" and "humble" terms to resemble serious proposals (b) made by people in who, his day, conventionally used such terms to deflect audience perceptions of author grandiosity or egoism, avoiding broadcasting their own brilliance through humble (c) and modest (d) expressions of it.

24. A: In the first benefit (paragraph 7), Swift writes of eliminating Catholics. In the second benefit (c), he identifies gaining a valuable commodity (p8). In the third (b), he emphasizes national monetary gain (p9) via cost-benefit analysis. In the fourth (a), he cites eliminating child-rearing expenses in addition to gaining sale proceeds (p10). In the fifth (d), he identifies commercial

benefits to taverns (p11). In the sixth (p12), he names gains of increasing marriage, care, and maternal competition, plus eliminating spousal abuse.

25. D: Swift was not endeavoring to write the perfect example of the political essay (a) form that was so popular in his time, but rather to parody it (b) as well as to show, through the specific "solution" he "proposes," how ineffectual all such political literature had been (c) to reform society. He attacks both British exploitation of Ireland and incompetent Irish leadership.

26. D: Swift cites considerable evidence, but does not prove his points logically (a) as his suggestion so clearly violates religious, moral, ethical, and humane principles. He parodies the ruthless logic of pseudoscientific social engineering reformers who reduced human suffering to statistics and commodities. While citing facts and figures, he is neither neutral nor objective (b). To criticize British and Irish societies for their failings, he adopts an ostensibly sincere tone to blame them for economic and social problems. His "plan" is not real, but designed to shock readers; hence he does not make his points positively (c), but negatively.

27. A: Swift was just as disgusted with the apathy of Irish subjects under British rule as he was with British mistreatment of Ireland and Irish poverty and suffering. He wanted to shock readers out of their indifference, to stimulate them to question their own values and be outraged enough to take true reformative action. He was passionate about economic, political, and other social wrongs, not about fame (b) or money (c). He was not simply trying to entertain; he wanted to alert readers to reality, not make them forget it (d).

28. C: Swift's meaning in this sentence is not literal, e.g., the landlords were already cannibalizing poor tenants (a) or indebted tenants owed their children to landlords (d) as food. While he does draw an analogy between the concepts of Britain's oppression of the Irish and of its eating them (b), this is not the best interpretation as it omits another part of Swift's meaning: that British oppression of the Irish, analogous to cannibalistic consumption, was compounded by rich Irish landlords' exploiting ("devouring") poor Irish tenants (c)—his country consuming its own resources and itself.

29. B: The proposer persona does not claim moral standards too high to participate in the proposal (a) or scientific objectivity (c) from which he would not descend, nor does he cite an attachment or unwillingness to sell his children (d). In fact, throughout the essay he reiterates a fundamental assumption that anybody with children the right age would sell them. Instead, he attributes his lack of vested interest in having only a child too old to eat and a wife too old to bear more (b).

30. C: The poor Irish population was Catholic (contributing to the overpopulation), while Swift was Protestant (a). Even readers lacking historical background knowledge can deduce this from Swift calling them "Papists" and describing them as "with whom we are... over-run," "the principal breeders," "our most dangerous enemies," and "hoping to take... advantage," while describing Protestants as "good." Swift/his persona never states nor implies wanting relief from his own children (b). However, despite their contrasts, both prioritize economics (c). Thus choice (d) is incorrect.

31. B: "Cross-posted" means the material was published on two different web pages, in this case on two federal websites (whitehouse.gov and ed.gov). The word "from" indicates it was originally posted on the White House Blog site and then also posted to the Department of Education blog site on the same date—not vice versa (a). "Cross-referenced" (c), (d) means that one article refers to another—not that the identical article appears in two places (b).

32. D: The source of the opening quotation is cited as Article 26 of the United Nations Declaration of Human Rights, an agreement among the many world members of the United Nations. Therefore it is not from a US federal government agency (a), a private educational company (b), or the United States Constitution (c), but from a document signed by global members of the UN.

33. B: According to this blog, worldwide youth responding to a UN survey the year before publication gave a good education higher priority than improvements in jobs (a), healthcare (c), infrastructure, and electricity (d). They did not give education equal importance (a) to anything else or secondary priority (c) to anything else, and it did not come after anything else (d) in importance.

34. A: The article states in its first paragraph (4) that, according to estimates from World Bank economists, individual income is 10-15 percent more for each year of more individual education. It does not state anywhere that individuals are hired 10-15 percent more per year of education (b), promoted 10-15 percent more often due to education (c), or that higher earners have 10-15 percent more education (d).

35. D: While the text does not explicitly state it, readers can logically infer that open-source and/or openly licensed educational materials are free of charge for use, supported by public funding (b). The text DOES explicitly state (paragraph 6), "Open licenses grant anyone the rights to revise, remix, and redistribute these educational materials" (c). Because (b) can be inferred, (c) is explicitly stated, and (a) is explicitly contradicted in the article, (d) is correct.

36. C: Lowering global education costs (a) is an important idea introduced in the first paragraph (4), but not most directly related to the title and summary (paragraph 2). The "ripple effect" to families and communities (b) named in the same paragraph refers to how education not only raises individual earnings, but spreads to benefit larger groups. This paragraph also presents evidence that young people highly value education (d)—another important idea. But none of these is as closely related to the title and summary as the idea of enabling more equal access to quality education (c).

37. C: This piece does not use the type of transition between its first and second paragraphs wherein the second paragraph's first sentence refers to the last sentence(s) of the first paragraph (a), nor does it continue the same thought from the first to second paragraph (b). However, it does not simply change the subject completely and abruptly (d). After a general discussion of the main idea, including supporting evidence in the first paragraph, the second paragraph introduces a related topic by identifying the date, co-hosts, and purpose (c) of a workshop on that idea.

38. B: In the third paragraph (6), the bloggers describe how open licenses materials enabled *offline* access to educational videos for learners and educators, i.e., they did not need Internet access (a) to view these. This paragraph also points out how open licensing enables one government or organization's investment to benefit others (b) who have equal access to open-source materials rather than stealing them (c); and has benefited over 2 million learners worldwide, *including* American prison inmates and Syrian refugees (d).

39. C: Collaboration between government AND civil society (a) is identified as part of an open education initiative, the second US Open Government Partnership National Action Plan (paragraph 5), including workshops with multinational participants. Empowering local communities is identified (p7) as affirming learner experiences and avoiding stereotypical assumptions, never as limited to these (b), (d), but empowering educators "to collaborate on and adapt textbooks *across*

local *and international borders*," enabling both preserving basic content and customizing specific features to reflect student cultural and ethnic diversity (c).

40. A: The first sentence of the last paragraph summarizes three "key national priorities" that open education further. The following sentences all forecast US government plans for the future (a) with open licensing rather than summarizing main points from preceding paragraphs (b), introducing new material at the end (c), or reaching any conclusion based on any preceding logical sequence (d).

Practice Test #3

Practice Questions

Questions 1 to10 pertain to the following scenario:
Physical activity is an important part of managing body weight.

1   Being physically active can help you achieve a healthy weight and prevent excess weight gain. However, physical activity is also important to all other aspects of your health. Benefits include sleeping better at night, decreasing your chances of becoming depressed, and helping you look good. When you are not physically active, you are more likely to have health problems, including heart disease, type 2 diabetes, and high blood cholesterol.

2   The amount of physical activity needed to manage body weight depends on calorie intake and varies a lot from person to person. Some adults will need to do more physical activity than others to manage body weight.

3   How much physical activity do you need to help manage body weight?

To start, adults should do the equivalent of 150 minutes (2 hours and 30 minutes) of moderate-intensity aerobic activity each week.
- If necessary, adults should increase their weekly minutes of aerobic physical activity gradually over time (while eating fewer calories) to meet weight loss goals.
- Some adults who need to lose weight may need to do more than the equivalent of 300 minutes (5 hours) per week of moderate-intensity activity to meet weight loss goals.

4   This may sound like a lot. However, your weight is a balance of the number of calories you eat and drink and the physical activity you do. Weight loss can be achieved by eating and drinking fewer calories OR by burning more calories in physical activity. The people with the greatest long-term success are doing BOTH – eating less and being more active. For example, walking 30 minutes each day and drinking one less soda each day are two small steps you can take that can have a big impact on your weight over time.

5   Get started increasing physical activity:

- Pick activities you like and that fit into your life.
- Be active with family and friends. Having a support network can help you stay active.
- Keep track of your physical activity and gradually increase how much you do over time. Use the SuperTracker, a journal, a log, or mark your activity on a calendar.
- If you are interested in a physical challenge to get you started, try the President's Challenge.

6   Stumbling blocks

Concerned about increasing physical activity? Below are some common "stumbling blocks" and ideas to help you overcome these barriers. Note: If you are on a mobile device, you may need to turn your phone 90 degrees to see the full chart.

"I dislike physical activity." "Running just isn't my idea of fun."	Pick activities that you like and start by doing what you can, at least 10 minutes at a time. Every bit adds up, and the health benefits increase as you spend more time being active. If one activity, like running, doesn't appeal to you, find something that does. There are lots of activities, such as: swimming, biking, walking, playing tennis, basketball, hiking, rollerblading, etc. The point is to get out there and move! Doing something is better than doing nothing.
"I don't have the energy to be active."	Daily activities like walking, gardening, and climbing up the stairs all count. Start with what you can do, even if that's just 10 minutes. You may even find yourself more energized after being active!
"I don't know the first thing about being active."	Physical activity simply means movement of the body that uses energy. You can choose moderate or vigorous intensity activities, or a mix of both, each week. Moderate physical activities include: walking briskly, bicycling, dancing, and golf. Vigorous physical activities include: running, jogging, swimming, basketball, and aerobics. Check out these tips for increasing physical activity.
"How do I know when I have gotten enough exercise for the day?"	For substantial health benefits, the 2008 Physical Activity Guidelines recommend that adults get at least 150 minutes (2 hours and 30 minutes) a week of moderate-intensity activity or 75 minutes (1 hour and 15 minutes) a week of vigorous-intensity aerobic physical activity, or an equivalent combination of moderate- and vigorous-intensity aerobic activity. Aerobic activity should be performed in episodes of at least 10 minutes, and preferably, it should be spread throughout the week.

--United States Department of Agriculture (USDA) website (www.choosemyplate.gov, 2015)

1. What benefit of physical activity does this text NOT specifically identify?
   a. Improved appearance
   b. Lower depression risk
   c. Improved sleep quality
   d. Improved muscle mass

2. What can physical activity help to accomplish, according to this text?
    a. It can help you maintain a healthy weight, but not lose weight.
    b. It can help your overall health but does not affect your weight.
    c. It can help you to avoid gaining excessive amounts of weight.
    d. It can help you lose weight, maintain it, and never gain weight.

3. What does this text say about physical inactivity relative to health?
    a. Being physically inactive increases the probability of health problems.
    b. Being physically inactive has no impacts on the status of your health.
    c. Health problems are more likely caused by too much exercise than by none.
    d. Health problems can cause physical inactivity rather than vice versa.

4. According to the text, what is true about physical activity necessary for weight management?
    a. Everybody needs the same amount of physical activity for managing weight.
    b. The amount of activity required varies among individuals to manage weight.
    c. The number of calories consumed does not affect activity to manage weight.
    d. It is impossible to determine a physical activity amount for managing weight.

5. This source identifies which amount of physical activity as a *beginning* for adult weight management?
    a. One-and-a-half hours of low-intensity activity every week
    b. Two-and-a-half hours of moderate aerobic activity weekly
    c. 250 minutes of high-intensity aerobic activity for every week
    d. More than 300 minutes of vigorous aerobic activity per week

6. The most successful long-term strategy for weight management is what, according to the source?
    a. Eating less with greater activity
    b. More activity regardless of diet
    c. Eating less regardless of activity
    d. Constant activity and diet levels

7. From the advice given in the first row of the chart of stumbling blocks, what can you infer?
    a. You should only choose from those activities it names.
    b. Many activities exist, but they must be effective ones.
    c. Even a few minutes of activity are better than nothing.
    d. You should choose an activity you enjoy, whatever it is.

8. For people who claim ignorance about being active, what response does the text offer?
    a. It offers a basic definition of physical activity, but no examples.
    b. It offers some examples of moderate but not vigorous activity.
    c. It offers a link for tips to increase physical activity, nothing else.
    d. It offers a definition, examples, and a link for additional advice.

9. What can you logically conclude based on the information provided in this source?
    a. The Physical Activity Guidelines cited are not from a government agency.
    b. The Physical Activity Guidelines give no minimum durations for aerobics.
    c. The Physical Activity Guidelines allow concentrating activity in a few days.
    d. The Physical Activity Guidelines advise distributing activity across a week.

10. Which of the following would be the best title for this text based on its content?
    a. Manage Our Body Weight
    b. Be Healthier and Happier
    c. Increase Physical Activity
    d. Prevent Health Problems

Questions 11 to20 pertain to the following scenario:

Investing in Teachers Instead of Prisons

SEPTEMBER 30, 2015

Arne Duncan, Secretary, US Department of Education

As prepared—speaker may have deviated from this version

1   I want to tell you about something I'm not proud of.

2   Early in my time as CEO of Chicago Public Schools, we set out to make our schools safer places for children and adults.

3   We knew that too many of our students were going to jail. So I asked if we could find out what time of day our kids were getting arrested.

4   I figured that if we knew when the arrests were occurring—after school, I suspected—we could target an intervention to keep kids more engaged.

5   I didn't expect the answer: that the majority of the arrests were occurring during the school day, in our school buildings, mostly for nonviolent misdemeanors.

6   Those calls to the police, to put kids in jail? We were making them.

7   We were responsible. We had met the enemy, and it was us.

8   No one had set out to criminalize the behavior of our students, or to start them down a path of incarceration. But those were the facts.

9   And they are bound up with another set of facts.

10   The fact that America has less than five percent of the world's population— and more than 20 percent of its inmates.

11   The fact that America locks up black people at a far higher rate than South Africa did at the height of Apartheid.

12   The fact that young men of color are six times more likely to be incarcerated than white males.

13   The fact that one out of every three black men in America is predicted to go to prison at some point in their lives—one in three—while just one in five of them receives a bachelor's degree.

14   Facing the facts on incarceration leaves us with no choice. We, as a country, must do more to change the odds.

15   And that's why I want to lay out an idea today that will strike some as improbable or impractical, but which I think is essential.

16   It's about setting a different direction as a society, a different priority—one that says we believe in great teaching early in our kids' lives, rather than courts, jails and prisons later.

17   The bet we're making now is clear. In the last three decades, state and local correctional spending in this country has increased almost twice as fast as spending on elementary and secondary education. Ask yourself, "What does that say about what we believe?"

18   Leaders at the state and local levels have the power to change that—to place a bet on getting it right with kids from the start, and on the power of great teaching in particular.

19   I'm not pretending for a second that schools can do this alone—that they can replace efforts to deal with poverty, hunger, homelessness, or other ills that affect our young people. But the facts about the impact of great teaching are too powerful to ignore.

20   I haven't met a parent yet who needed to be convinced that it was important for her child to have a great teacher. Parents intuitively know what research tells us.

21   A mountain of evidence makes clear not just that teachers are the most important factor in a school, but how important they are—so much so that kids who have great teachers end up with months' worth more learning than kids who don't.

22   And the benefits of a great teacher prove out in life, not just in school. A single year with an excellent teacher rather than an ineffective one—a single year—has been shown to have benefits in lifetime earnings of a quarter-million dollars or more for that class—and a measurable impact on their likelihood of attending college, and of having a child in their teenage years.

23   The linkage between education, or a lack thereof, and incarceration is powerful.

24   More than two-thirds of state prison inmates are high school dropouts. And an African-American male between the ages of 20 and 24 without a high school diploma or GED has a higher chance of being imprisoned than of being employed.

25   Today, our schools suspend roughly three and a half million kids a year, and refer a quarter of a million children to the police each year. And the patterns are

even more troubling for children of color —particularly boys—and for students with disabilities.

26   We cannot lay our incarceration crisis at the door of our schools. But we have to do our part to end the school to prison pipeline.

27   So here's an idea for how you put a new emphasis on schools rather than jails.

28   If our states and localities took just half the people convicted of nonviolent crimes and found paths for them other than incarceration, they would save upwards of $15 billion a year.

29   If they reinvested that money into paying the teachers who are working in our highest-need schools and communities—they could provide a 50 percent average salary increase to every single one of them. Specifically, if you focused on the 20 percent of schools with the highest poverty rates in each state, that would give you 17,640 schools—and the money would go far enough to increase salaries by at least 50 percent.

30   In our schools, reducing the number of our young people who end up behind bars, fundamentally, is about changing the odds for our most underserved students. That means following through on the difficult but vital work of turning around chronically low performing schools, and helping educators continue crucial progress in cutting dropout rates and improving graduation rates, which today are at historic highs. It means ensuring that all students—including and especially those in low-income communities of color—have access to high standards, aligned to the expectations of the real world, and challenging coursework that prepares them for college—without time lost to remediation.

31   It means expanding the opportunity of quality preschool, whose power to reduce incarceration is well-established. It means giving teachers the preparation and support they need to succeed—especially in high need schools. And it means ensuring that children go to school free from fear—whether from gun violence or bullying or racial or sexual harassment or assault. None of that work is new; all of it is essential to changing the odds.

32   Unfortunately, some in this country would have us move in exactly the opposite direction—by cutting the funds that states and districts so desperately need to make opportunity real for our kids. That's exactly what Republican budget proposals would do. As compared to the President's budget, they would cut funds for vulnerable students, support for teachers, job training, and preschool opportunities that we know—we know—help our young people become productive citizens rather than wasting years behind bars. It is the foundation upon which academic success can be built.

33   All the ideas I've talked about today are part of that same fight. Yes, it's about educational and economic opportunity. But it's bigger than that. It's a fight to increase social mobility. It's a fight for social justice. For too many of our children today, it can literally mean the difference between life and death.

34   Our children and our country deserve a different bargain, a different set of priorities. And, when we bet on the extraordinary potential of ALL of our children, when we bet on the transformative power of teachers, we cannot lose.

11. What does Secretary Duncan identify as a main source of student arrests in Chicago Public Schools?
    a. Criminal activities by students outside of school days
    b. A large proportion of violent offenses during school
    c. Schools' reporting students for nonviolent offenses
    d. Students' violent crimes during truancy from school

12. The "facts on incarceration" (paragraph 14) cited in this text include which of the following?
    a. America's proportion of prisoners in the world is over four times its proportion of the world population.
    b. America's rate of incarcerating black people is second only to South Africa's at apartheid's extreme.
    c. America's incarceration of young black men is three times more probable than that of white males.
    d. America's black males are projected to be imprisoned five percent more than to be given bachelor's degrees.

13. Which of the following best expresses the main idea of this text?
    a. The American prison system is racially biased.
    b. Prioritizing education can lower incarceration.
    c. America's incarceration crisis is the schools' fault.
    d. Great education has huge economic benefits.

14. What examples are included in these excerpts of how local and state governments can shift emphasis from prisons to schools?
    a. Paying more to teachers in the poorest schools and communities
    b. Doing (c) to fund also doing (a), but (d) is not used as an example
    c. Saving money through alternatives to prison for nonviolent crime
    d. Reallocating funding from prison facilities to educational facilities

15. Which literary/rhetorical device does Duncan use in paragraphs 30 and 31 to create emphasis?
    a. Parallel structure
    b. Circumlocution
    c. Euphemisms
    d. Hyperbole

16. Among these improvements that Duncan calls for as essential to "changing the odds" for underserved students, which one does he identify with a known ability to prevent prison time?
    a. Enhancing professional development for teachers
    b. Enhancing support of high-need schools' teachers
    c. Enhancing early childhood education opportunities
    d. Enhancing safer school environments for students

17. What can you conclude about the speaker's point of view from paragraph 32?
    a. He opposes Democratic budget proposals to cut education funding.
    b. He opposes bipartisan budget proposals that cut education funding.
    c. He opposes the president's budget, as it will cut education funding.
    d. He opposes Republican budget proposals to cut education funding.

18. In calling for his audience to question and reevaluate their beliefs, Duncan says, "What does that say about what we believe?" To which of these does he refer?
    a. Federal and state spending have increased equally for corrections and for schools in 30 years.
    b. Federal, state, and local spending increased 50 percent more for corrections than schools in 30 years.
    c. Local and state spending has increased nearly twice as much for corrections as it has for schools in 30 years.
    d. Federal, state, and local spending have decreased for schools, but not corrections, in 30 years.

19. What does Duncan say about things that are all "part of that same fight"?
    a. The fight is for educational opportunity, not economic opportunity.
    b. The fight is for increasing social mobility, not to attain social justice.
    c. The fight is for educational and economic opportunities, not social ones.
    d. The fight is for many children, a fight that determines life or death.

20. How can you best characterize the attitude or tone of the concluding paragraph?
    a. Given the serious challenges named, it is realistically cautious.
    b. Given the serious challenges named, it is inspiringly positive.
    c. Given the serious challenges named, this is suitably negative.
    d. Given the serious challenges named, it is objectively neutral.

Questions 21 to30 pertain to the following scenario:

Enjoy Foods from Many Cultures

10 tips to wisely celebrate healthier foods and customs

Print in English   Print in Spanish

As a diverse Nation, we can embrace our cultural traditions for the foods we love and still prepare them in healthier ways. This involves being creative with favorite recipes by substituting foods and ingredients that are less healthy with flavorful and appealing choices that still help remind us of our treasured food ways.

1. Cook with others
Learn about cooking different traditional or regional foods from others who use authentic recipes and ingredients and explore ways to improve the nutrition of some of your own family favorites. Cooking dishes at home allows you to add variety to meals. If needed, adapt recipes by cutting back on gravies, creams, and sauces; adding more vegetables; or baking instead of frying.

2. Blend cultures

Many popular foods and beverages in America blend the cuisines of many cultures. Celebrate our Nation's diversity and be inspired by dishes that include more fruits, vegetables, whole grains, beans, seafood, lean meats, and low-fat dairy.

3. Add a touch of spice

Combinations of herbs and spices often remind us of dishes from our own heritage or our favorite ethnic food. Add flavor to meals with herbs and spices, such as chili, garlic, ginger, basil, oregano, curry, or cilantro, which can replace salt and saturated fat.

4. Use familiar foods to create exotic dishes

Use foods you know and prepare new recipes, such as adding curry to chick peas, cilantro to brown rice, or mango to your salad or smoothie. Make half your plate fruits and vegetables.

5. Find the salt and sodium and go with lower numbers

All packaged foods are labeled to show amounts of sodium. Use "low-sodium" soy sauce, or broth or canned beans labeled "no salt added." Check nutrition labels and use products that are lower in sodium or are salt-free.

6. Think about beverages

Many cultures offer tasty beverages, such as fruit drinks, alcoholic drinks, rich coffees, and sweet teas. Consider using frozen fruits to create a great tasting smoothie, or adding spices, low-fat dairy, and small amounts of sugar to make beverages. When buying prepared beverages, choose items with less sugar and fat. To manage calories, drink water or other unsweetened beverages instead of sugary drinks.

7. Delight in cultural gatherings

Celebrate traditions, especially those that help you stay physically active. Have fun with traditional dances, sports, and games that make you move. Balance what you eat with regular physical activity.

8. Show children what's important

Children learn to cook from their elders. Show kids how meals and dishes from various traditions are prepared. Let them taste foods they made, as you share related stories and customs from your own heritage or expose them to other cultures, but consider ways to cut back on high-calorie foods and ingredients.

9. Make smart choices when dining out

Eating out offers tempting new dishes that make it easy to overeat. Choose lower calorie dishes, such as stir fries, kabobs, or whole-wheat pastas with tomato sauce. Split a dish or ask for a take-home container at the start of a meal to save part of what's served on your plate.

10. Remember, all types of foods fit on MyPlate
MyPlate is designed to remind Americans to eat healthfully, using foods from the food groups. The MyPlate website provides practical information, tips, tools, and recipes that will help you build a healthier diet.
- See more at: http://www.choosemyplate.gov/ten-tips-enjoy-foods-from-many-different-cultures

21. What does the text recommend for cooking at home and with others?
    a. Meals tend to have less variety when cooked at home.
    b. Cooking with others enables learning authentic recipes.
    c. Cooking with others makes your recipes less nutritious.
    d. Ingredients and preparation should never be changed.

22. How can Americans celebrate cultural diversity in cuisine, according to the text?
    a. By getting inspiration from foods popular in America from multicultural sources
    b. By researching, cooking, and consuming only foods and drinks from other cultures
    c. By preparing only authentic recipes from other cultures, regardless of contents
    d. By not cooking at home, but eating at restaurants and homes of other cultures

23. According to the textual evidence, what is true about flavorings and seasonings in cooking?
    a. There is no way that herbs can take the place of salt.
    b. Spices require saturated fat to deliver the full flavors.
    c. Herbs and spices can recall favorite ethnic food tastes.
    d. Herbs and spices add just as much sodium as salt does.

24. Which of the following best expresses the main idea of this text?
    a. Americans need to be more adventurous with food.
    b. Other cultures have healthier diets than America.
    c. It is possible to celebrate diverse cuisine nutritiously.
    d. Multicultural dishes must be adapted to be healthy.

25. To create exotic tastes in home-cooked meals, what does this source recommend?
    a. Following new recipes that contain only exotic ingredients
    b. Adding exotic ingredients to familiar foods in new recipes
    c. Substituting more familiar ingredients into exotic recipes
    d. Adding one exotic herb or spice to every familiar recipe

26. What can you conclude from the advice given in this source?
    a. It is impossible to determine sodium levels in packaged ethnic foods.
    b. Tasty cultural drinks have no alternatives with lower sugar and/or fat.
    c. Calories in sugary drinks do not count the same way as calories in food.
    d. Even when ethnic foods are prepackaged, healthy choices are possible.

27. Relative to traditional cultural events, what can you infer from the text?
    a. Balancing food and physical activity applies to these events.
    b. Cultural celebrations offer more food than physical activity.
    c. Certain cultural events involve physical activity but no food.
    d. Physical activity is unnecessary if foods are healthy enough.

28. What do the authors advise adults to do with children regarding cultural food traditions?
    a. Adults should show children how to make traditional dishes and/or meals.
    b. Adults should let children taste different foods, but not make them.
    c. Adults should teach children to cook without adding customs and/or stories.
    d. Adults should teach children authentic recipes without modifications.

29. What inferences can you draw from the tip about eating out and choosing wisely?
    a. Larger portion sizes at restaurants make it impossible to eat a healthy diet.
    b. Stir-fries and kabobs have as many calories as any other restaurant dishes.
    c. Tomato sauce at restaurants has equal calories to creamy sauces or gravies.
    d. Diners can pack take-home before eating or share dishes when eating out.

30. According to the USDA, what proportion of food on your plate should be vegetables and fruits?
    a. A third
    b. Half
    c. A quarter
    d. Unknown

Questions 31 to 40 pertain to the following scenario:

More than 50 Corinthian Campuses Transition to Nonprofit Status under Zenith Education Group

Zenith has agreed to implement a series of improvements to improve outcomes, strengthen career training, and ensure accountability and transparency

FEBRUARY 3, 2015

Contact: Press Office, (202) 401-1576, press@ed.gov

1   Zenith Education Group, a newly created nonprofit provider of career school training, announced earlier today that it had finalized its acquisition of more than 50 Everest and WyoTech campuses from Corinthian Colleges Inc., a transaction that was first announced in November. The deal will allow nearly 30,000 students to pursue their career goals without disruption, and will give those students the opportunity to complete their education under new management that is set to implement a new plan to improve the education of its students.

2   "We recognize the hard work that thousands of students have undertaken to improve their lives and we want to do whatever we can to make sure those efforts don't go to waste. That's why the Department has kept students' best interests at heart in every decision made about Corinthian," said Under Secretary Ted Mitchell. "We're confident students will be safeguarded by the strong and bold commitments Zenith has made, which include offering students high-quality career training and counseling, improving affordability by reducing tuition and providing grant aid to students, and focusing on student outcomes."

3   In June, the Office of Federal Student Aid (FSA) office placed Corinthian on an increased level of financial oversight after the company failed to respond to the

Department's repeated requests for answers about questionable practices. Following further investigation, the Department ordered the for-profit company to sell and prepare to wind down all of its programs. After a diligence process, Corinthian and ECMC Group, of which Zenith is a member, agreed in November to the purchase and sale of approximately 50 Corinthian schools. The Department supported Zenith's purchase and by stepping in to avoid a sudden shutdown of Corinthian, the Department ensured that students had the opportunity to continue their education with minimal disruption and with significant savings in taxpayer investments. Between the fall and today, Zenith acquired the approvals of the state authorizing agencies and accreditors of the schools it is acquiring.

4   As part of the terms of the sale, the parties agreed to pay $12 million in up-front payments that will be used to benefit Corinthian students and up to an additional $17.25 million in earn-out payments to the Department over the next seven years that will also be used to benefit Corinthian students. The Department is proud to announce today that, in conjunction with the Consumer Financial Protection Bureau, it is using a portion of those proceeds for more than $480 million in loan forgiveness for borrowers who took out Corinthian's high-cost private student loans. The hundreds of millions of dollars' worth of private loan forgiveness will serve to help past Corinthian students also make a fresh start.

5   In addition to the immediate changes announced today, Zenith also agreed to a series of conduct provisions as well as previously announced plans to voluntarily hire an independent monitor to ensure Zenith operates with integrity and transparency and in compliance with federal regulations and agree with several conduct provisions to protect students.

6   Furthermore, in the months since the announcement of the sale, Zenith has agreed to implement a series of improvements to improve outcomes, strengthen career training, and ensure accountability and transparency. These improvements include a student choice program (including refund options) that will apply to approximately 40 percent of its current students; an immediate 20 percent tuition cut and new scholarships and grants; a pledge to adhere to the Department's gainful employment rules and a renewed commitment to accountability and transparency which will be governed by their independent monitor.

7   To ensure that students understand the transaction and its ramifications, starting today, FSA will also reach out directly to the approximately 30,000 former Corinthian students who are now enrolled at Zenith to inform them of the ownership change and what the transition means for them. Additional information and updates, including documents relating to the terms of the deal, will be available at www.studentaid.ed.gov/Corinthian.

8   Throughout, the Department has sought a wind down of Corinthian Colleges that protects students, protects the investment taxpayers have made in their success, and creates opportunities for students to finish what they started. The Department has also sought a resolution that, where possible, establishes a strong and ongoing platform for high quality career education in the future. Today's announcement by Zenith and Corinthian is a major and positive step in these directions.

This release has been updated to clarify terms of the payment and earn-out.

31. According to this text, what can you conclude about Zenith Education Group?
    a. It is a commercial career school training provider.
    b. It is an education organization with a long history.
    c. It recently purchased colleges from a corporation.
    d. Its purchases did not involve the Department of Education.

32. From the evidence provided, you could infer that, across all campuses bought from Corinthian by Zenith, the average number of students per campus would be what?
    a. Approximately 800
    b. Approximately 600
    c. Approximately 500
    d. No evidence given

33. Who is Ted Mitchell?
    a. He is the Secretary of the US Department of Education (ED)
    b. A blogger for ED's official blog, but no job title given
    c. Under Secretary of the ED
    d. Under Secretary of the new Zenith Education Group

34. Which office raised the level of financial oversight on Corinthian Colleges?
    a. The US Department of Education (ED)
    b. The ECMC Group that includes Zenith
    c. The US ED Office of Financial Oversight
    d. The Office of Federal Student Aid (FSA)

35. The main idea of this piece is best represented in which of the following?
    a. In the subtitle
    b. The main title
    c. Paragraph 1
    d. Paragraph 7

36. In the quotation from Ted Mitchell, which word choice is most descriptive to convey approval of Zenith?
    a. "Bold"
    b. (a) and (c)
    c. "Strong"
    d. "Decision"

37. Who is collaborating to relieve students of expensive private student loan debt?
    a. Corinthian Colleges, Inc.; ECMC Group; and ECMC's member, Zenith Education Group
    b. The US Department of Education (ED) and the Consumer Financial Protection Bureau
    c. The ED and the Office of Federal Student Aid (FSA)
    d. Corinthian Colleges, Zenith Education, Consumer Financial Protection Bureau (CFPB)

38. What can you logically conclude from the text about the student loan forgiveness described?
    a. The government wants to remediate Corinthian's excessive charges for students.
    b. The government wants to give students a fresh start because loans are always costly.
    c. The government wants to give students additional benefits from its own Department of Education funds.
    d. The government wants to afford relief by forgiving parts of federal student loans.

39. Among improvements to which Zenith has agreed, which one is identified as having been voluntary on Zenith's part?
    a. New grants and scholarships
    b. Immediate tuition reduction
    c. Hire an independent monitor
    d. Adhere to conduct provisions

40. According to this text, what is true about the motivations and goals of the Department of Education (ED) relative to this sale?
    a. ED has worked to avert disrupting education and save taxpayer investments.
    b. ED secured a resolution for future career education quality including this deal.
    c. ED's involvement with this deal has aimed only to avert education disruption.
    d. ED's involvement with this deal has aimed only to save taxpayer investments.

Constructed Response

Read the passages and examine the graphic below, and then answer the essay questions that follow.

PASSAGE A

Thank you for taking the time to express your support of H.R. 1095, the Battlefield Excellence through Superior Training (BEST) Practices Act. I was glad to introduce this bill and am hopeful that it will be signed into law.

As a member of the House Armed Services Committee, I assure you that the safety and security of our armed service members is my top priority. I introduced the BEST Practices Act on February 26, 2015. The bill is currently pending before the House Armed Services Committee for further deliberation. This landmark bill would end the use of live animals for research in both combat trauma injuries and chemical and biological casualty management exercises. Currently, the U.S. Department of Defense uses live monkeys to train medical personnel to treat casualties of chemical and biological agent attacks and uses live goats and pigs to teach physicians, medics, corpsmen, and other personnel methods to respond to severe battlefield injuries. Like you, I believe that animals deserve to be treated humanely.

Our troops risk their lives on a daily basis to ensure the safety of all Americans. They deserve the best medical treatment available. If enacted, this bill will phase in the use of human-based methods for combat trauma training and chemical casualty courses. These methods include the superior education and preparation of military personnel through the use of state-of-the-art medical simulators, immersion training in civilian and military trauma centers, and other human-based methods of education. This bill will provide quality training for our soldiers and ensure the humane treatment of our animals.

This is an important issue. In addition to sponsoring this legislation during the 111th and 112th Congresses, I previously wrote a letter to the Army Surgeon General urging the military to phase out the use of live animals in trauma training. Fourteen other members of Congress signed this letter. I am hopeful that H.R. 1095 will soon come to the floor of the House of Representatives for a vote.

Again, thank you for taking the time to express your thoughts about the BEST Practices Act. If you have any questions or comments in the future, please visit my office online at www.hankjohnson.house.gov .

Sincerely,

Henry C. "Hank" Johnson, Jr.
Member of Congress

PASSAGE B

Thank you for contacting me regarding S.587, the "Battlefield Excellence through Superior Training Practices Act." I always enjoy the opportunity to hear from my fellow Georgians.

On February 26, 2015, Senator Wyden introduced S.587. If enacted, this legislation would take steps to eliminate the use of live animals in military combat and medical training exercises by substituting more humane alternatives. I hold in high regard my duty as a member of the Senate to ensure our military personnel are properly trained by the time they deploy to the line of duty. As your Senator, I will do my best to ensure that our military receives the best training possible at a reasonable cost to the taxpayers while maintaining respect for the well-being of people and animals alike.

Again, thank you for taking the time to contact me about this issue. Your thoughts are important to me, and I will keep them in mind as the Senate considers legislation pertaining to the training and readiness of our military.

Kindest regards,

David Perdue
United States Senator

S. 587: Battlefield Excellence through Superior Training Practices Act

Nation

| 3 SUPPORTING | 100% |
| 0 OPPOSING | 0% |

Bill Summary
2/26/2015--Introduced.

Battlefield Excellence through Superior Training Practices Act or the BEST Practices Act

Requires the Department of Defense (DOD), no later than: (1) October 1, 2018, to develop, test, and validate human-based training methods for training members of the Armed Forces in the treatment of combat trauma injuries, with the goal of replacing live animal-based training methods; and (2) October 1, 2020, to only use human-based training methods for such purposes.

Prohibits the use of animals in such training after the latter date, but permits DOD to exempt a particular command or training method from human-based training method requirements for up to one year if the human-based methods will not provide an educationally equivalent or superior substitute for live animal-based training methods. Allows exemption periods to be renewed.

Requires DOD to submit an annual report to Congress regarding the development and implementation of the human-based training methods, including the justifications for any exemptions.

1. In an approximately 100- to 200-word essay, compare and contrast the positions of both passages. Identify to which part of Congress each version of this bill was introduced from each passage. Include whether they seem to agree, disagree, or both; which evidence is supplied to support their statements; whether evidence is sufficient or insufficient; why you think each supplies more or less evidence; how relevant and valid the evidence in either passage is; and examples from each passage to back up your evaluations. Write for an adult, educated audience, using your own words except in quotations. Edit your final draft to fit all standard American English writing conventions.

2. In an essay approximately 100-200 words long, explain how the information in the graphic, including the bill summary, is related to Passage A, e.g., whether either supports or refutes the other. Give examples to support what you explain. Write as if you are addressing an educated adult audience. Other than quotations, use your own words. Ensure that your final, edited draft complies with all writing conventions for standard American English.

3. Compose an essay of roughly 400-600 words to support a claim evaluating the benefits and considerations of phasing in only human-based methods for training armed services personnel to treat combat trauma injuries. Fully develop an argument supporting the claim. Your claim should show: (1) knowledge and comprehension of this subject, (2) logical and valid reasoning related to and building upon the arguments and/or information in the sources, (3) enough pertinent evidence from all three sources to support it, and (4) at least one counterclaim you can predict and your response to it. Write your essay for educated adults as the target audience. Throughout the composition, consistently use an appropriate tone, suitable style, and language that is specific and clear. Except for quotations, write in your own words. Edit your final draft to fit all standard American English writing conventions.

Answers and Explanations

1. D: Section 1 of this text identifies benefits of physical activity including looking better (a), less likelihood of depression (b), and better quality of sleep (c). It does NOT identify improved muscle mass (d) as a benefit. Also, not all physical activity increases muscle mass. For example, swimming can increase aerobic capacity, endurance, flexibility, and muscle strength, but not muscle mass because it is not a weight-bearing exercise.

2. C: According to this text, physical activity can "help you achieve a healthy weight," i.e., either maintain a healthy weight OR lose weight (a), improves overall health AND is important to weight management (b), and can prevent gaining excessive weight (c). However, it does NOT say physical activity can prevent you from ever gaining weight (d), which generally requires a combination of diet and exercise.

3. A: The last sentence in paragraph 1 states that health problems including heart disease, type 2 diabetes, and high blood cholesterol are more likely when you are not physically active. Therefore it is untrue that physical inactivity has no impacts on health status (b), and also by implication that health problems are less likely from no exercise than too much (c). Because physical inactivity can cause health problems, choice (d) is also incorrect.

4. B: The text states that how much physical activity is required for managing weight "varies a lot from person to person," making (a) incorrect; and "depends on calorie intake," making (c) incorrect. The text also provides general guidelines, including a beginning amount, a direction to increase this gradually if needed, and a larger amount some adults who want or need to lose weight will have to exceed for weight loss, making choice (d) incorrect.

5. B: The source advises adults to *begin* by getting two-and-a-half hours, i.e., 150 minutes, of moderate-intensity aerobic activity every week. Therefore, (a) is neither enough time nor intensity, and (c) and (d) are both more in time and intensity than recommended to *start* with. Also, more than 300 minutes of *moderate*-intensity, NOT high-intensity aerobic activity is what the source says *some* adults may need to exceed for meeting weight loss goals.

6. A: In paragraph 4, the source states that, while weight loss can be attained through consuming less (c) OR burning more calories through being physically active (b), "the people with the greatest long-term success are doing BOTH—eating less and being more active." Because they decrease consumption and increase activity, maintaining the same levels of each (d) is incorrect.

7. D: The text identified gives a number of activities as examples to show there are many, but does NOT say you should only choose from among these (a), or that they must be effective (b). It also says in its last sentence, "Doing something is better than doing nothing." Thus (c) is incorrect. The first sentence begins, "Pick activities that you like..." So you can infer that whatever activity you choose, it is important that it be something you enjoy (d).

8. C: The third row in the chart of stumbling blocks and corresponding suggestions offers a simple definition of physical activity; choices of moderate intensity, vigorous intensity, or a combination of both; some examples of each (a), (b); and also a link to a page of tips for increasing physical activity (d).

9. D: The fourth row in the stumbling blocks and ideas chart cites the 2008 Physical Activity Guidelines. Because the text is identified as from the USDA website, you can logically conclude these

Guidelines it cites ARE also from a government agency (a). (They are, in fact, from health.gov.) As the text specifies "episodes of at least 10 minutes" for aerobic activity, you can logically conclude this comes from the cited guidelines (b). The same applies to the advice of spreading activity over the week (d), not concentrating it into a few days (c).

10. C: "Increase Physical Activity" is the actual title of this web page, reflecting its content. Choice (a) is not the best title: while the subtitle states, "Physical activity is an important part of managing body weight," the content is primarily about increasing physical activity, not managing body weight. Although it identifies better health and less chance of depression as benefits of physical activity, using these as the title (b) would not identify the content as accurately. The same applies to (d): this is a benefit of physical activity, but does not identify the main content.

11. C: In paragraphs 5-6, Duncan identifies the school personnel themselves' reporting students, "mostly for nonviolent misdemeanors," as a main source of student arrests in Chicago Public Schools rather than student criminal activity outside school hours (a), violent offenses by students during school (b), or violent crimes committed by students truant from school (d).

12. A: The text cites the facts that America contains less than five percent of the world's population, but over 20 percent of its prisoners (paragraph 10); that America's rate of incarcerating black people is currently "*far higher*" (p11) than South Africa's at the height of apartheid (b), not second to it; that America's incarceration of young black men is SIX times likelier than of white males (p12), not three (c); and that one in three (c. 33 percent) of America's black males are projected to be imprisoned at some point vs. one in five (20 percent) to get bachelor's degrees (p13)—i.e., roughly 13 percent more, not five percent more (d).

13. B: This text's main idea is best-expressed as "prioritizing education can lower incarceration rates"—hence the title. While Duncan cites statistics which could support a position that the American prison system is racially biased (a), OR that black males are highly overrepresented in the prison system, these are both just evidence supporting the main idea. Duncan states (paragraph 26), "We cannot lay our incarceration crisis at the door of our schools" (c). He cites a great education's economic benefits in life (p22), but these are also supporting details, not the main idea (d).

14. B: Duncan gives the example of saving money by not incarcerating nonviolent offenders (c) in paragraph 28, and explains in paragraph 29 how those savings could be reinvested in 50 percent salary increases for every teacher in the poorest schools and communities (a). However, he never gives choice (d) as an example, thus choice (b) is correct.

15. A: In these two paragraphs, Duncan repeatedly begins sentences and clauses with "that means" and "it means" to emphasize each of the specific actions needed to end the school-to-prison pipeline. He does not "talk around" his meaning by using unnecessarily complex wording (b); substitute indirect descriptions for more factual ones (c); or unrealistically, overly exaggerate the facts (d).

16. C: In paragraph 31, Duncan refers to giving teachers needed preparation (a) and support, particularly in high-need schools (b); enabling students to attend school without fear (d); and expanding quality preschool opportunities (c) as among essential ingredients to "changing the odds" for underserved students. Of these, he identifies extending more early childhood education opportunities through quality preschools (c) as having a "power to reduce incarceration" that is "well-established."

17. D: In paragraph 32, Duncan states that "cutting the funds that states and districts so desperately need to make opportunity real for our kids" is "exactly what Republican budget proposals would do." He does not attribute this to Democratic budget proposals (a) or bipartisan ones (b). In criticizing Republican budget proposals for cutting educational funds, he *contrasts* them with the president's budget (c), not criticizes it.

18. C: Duncan refers to the fact he cites in the same paragraph (17) that, over the past 30 years, local and state spending for corrections increased nearly twice as much as for schools. He wants his audience to recognize this as a sign of misplaced priorities. He does not cite equal increases in federal and state spending for corrections and schools (a); increases in federal, state, and local spending for corrections 50 percent more than for schools (b), but almost 100 percent more; or decreases in federal, state, and local spending for schools, but not corrections (d).

19. D: In paragraph 33, Duncan describes "that same fight" as including educational AND economic opportunity (a) to increase social mobility AND for social justice (b), (c); and "for too many of our children today, it can literally mean the difference between life and death" (d). (In some elided portions, he earlier gave examples of school shootings and other mass violence, and contrasted student paths leading to success with trajectories ending in prison or death, adding weight to the life-and-death statement here.)

20. B: After describing serious challenges but also proposing various solutions, citing recent successes (not all included in the excerpted passages), and calling for action, Duncan concludes with an inspiringly positive tone: "When we bet on the extraordinary potential of ALL of our children, when we bet on the transformative power of teachers, we cannot lose." Such a firmly optimistic attitude cannot be described as cautious (a), negative (c), or neutral (d).

21. B: The USDA recommends cooking with others to learn authentic dishes from other cultures as a way of expanding your repertoire of recipes and ingredients. Tip #1 recommends exploring ways to make favorite recipes more nutritious as a part of cooking with others (c). It points out that cooking at home enables giving meals *more* variety, not less (a); and *advises* changing ingredients by reducing fats, increasing vegetables, and/or preparation by baking, not frying, as needed (d) to improve nutrition.

22. A: The text encourages readers to take inspiration from dishes with nutritious ingredients that are popular in America and combine multicultural cuisines. It does NOT tell readers to prepare and eat only foods and drinks from other cultures (b), to cook only other cultures' authentic recipes even if the contents are not nutritionally sound (c), or only to eat at restaurants and homes of other cultures instead of cooking at home (d).

23. C: The text advises using herbs and spices, which it says *can* replace salt (a) and saturated fat (b). Moreover, it points out that certain herb and spice combinations can produce tastes that remind us of our favorite ethnic foods (c). Herbs and spices do not add sodium like salt does (d), and there is no textual evidence otherwise.

24. C: Although this text encourages Americans to be more adventurous with food, this is not its main idea (a); as one aspect of nutritiously celebrating diverse cuisine (c) is supporting information. The text never says other cultures have healthier diets than America (b), so it cannot be a main idea. It recommends adapting some authentic multicultural dishes *"if needed"* to be healthier, but never says they all *must* be adapted to be healthy (d).

25. B: This source recommends making new recipes by combining familiar and exotic ingredients, like adding mangos to smoothies and salads, cilantro to brown rice, or curry to chickpeas rather than following recipes with only exotic ingredients (a), making familiar food substitutions for exotic ones in recipes (c), or adding only one exotic flavoring per familiar recipe (d).

26. D: You can conclude this from the advice that healthy choices are always possible. This can be done by selecting packaged ethnic foods with zero, low, or reduced sodium, which *is* always labeled on all packaged foods (a); and selecting prepared drinks with less sugar and/or fat (b), drink water, or make beverages with zero or less sugar and fat. It is not true that calories in sugary drinks count differently than calories in food (c).

27. A: Tip #7 advises readers to "Balance what you eat with regular physical activity." This is not just advice for cultural events, but part of the USDA's overall advice for healthy lifestyle. The authors reiterate this advice here to show it applies to cultural celebrations as well. They do not say cultural celebrations offer more food than physical activity (b) or physical activity without food (c). Because they advise balancing food and activity, choice (d) is incorrect.

28. A: The authors advise adults to show children how to make culturally traditional dishes and meals because children learn to cook from adults. They advise adults to let children *both* make and taste these foods (b) to learn by doing, to share customs and stories related to the foods (c) as they prepare and taste them, and to consider ways of modifying recipes with high-calorie ingredients (d).

29. D: While restaurants do typically serve larger portions, this does not make it impossible to eat out with healthy choices (a). As the text points out, diners can pack part of their meals to take home before starting to eat, or share a dish with a friend. Because the authors identify stir-fries and kabobs as examples of lower-calorie dishes, you can infer they do NOT have as many calories as other dishes (b). The same applies to tomato sauce (c), which has less fat than creamy sauces and gravies.

30. B: The USDA's recommendation is to make one-half the food on your plate vegetables and fruits, not one-third (a) or one-quarter (c). This is repeated throughout its choosemyplate.gov web pages, including in the list reproduced here under tip #4. Therefore, choice (d) is incorrect.

31. C: This press release identifies Zenith as a non-profit (a) career school training provider that has been "newly created" (b) and recently purchased over 50 college campuses from the Corinthian Colleges for-profit corporation (c), and that these purchases had the support of the US Department of Education (d).

32. B: The text identifies over 50 campuses and almost 3,000 students. Dividing 3,000 by 50 would yield an *average* of approximately 600 students per campus. (Of course, this is just an average; each campus could have many more or fewer students.) Therefore, choices (a) and (c) are incorrect, and because an average can be computed from the evidence, (d) is also incorrect.

33. C: Arne Duncan is Secretary of the Department of Education (ED), not Ted Mitchell (a). Mitchell authored this particular post for ED's official blog site, but his job title IS noted at the end of the article (b). Mitchell is identified as Under Secretary in the second paragraph (c) of the US Department of Education (ED), which issued this release, NOT Under Secretary of Zenith Education Group (d), as can be determined from paragraph 3.

34. D: According to this text, the Office of Federal Student Aid (FSA) raised financial oversight levels on Corinthian Colleges after Corinthian did not answer the Department of Education's (ED) questions. ED ultimately ordered Corinthian to sell because of its questionable practices and unresponsiveness, but ED did not increase financial oversight (a). The ECMC Group, which includes Zenith (b), agreed for Zenith to buy Corinthian's schools, but had nothing to do with financial oversight before purchase. There is no such thing as a US ED Office of Financial Oversight (c).

35. A: The subtitle focuses on the improvements Zenith agreed to implement that will ensure transparency and accountability as well as better outcomes. The main title (a) focuses on the transition from for-profit to nonprofit status. Readers may infer that greater transparency, accountability, and outcomes are attributable to nonprofit status, but the former comprise the main idea rather than the latter. Paragraph 1 (c) introduces and summarizes the transition. Paragraph 7 (d) informs how FSA will notify students of the transition and provides a link to more updates and/or information.

36. B: The adjectives "bold" (a) and "strong" (c) both convey Mitchell's attitude that he and the Department of Education (ED) approve of Zenith's commitments to students. The noun "decision" (d) is more neutral, simply identifying every determination or choice ED has made about Corinthian.

37. B: The US Department of Education and the Consumer Financial Protection Bureau are the government agencies collaborating to forgive Corinthian's former expensive private student loans to benefit students. One would not expect Corinthian to participate (a), (d) as it was the source of those expensive private loans. As a nonprofit, Zenith would not have the funds for such loan forgiveness (a), (d). The Office of Federal Student Aid (FSA) (c) is only identified in this text as having increased financial oversight of Corinthian before the sale (paragraph 3), contacting students about the change, and providing further information and updates online (p7).

38. A: Because the text describes Corinthian's (former) private student loans as "high-cost" (paragraph 4), you can logically assume that the government's forgiveness of these loans is to remediate the excessive charges for students—not simply because all student loans are always expensive (b). The Department of Education (ED) is not using its own funds for this (c); the text indicates that the funds come from payments to ED from the parties to the sale. ED is forgiving only those private loans from Corinthian, NOT any parts of federal loans (d).

39. C: According to the information (paragraphs 5-6), Zenith has agreed to implement improvements that include offering new grants and scholarships (a), an immediate 20 percent reduction in tuition (b), and adhering to "several conduct provisions [d] to protect students." The only improvement identified as voluntary on Zenith's part is its "previously announced plans to *voluntarily* hire an independent monitor" (p5).

40. A: In most paragraphs throughout the text, the authors reinforce the Department of Education's (ED) goals of preventing students' education from being disrupted by substituting a sale of ownership for a shutdown, AND of saving and protecting taxpayer investments in student success (paragraphs 3, 7)—not just one (c) or the other (d). They add that ED has also "*sought*—NOT secured (b) a resolution for future career education quality." They describe this deal as "a major and positive step in these directions"—NOT as part of the resolution (b) it has sought.

Practice Test #4

Practice Questions

Questions 1 to10 pertain to the following scenario:

Making a Difference for National Hispanic Heritage Month

October 8, 2015

By: Mary K. Wakefield, Ph.D., RN, HHS Acting Deputy Secretary

1   Just recently, Secretary Burwell met with the leadership of the United Farm Workers and Farmworker Justice. There is so much we can learn from these leaders today, and from their predecessors.

2   In 1970, fresh from successfully organizing grape farmworkers, the charismatic chair of the new United Farm Workers Organizing Committee drove hurriedly from San Jose, California to Salinas. Talking to a reporter in the car, he said, "I've always maintained that it isn't the form that's going to make the difference. It isn't the rule or the procedure or the ideology, but it's human beings that will make it."

3   César Chávez's words ring true today, and during National Hispanic Heritage Month, which takes place from September 15 to October 15, we celebrate the impact that Hispanics have made to the very fabric of our nation's history.

4   And as HHS works toward transforming our health system to one that puts consumers at the center of their care, we're promoting outreach methods to expand care within the Hispanic community, such as working with *promotores de salud*.

5   Promotores de salud are community health workers who educate members of their community about the programs, services and resources that are available to them in order to make better, more informed decisions about their family's health. As trusted members of their community who share similar cultural backgrounds and speak the same language, promotores de salud work with individuals and communities to understand how culture, language and lifestyles contribute to their health decisions.

6   Through the HHS Action Plan to Reduce Racial and Ethnic Health Disparities, we are supporting efforts by promotores de salud, our Office of Minority Health and the Promotores de Salud Steering Committee, to help teach communities about ways to keep us and our loved ones healthy. This means a focus on wellness visits and other important services like cancer screenings. It means promoting heart health and helping connect people to the resources they need to prevent and manage chronic diseases, like diabetes, which are still more prevalent among Hispanics than among non-Hispanic whites. Promotores de salud are helping to improve the health of the communities they serve.

7   The tradition of promotores de salud is based on the idea that health isn't just about tests and pills. It comes from a holistic approach to health that meets people where they are, and recognizes the value of sharing healthy habits and creating healthy environments to generate better health decisions and outcomes.

8   Today, we know that despite enormous progress, Hispanics are still more likely to be uninsured than any other racial or ethnic group. Furthermore, they suffer from chronic illnesses like asthma, diabetes and cervical cancer at disproportionately high levels.

9   As we look to transform our nation's health care system into one that works for all Americans, we want to put individuals at the center of their care. And thanks to the Affordable Care Act, we're making progress.

10   Since the passage of the Affordable Care Act, about 17.6 million uninsured people have gained health coverage, including 4.0 million Hispanics. For the Hispanic community, the rate of uninsurance has dropped by 11.5 percentage points. That means that there are now more Hispanics that can see their clinician on a routine basis, get treated early for the onset of a chronic disease, or seek emergency care that is affordable and of high quality.

11   And with new protections, coverage is now better for everyone, no matter where you buy your insurance. Preventive services at no extra cost, like annual checkups, certain cancer screenings, and vaccinations, can go a long way toward closing the health gap that still persists in the Hispanic community.

12   Hispanic families across the country now have the security that comes with health coverage. They can rest a little easier at night, because they know a sickness or an accident won't bankrupt them or their family.

13   But there's still more to do. Open Enrollment is less than one month away, when individuals can shop for new insurance on the Marketplace or find a plan that better fits their families' needs. And as more Americans get covered, we have to make sure they know how to use that coverage as well, by connecting with providers and taking advantage of their benefits.

14   This National Hispanic Heritage Month, let's all agree to be the human beings that César Chávez called on to make a difference, by spreading the word about where Hispanic families can go to obtain affordable coverage and learning about and using new benefits that can keep us all healthier.

15   The next Open Enrollment begins November 1 and runs through January 31, 2016.

16   For more information, visit HealthCare.gov (https://www.healthcare.gov/) or CuidadoDeSalud.gov (https://www.cuidadodesalud.gov/es/).

17   You can also find assistance in your own community at localhelp.healthcare.gov, or calling 1-800-318-2596 (TTY: 1-855-889-4325). Operators are standing by, day or night, in Spanish and in English.

--Blog from the website of the US Department of Health and Human Services (HHS) (October 8, 2015)

1. Where in this text is the "charismatic chair of the new United Farm Workers Organizing Committee" described in paragraph 2 first identified by name?
    a. Paragraph 2
    b. Paragraph 3
    c. Paragraph 4
    d. Not identified

2. The author quotes Chávez making the point that which of the following make the difference in organizing and other social reform efforts?
    a. The rules that people follow
    b. The procedures people follow
    c. The people who participate
    d. The ideology guiding people

3. According to the text, what do Americans celebrate during National Hispanic Heritage Month?
    a. The impact of Hispanics on American history
    b. The impact of American history on Hispanics
    c. The holidays that are celebrated by Hispanics
    d. The cultural heritage that only Hispanics have

4. Based on the textual evidence, when is National Hispanic Heritage Month?
    a. During October
    b. During November
    c. During September
    d. (a) and (c), not (b)

5. Readers unfamiliar with Spanish can determine from the surrounding context and/or some knowledge of etymology that *promotores de salud* literally means which of the following?
    a. "Promoters of health"
    b. "Community workers"
    c. "Advertisers of salad"
    d. "Producers of rooms"

6. According to the author, the *promotores de salud* tradition originates from which of these?
    a. Early diagnosis and treatment
    b. Taking medication as directed
    c. A scientific approach to health
    d. A holistic orientation to health

7. What can you logically infer or conclude from the description of Hispanics' status relative to health insurance and chronic illness?
    a. These differences are completely due to a lack of American educations.
    b. These differences in illness are entirely due to lacking health insurance.
    c. These differences are related to socioeconomic and immigration status.
    d. These differences are not attributable to anything without information.

8. Which of the following best describes the overall tone, attitude, and viewpoint of the author?
    a. Positive but not complacent
    b. Negative but not hopeless
    c. Passionate but impractical
    d. Neutral but informational

9. Of the following, which is an important idea related to American healthcare reform that the author refers to twice in this piece?
    a. Benefit-centered healthcare
    b. Nurses-centered healthcare
    c. Patient-centered healthcare
    d. Doctor-centered healthcare

10. What does the concluding paragraph (14) accomplish most?
    a. It summarizes each of the points made in the preceding paragraphs.
    b. It invites readers to inform Hispanics and themselves about the ACA.
    c. It ties in the ending with the important idea from the quotation in p2.
    d. It accomplishes (b) and (c) effectively, but it does not accomplish (a).

Questions 11 to20 pertain to the following scenario:
Getting Ready for the Next Open Enrollment

September 22, 2015

By: Nicholas Garlow, HHS (Public Affairs)

1   Mark your calendars. Open Enrollment for 2016 health coverage begins November 1.

2   Today, Secretary Burwell visited the Howard University College of Medicine to reflect on the progress made under the Affordable Care Act and to preview the work ahead of us during the third Open Enrollment period.

3   Secretary Burwell also broke some news during her speech on the impact the Affordable Care Act has had for millions of Americans.

4   View image on Twitter (http://twitter.com/SecBurwell/status/646328750372704256/photo/1)

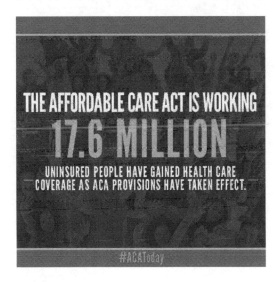

 **Sylvia Burwell**
✔@SecBurwell
News → about 17.6M Americans have gained coverage as #ACA provisions have taken effect. #ACAToday #ACAisWorking
10:22 AM - 22 Sep 2015
374374 Retweets
265265 Favorites

5   Check out some of the issues the Secretary touched on during her speech this morning.

6   *"Five years in, millions of people have new coverage and the annual uninsured rate has been reduced to its lowest levels on record... The Marketplace offered a product that millions of consumers wanted... The private sector has actually added 13.1 million jobs over 66 straight months of job growth. Our unemployment rate is at its lowest level since April of 2008. And we have not seen the creation of a "part-time economy."*

7   *"When we look at the evidence, the Affordable Care Act is delivering on access, affordability and quality."*

8   *"According to a study we are releasing today, as the ACA's coverage provisions took effect, an estimated 17.6 million Americans have gained coverage. And this progress has been even bigger for people of color: The uninsured rate among African-American adults has declined by more than 10 percentage points, compared to about 7.7 for the total population."*

9   *"The ACA is about more than the Marketplace. People are beginning to understand that the ACA is improving their care no matter where they buy their insurance. With new protections and required benefits, like preventive services at no extra cost, it's improved the quality of coverage for all Americans."*

10   *"The questions that surrounded this law a year ago have been answered, and now we have a new opportunity in front of us: building on this progress."*

11   *"We have three main goals this year: improve the consumer experience, retain our current customers, and increase new enrollment. Current Marketplace customers express satisfaction with their coverage and we expect most to come back. And we believe we can continue to connect people with the coverage they need and bring the number of uninsured down."*

12   *"All of us in this room have an important power, and with it an opportunity to empower others. And we know that there can be no power without health. It is the foundation of our lives. It affects our educations, our safety, and our economic opportunities. Until we know all Americans have a chance to find affordable coverage, quality care, and the tools to make the best decisions for their health, we will struggle as a nation to move forward."*

13   You can read Secretary Burwell's full remarks at http://www.hhs.gov/about/leadership/secretary/speeches/2015/access-affordability-quality-progress-aca.html. Remember to follow the Secretary on Twitter @SecBurwell. You can join the conversation around today's speech using #ACAToday.

14   Secretary Burwell Previews Third Open Enrollment

[NOTE: AT THIS LOCATION IN THE ARTICLE IS AN EMBEDDED YOUTUBE VIDEO OF SECRETARY BURWELL'S 17-MINUTE SPEECH ON THE SUBJECT. THE LINK TO THAT VIDEO: https://www.youtube.com/watch?v=bmeeb9-P94c]

0:00 / 17:16

15   Remember, Open Enrollment for 2016 coverage starts November 1, 2015. Sign up for HealthCare.gov (https://www.healthcare.gov/) text and email reminders to stay informed.

16   We're getting ready for the third Open Enrollment http://www.hhs.gov/blog/2015/09/22/getting-ready-next-open-enrollment.html #ACAToday#ACAisWorking

11. Who posted this blog?
    a. Sylvia Burwell, the Secretary of the Department of Health and Human Service (HHS)
    b. Nicholas Garlow, HHS Under Secretary
    c. Nicholas Garlow, HHS Public Affairs Department.
    d. Whoever posted it is not identified here.

12. Even without background information, what can you logically infer about the connection between paragraph 2 and paragraph 8?
    a. There is no connection other than their being in the same article.
    b. Howard University is among America's historically black colleges.
    c. Students in medical college have a special interest in health laws.
    d. You can logically infer both (b) and (c); therefore, (a) is incorrect.

13. Among several ways this piece leverages Internet technology for support, which one LEAST directly involves social networking websites?
    a. A copy of a tweet posted by Secretary Burwell on Twitter
    b. An included YouTube video of Secretary Burwell's speech
    c. A prepared tweet with link and hashtags for users to share
    d. A link to subscribe to get text message and email updates

14. According to the evidence given, which of the following is a result of passing the Affordable Care Act?
    a. The lowest unemployment rate in over seven years
    b. The lowest yearly uninsured rate in over five years
    c. The millions of jobs added for four years of growth
    d. The creation of the predicted "part-time economy"

15. From statistics cited in the text, what has been the ACA's impact for African-American adults?
    a. Their rate of uninsured has decreased equally with that of the total population.
    b. Their rate of uninsured has decreased more than it has for the total population.
    c. Their rate of uninsured has decreased slightly less than for the total population.
    d. Their rate of insured has increased by twice as much as for the total population.

16. Which of the following did the Secretary say about the Affordable Care Act?
    a. It is improving healthcare irrespective of where consumers purchase health insurance.
    b. It is improving healthcare for consumers who bought it through the Marketplace.
    c. It is improving healthcare only as a result of the new protections that it gives consumers.
    d. It is improving healthcare; however, free preventive services were always requirements.

17. Of the following, which is NOT defined as one of the Department of Health and Human Services' main goals for the coming year?
   a. To expand new health insurance enrollments
   b. To keep the existing Marketplace customers
   c. To lower health insurance premiums further
   d. To better Marketplace consumer experience

18. Which of these best expresses the main idea of the speech excerpts here?
   a. The last hashtag from paragraph 16
   b. The title of this blog post
   c. The first paragraph, i.e., paragraph 1
   d. The facts presented in paragraph 8

19. In what terms does the Secretary represent health and national progress in paragraph 12?
   a. Health and national progress are both depicted in positive terms
   b. Health in positive terms and national progress in negative terms
   c. Health in negative terms and national progress in positive terms
   d. Health and national progress are both shown in negative terms

20. How can this article's readers access an online print copy of the entire speech to read?
   a. By clicking on the first link supplied in paragraph 13
   b. By clicking on the link that is found in paragraph 14
   c. By clicking on the second link given in paragraph 13
   d. By clicking on the third link offered in paragraph 13

Questions 21 to30 pertain to the following scenario:

The Gift of the Magi

By O. Henry (1905, 1906)

[Jim and Della are an impoverished young married couple. As the story opens, it is approaching Christmas Eve, and Della has been crying because she only has $1.87 to buy Jim a present. Here the story continues:]

1   Now, there were two possessions of the James Dillingham Youngs in which they both took a mighty pride. One was Jim's gold watch that had been his father's and his grandfather's. The other was Della's hair. Had the Queen of Sheba lived in the flat across the airshaft, Della would have let her hair hang out of the window some day to dry just to depreciate Her Majesty's jewels and gifts. Had King Solomon been the janitor, with all his treasures piled up in the basement, Jim would have pulled out his watch every time he passed, just to see him pluck at his beard from envy.

2   So now Della's beautiful hair fell about her, rippling and shining like a cascade of brown waters. It reached below her knee and made itself almost a garment for her. And then she did it up again nervously and quickly. Once she faltered for a minute and stood still while a tear or two splashed on the worn red carpet.

3   On went her old brown jacket; on went her old brown hat. With a whirl of skirts and with the brilliant sparkle still in her eyes, she fluttered out of the door and down the stairs to the street.

4   "Will you buy my hair?" asked Della.

5   "Twenty dollars," said Madame, lifting the mass with a practised hand.

6   "Give it to me quick," said Della.

7   She found it at last. It surely had been made for Jim and no one else. There was no other like it in any of the stores, and she had turned all of them inside out. It was a platinum fob chain simple and chaste in design, properly proclaiming its value by substance alone and not by meretricious ornamentation--as all good things should do. It was even worthy of The Watch. As soon as she saw it she knew that it must be Jim's. It was like him. Quietness and value--the description applied to both. Twenty-one dollars they took from her for it, and she hurried home with the 78 cents. With that chain on his watch Jim might be properly anxious about the time in any company. Grand as the watch was, he sometimes looked at it on the sly on account of the old leather strap that he used in place of a chain.

8   The door opened and Jim stepped in and closed it. He looked thin and very serious. Poor fellow, he was only twenty-two--and to be burdened with a family! He needed a new overcoat and he was without gloves.

9   Jim stepped inside the door, as immovable as a setter at the scent of quail. His eyes were fixed upon Della, and there was an expression in them that she could not read, and it terrified her. It was not anger, nor surprise, nor disapproval, nor horror, nor any of the sentiments that she had been prepared for. He simply stared at her fixedly with that peculiar expression on his face.

10   "Jim, darling," she cried, "don't look at me that way. I had my hair cut off and sold it because I couldn't have lived through Christmas without giving you a present. It'll grow out again--you won't mind, will you? I just had to do it. My hair grows awfully fast. Say 'Merry Christmas!' Jim, and let's be happy. You don't know what a nice--what a beautiful, nice gift I've got for you."

11   "You've cut off your hair?" asked Jim, laboriously, as if he had not arrived at that patent fact yet, even after the hardest mental labour.

12   "Cut it off and sold it," said Della. "Don't you like me just as well, anyhow? I'm me without my hair, ain't I?"

13   Jim looked about the room curiously.

14   "You say your hair is gone?" he said, with an air almost of idiocy.

15   "You needn't look for it," said Della. "It's sold, I tell you--sold and gone, too. It's Christmas Eve, boy. Be good to me, for it went for you. Maybe the hairs of my

head were numbered," she went on with a sudden serious sweetness, "but nobody could ever count my love for you. Shall I put the chops on, Jim?"

16   Out of his trance Jim seemed quickly to wake. He enfolded his Della. For ten seconds let us regard with discreet scrutiny some inconsequential object in the other direction. Eight dollars a week or a million a year--what is the difference? A mathematician or a wit would give you the wrong answer. The magi brought valuable gifts, but that was not among them. This dark assertion will be illuminated later on.

17   Jim drew a package from his overcoat pocket and threw it upon the table.

18   "Don't make any mistake, Dell," he said, "about me. I don't think there's anything in the way of a haircut or a shave or a shampoo that could make me like my girl any less. But if you'll unwrap that package you may see why you had me going a while at first."

19   White fingers and nimble tore at the string and paper. And then an ecstatic scream of joy; and then, alas! a quick feminine change to hysterical tears and wails, necessitating the immediate employment of all the comforting powers of the lord of the flat.

20   For there lay The Combs--the set of combs, side and back, that Della had worshipped for long in a Broadway window. Beautiful combs, pure tortoise-shell, with jewelled rims--just the shade to wear in the beautiful vanished hair. They were expensive combs, she knew, and her heart had simply craved and yearned over them without the least hope of possession. And now, they were hers, but the tresses that should have adorned the coveted adornments were gone.

21   But she hugged them to her bosom, and at length she was able to look up with dim eyes and a smile and say: "My hair grows so fast, Jim!"

22   And then Della leaped up like a little singed cat and cried, "Oh, oh!"

23   Jim had not yet seen his beautiful present. She held it out to him eagerly upon her open palm. The dull precious metal seemed to flash with a reflection of her bright and ardent spirit.

24   "Isn't it a dandy, Jim? I hunted all over town to find it. You'll have to look at the time a hundred times a day now. Give me your watch. I want to see how it looks on it."

25   Instead of obeying, Jim tumbled down on the couch and put his hands under the back of his head and smiled.

26   "Dell," said he, "let's put our Christmas presents away and keep 'em a while. They're too nice to use just at present. I sold the watch to get the money to buy your combs. And now suppose you put the chops on."

27   The magi, as you know, were wise men--wonderfully wise men--who brought gifts to the Babe in the manger. They invented the art of giving Christmas presents. Being wise, their gifts were no doubt wise ones, possibly bearing the privilege of exchange in case of duplication. And here I have lamely related to you the uneventful chronicle of two foolish children in a flat who most unwisely sacrificed for each other the greatest treasures of their house. But in a last word to the wise of these days let it be said that of all who give gifts these two were the wisest. Of all who give and receive gifts, such as they are wisest. Everywhere they are wisest. They are the magi.

21. What effects do the references to the Queen of Sheba and King Solomon (paragraph 1) accomplish?
    a. They emphasize Jim and Della's pride using exaggerated comparisons.
    b. They introduce an impression of grandeur to an incongruous context.
    c. They establish the story and its two main characters in a Biblical setting.
    d. They accomplish the effects in (a) and (b) rather than the effect in (c).

22. The word choice of repeating "brown" in paragraphs 2-3 achieves which of the following?
    a. Comparison
    b. Alliteration
    c. A contrast
    d. Emphasis

23. Which of these best describes the author's purpose in describing Jim in paragraph 8?
    a. He was showing the effects that poverty had had upon Jim.
    b. He was painting a picture so readers felt they knew Jim well.
    c. He was eliciting reader sympathy for Jim instead of for Della.
    d. He was showing how Jim was affected by marriage to Della.

24. In paragraph 9, O. Henry describes an expression in Jim's eyes that "terrified" Della as "not anger, nor surprise, nor disapproval, nor horror, nor any of the sentiments that she had been prepared for." What does that expression *most* signify?
    a. Jim was simply in shock at seeing Della without her long hair.
    b. Jim was simply trying to process the couple's cross purposes.
    c. Jim was transfixed at Della's beauty with the shorter haircut.
    d. Jim still could not believe how much his gift for Della had cost.

25. The author describes Jim as saying, "'You've cut off your hair?'… laboriously, as if he had not arrived at that patent fact yet, even after the hardest mental labour"; looking "about the room curiously"; and repeating, 'You say your hair is gone?'… with an air almost of idiocy"; and being in a "trance." What is the reason for these reactions?
    a. O. Henry was showing that Jim had a good character, but was not very bright.
    b. O. Henry was showing that hunger had made it hard for Jim to grasp changes.
    c. O. Henry was showing that Jim had trouble reconciling Della's actions with his own.
    d. O. Henry was showing that Jim generally could not cope with the unexpected.

26. Which literary device did O. Henry use prominently in this story's plot?
    a. Tragic irony
    b. Verbal irony
    c. Dramatic irony
    d. Situational irony

27. In which of the following descriptions from paragraph 20 does the author use language to show that, despite their expense, the combs' beauty and value were surpassed by the beauty and value of Della's hair?
    a. "For there lay The Combs—the set of combs, side and back, that Della had worshipped long in a Broadway window."
    b. "They were expensive combs, she knew, and her heart had simply craved and yearned over them without the least hope of possession."
    c. "And now, they were hers, but the tresses that should have adorned the coveted adornments were gone."
    d. "Beautiful combs, pure tortoise shell, with jewelled rims—just the shade to wear in the beautiful vanished hair."

28. Which of the following quotations from these passages is most similar to foreshadowing?
    a. "So now Della's beautiful hair fell about her rippling and shining like a cascade of brown waters."
    b. "Jim stopped inside the door, as immovable as a setter at the scent of quail."
    c. "And then Della leaped up like a little singed cat and cried, 'Oh, oh!'"
    d. "This dark assertion will be illuminated later on."

29. How could you best characterize Jim's response to the realization that each of them had sold the object of the other's gift?
    a. Heartbroken, but resigned to a sad situation
    b. Disappointed, yet accepting of a harsh reality
    c. Resilient, prioritizing love above material gifts
    d. Unsurprised, as he was used to their poverty

30. Why does O. Henry describe the two main characters as "the magi"?
    a. Because they both came home, each bearing a gift
    b. Because they both would rather give than receive
    c. Because they were really unwise, "foolish children"
    d. Because they also got Christmas gifts for the "Babe"

Questions 11 to20 pertain to the following scenario:
The Little Match Girl

By Hans Christian Andersen (1845)

1   Most terribly cold it was; it snowed, and was nearly quite dark, and evening-- the last evening of the year. In this cold and darkness there went along the street a poor little girl, bareheaded, and with naked feet. When she left home she had slippers on, it is true; but what was the good of that? They were very large slippers, which her mother had hitherto worn; so large were they; and the poor little thing lost them as she scuffled away across the street, because of two carriages that rolled by dreadfully fast.

2   One slipper was nowhere to be found; the other had been laid hold of by an urchin, and off he ran with it; he thought it would do capitally for a cradle when he some day or other should have children himself. So the little maiden walked on with her tiny naked feet, that were quite red and blue from cold. She carried a quantity of matches in an old apron, and she held a bundle of them in her hand. Nobody had bought anything of her the whole livelong day; no one had given her a single farthing.

3   She crept along trembling with cold and hunger--a very picture of sorrow, the poor little thing!

4   The flakes of snow covered her long fair hair, which fell in beautiful curls around her neck; but of that, of course, she never once now thought. From all the windows the candles were gleaming, and it smelt so deliciously of roast goose, for you know it was New Year's Eve; yes, of that she thought.

5   In a corner formed by two houses, of which one advanced more than the other, she seated herself down and cowered together. Her little feet she had drawn close up to her, but she grew colder and colder, and to go home she did not venture, for she had not sold any matches and could not bring a farthing of money: from her father she would certainly get blows, and at home it was cold too, for above her she had only the roof, through which the wind whistled, even though the largest cracks were stopped up with straw and rags.

6   Her little hands were almost numbed with cold. Oh! a match might afford her a world of comfort, if she only dared take a single one out of the bundle, draw it against the wall, and warm her fingers by it. She drew one out. "Rischt!" how it blazed, how it burnt! It was a warm, bright flame, like a candle, as she held her hands over it: it was a wonderful light. It seemed really to the little maiden as though she were sitting before a large iron stove, with burnished brass feet and a brass ornament at top. The fire burned with such blessed influence; it warmed so delightfully. The little girl had already stretched out her feet to warm them too; but-- the small flame went out, the stove vanished: she had only the remains of the burnt-out match in her hand.

7   She rubbed another against the wall: it burned brightly, and where the light fell on the wall, there the wall became transparent like a veil, so that she could see into the room. On the table was spread a snow-white tablecloth; upon it was a splendid porcelain service, and the roast goose was steaming famously with its stuffing of apple and dried plums. And what was still more capital to behold was, the goose hopped down from the dish, reeled about on the floor with knife and fork in its breast, till it came up to the poor little girl; when--the match went out and nothing but the thick, cold, damp wall was left behind. She lighted another match. Now there she was sitting under the most magnificent Christmas tree: it was still larger, and more decorated than the one which she had seen through the glass door in the rich merchant's house.

8   Thousands of lights were burning on the green branches, and gaily-colored pictures, such as she had seen in the shop-windows, looked down upon her. The

little maiden stretched out her hands towards them when--the match went out. The lights of the Christmas tree rose higher and higher, she saw them now as stars in heaven; one fell down and formed a long trail of fire.

9   "Someone is just dead!" said the little girl; for her old grandmother, the only person who had loved her, and who was now no more, had told her, that when a star falls, a soul ascends to God.

10   She drew another match against the wall: it was again light, and in the lustre there stood the old grandmother, so bright and radiant, so mild, and with such an expression of love.

11   "Grandmother!" cried the little one. "Oh, take me with you! You go away when the match burns out; you vanish like the warm stove, like the delicious roast goose, and like the magnificent Christmas tree!" And she rubbed the whole bundle of matches quickly against the wall, for she wanted to be quite sure of keeping her grandmother near her. And the matches gave such a brilliant light that it was brighter than at noon-day: never formerly had the grandmother been so beautiful and so tall. She took the little maiden, on her arm, and both flew in brightness and in joy so high, so very high, and then above was neither cold, nor hunger, nor anxiety-- they were with God.

12   But in the corner, at the cold hour of dawn, sat the poor girl, with rosy cheeks and with a smiling mouth, leaning against the wall--frozen to death on the last evening of the old year. Stiff and stark sat the child there with her matches, of which one bundle had been burnt. "She wanted to warm herself," people said. No one had the slightest suspicion of what beautiful things she had seen; no one even dreamed of the splendor in which, with her grandmother, she had entered on the joys of a new year.

31. On what occasion is this story's setting, and what is its significance to the story?
    a. Christmas Eve; celebration and the promise of gifts
    b. New Year's Eve; celebration and a brand new start
    c. Thanksgiving; celebration and feasts of much food
    d. Easter; celebration, rebirth, and the ending of cold

32. From which word choices in paragraph 1 can the reader *infer* that the little girl was impoverished?
    a. "Bareheaded"
    b. "A poor little girl"
    c. "With naked feet"
    d. (a) and (c), not (b)

33. If you did not know the story's title, where in the text is evidence from which you could logically conclude that the little girl was trying to sell matches?
    a. Paragraph 1
    b. Paragraph 2
    c. (b), then (d)
    d. Paragraph 5

34. According to the text, why did the little girl stay outside rather than go home?
    a. Because she was homeless and had nowhere to go
    b. Because it was also just as cold and drafty at home
    c. Because her father beat her if she made no money
    d. Because (b) and (c) were deterrents; (a) is not true

35. What is the best explanation for the things the little girl saw in paragraphs 6-8?
    a. She imagined the things she wished for the most.
    b. She hallucinated, delirious from cold and hunger.
    c. She really saw those things, as the fire was magic.
    d. She saw those visions the moment before dying.

36. What is the primary effect of the descriptive writing in paragraphs 6-8?
    a. It gives the author a chance to show off his skills for writing descriptively.
    b. It draws readers in, making the visions and their loss more real to them.
    c. It entertains readers with vivid imagery, distracting them from a sad tale.
    d. It presents the details of comfort and happier times from the girl's past.

37. In paragraph 9, what is an important function of the little girl's statement?
    a. It identifies the significance of the falling star.
    b. It foreshadows what will happen at the end.
    c. It shows the girl was imagining the falling star.
    d. It signals the death of the girl's grandmother.

38. From the textual evidence, which of the following is true?
    a. Nobody had loved the little girl except for her grandmother.
    b. The little girl's parents loved her, but they were gone now.
    c. Everybody loved the little girl, but they were all just as poor.
    d. The grandmother was the only one left alive to love the girl.

39. "'She wanted to warm herself,' people said." (Paragraph12) What is most accurate about this quotation?
    a. It is false; she wanted to keep seeing her grandmother.
    b. It is true, but by itself was not the girl's only motivation.
    c. It affirms both her external behavior and internal need.
    d. It demonstrates the pity that everyone had always felt.

40. Regarding the author's purpose, what best describes the story's ending?
    a. It is simply a sad ending because the child has died.
    b. It is a happy ending in that the child was now happy.
    c. It is an ambiguous ending not telling her final status.
    d. It is an ironic ending, unexpected based on the rest.

Constructed Response

Read the passages and examine the graphic below, and then answer the essay questions that follow.

SUPPLEMENTARY BACKGROUND INFORMATION:

On June 25, 2013, the United States Supreme Court held that it is unconstitutional to use the coverage formula in Section 4(b) of the Voting Rights Act to determine which jurisdictions are subject to the preclearance requirement of Section 5 of the Voting Rights Act, Shelby County v. Holder, 133 S. Ct. 2612 (2013). The Supreme Court did not rule on the constitutionality of Section 5 itself. The effect of the Shelby County decision is that the jurisdictions identified by the coverage formula in Section 4(b) no longer need to seek preclearance for the new voting changes, unless they are covered by a separate court order entered under Section 3(c) of the Voting Rights Act.

(United States Department of Justice (DOJ), updated August 8, 2015)

PASSAGE A

Thank you for contacting me to express your support preserving the right to vote. I welcome feedback from my constituents and I appreciate your interest in this issue. I am sure you will be happy to know that I agree with you and will do all I can to preserve this fundamental right.

Voting is a fundamental aspect of our democratic system and federal law guarantees free exercise of this vital right. Protecting our Constitutional rights is one of the primary reasons I sought a seat on the House Judiciary Committee from my very first day in Congress. It is vitally important that our nation's elections are secure and that all Americans have confidence that their vote will be protected and counted accurately.

Our nation was founded on the principle of democracy and that everyone's vote is equally important. Indeed, women and African Americans fought long and valiant fights to secure their inalienable right to vote and in this context it seems wholly un-American to deny the citizens of our nation the right to be heard at the ballot box. During my time in Congress, I have been a staunch advocate of legislation to improve voter access to the ballot box and I will continue support initiatives to ensure the integrity of our elections. I am glad we can agree on this issue and am proud to be your Representative in Congress.

I am eager to hear from you and I look forward to working with you in the future. For more information, please visit my office online at http://hankjohnson.house.gov/, where you may sign up to receive my e-newsletter. Thank you again for contacting me.

Sincerely,

Henry C. "Hank" Johnson, Jr.
Member of Congress

PASSAGE B

Thank you for contacting me about legislation to amend the Voting Rights Act of 1965. I always appreciate the opportunity to hear from my fellow Georgians.

The right to vote is among the most fundamental rights guaranteed to all Americans, and voting rights legislation must reflect the realities of modern American society. Section 4 of the Voting Rights Act of 1965 contained a formula used to determine which state and local governments had to receive permission from the federal government in order to make changes to their voting laws. In *Shelby County v. Holder*, the United States Supreme Court invalidated the Section 4 formula on the grounds that it was based on decades-old practices that are no longer relevant in America today.

The Supreme Court further stated that it was unconstitutional for Congress simply to rely on past practices in order to justify treating some state and local governments differently from others. Therefore, as Congress continues to debate the Voting Rights Amendment Act of 2015 and the Voting Rights Advancement Act of 2015 in the wake of the *Shelby* decision, it is important that any changes to Section 4 reflect contemporary realities, not 50-year-old practices and data.

Again, thank you for taking the time to contact me about this issue. Your thoughts are important to me, and I will keep them in mind whenever the Senate considers legislation to amend the Voting Rights Act of 1965.

Kindest regards,

David Perdue
United States Senator

<u>**GRAPHIC**</u>

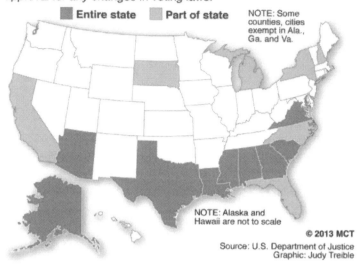

Voting Rights Act states

States with a history of discriminatory voting practices that are subject to Section 5 of the Voting Rights Act; states require federal approval for any changes in voting laws.

■ Entire state ■ Part of state

NOTE: Some counties, cities exempt in Ala., Ga. and Va.

NOTE: Alaska and Hawaii are not to scale

© 2013 MCT
Source: U.S. Department of Justice
Graphic: Judy Treible

1. Write an essay roughly 100-200 words long comparing and contrasting the two passages. Identify what each one claims. Identify what kinds of evidence each uses to support their claims. Evaluate how sufficient, pertinent, and valid the evidence is in each. Provide examples from both passages to support your evaluations. Write for an adult, educated audience. Except for quotations, use your own words. Edit your final draft to follow all standard American English writing conventions.

2. Compose an essay around 100 to 200 words long explaining how the information in the graphic adds to and counters or supports the statements in Passage B regarding Sections 4 and 5 of the Voting Rights Act. Use the Supplementary Background Information provided above the passages as needed, including applying, paraphrasing, and/or quoting it. Include examples from the graphic and the passage to support your statements. Write for a target audience of well-educated adults. Other than quotations, write in your own words. Edit your final draft to follow all standard American English writing conventions.

3. Write a roughly 400- to 600-word essay in which you develop an argument fully to support a claim evaluating positive and negative aspects of the Supreme Court's decision in *Shelby County v. Holder* and amendments to the Voting Rights Act. In your argument, include: (1) a claim showing knowledge and comprehension of the subject, (2) valid and logical reasoning that applies and elaborates upon the facts and arguments in the sources given, (3) enough pertinent evidence from all sources provided to support your claim, and (4) at least one counterclaim you can predict and how you respond to it. Other than quoting provided sources, write in your own words. Address a hypothetical audience that is adult and well-educated. Throughout your essay, consistently apply suitable tone and style and specific, clear wording and phrasing. Edit your final draft to fit all standard American English writing conventions.

Answers and Explanations

1. B: Though some readers have already identified the name by the description in paragraph 2, César Chávez is named in paragraph 3, not in the same paragraph (a) or in paragraph 4 (c). Therefore, it is incorrect that he is not identified (d) in any paragraph.

2. C: In paragraph 2, the author quotes Chávez saying, "I've always maintained that it isn't the form that's going to make the difference. It isn't the rule (a) or the procedure (b) or the ideology (d), but it's human beings (c) that will make it."

3. A: The text states in paragraph 3 that, during National Hispanic Heritage Month, Americans ("we") celebrate "the impact that Hispanics have made to the very fabric of our nation's history." It does not identify the month as for celebrating the impact of American history upon Hispanics (b), the holidays that Hispanics celebrate (c), or the cultural heritage exclusive to Hispanics (d).

4. D: National Hispanic Heritage Month is identified in paragraph 3 of the text as being from September (c) 15 to October (a) 15. Therefore, it lasts for a month's duration but spans two calendar months, and it is not celebrated during November (b).

5. A: Without knowing Spanish, readers can observe *promotores* is a cognate with English *promoters* (they share the same Latin root). They may recognize *salud* as a popular toast, or determine its meaning from the surrounding context: the entire piece is about health, and the very next paragraph (5) defines *promotores de salud* as "community *health* workers." However, choice (b) is incorrect by omitting "health," and moreover is not the phrase's literal meaning. *Salud* is not related to English *salad* (c) or *sala*, which is Spanish for "room" (d).

6. D: The author explains in paragraph 7 that this tradition is "based on the idea that health isn't just about tests (a) and pills (b). It comes from a holistic approach to health" (d). She does not mention a scientific approach (c), but focuses on creating healthy environments and sharing healthy habits, which will both lead to better decisions related to health and better health results.

7. C: Having less insurance and more chronic illness is not completely due to lack of American education (a), and although lacking health insurance contributes to illness, it is not the only factor (b). In addition to culture, lifestyle, etc., health insurance gaps and disproportionate chronic illness rates are also related to the lower socioeconomic and/or immigrant status of many Hispanics in the USA (c). Though any assertion should be supported, the target audience of this blog can logically make this inference/conclusion without additional information (d) through awareness of these statuses.

8. A: The author demonstrates positive tone and attitude by identifying ways *promotores de salud* improve communities' health; asserting "thanks to the Affordable Care Act, we're making progress" (paragraph 9); citing supporting statistics of more Hispanic health coverage (p10); identifying additional ACA benefits (p11-12); and concluding with a proactive recommendation (p14). She is not complacent, identifying needed improvements (p8, 13). Her overall tone is not negative (b). She offers practical (c) information and assistance resources (p15-17). While the text is informative, its tone is positive, not neutral (d).

9. C: Patient-centered healthcare is an important idea for American healthcare reform, of which improving healthcare coverage, knowledge, understanding, and applications for Hispanics is a part. In paragraph 4, the author includes Hispanic community outreach in the Department of Health and

Human Services' efforts to transform America's health system so it "puts consumers at the center of their care," and in paragraph 9 reiterates that "we want to put individuals at the center of their care." This reform vision is not for healthcare with benefits (a), nurses (b), or doctors (d) at its center, but patients and consumers.

10. B: The concluding paragraph (the prose conclusion, before the three additional, informational-only paragraphs) is NOT meant to and does NOT summarize all points made earlier (a). It does invite readers to inform Hispanic families and themselves about how to access health insurance through the ACA, and both learn about and utilize the new benefits (c). It also achieves symmetry and closure by referencing the Chávez quotation from paragraph 2 (d) that human beings make the difference, and encouraging readers to be those human beings by doing the things in (c).

11. C: Nicholas Garlow of the Department of Public Affairs within the US Department of Health and Human Services (HHS) is identified as the person who posted this blog on the official HHS blog site; therefore, choice (d) is incorrect. He is NOT Under Secretary of HHS (b). While Garlow posted it, the majority of the blog's content is taken from HHS Secretary Burwell's (a) speech at Howard University.

12. D: There is definitely a connection between these two paragraphs, so (a) is incorrect. First, Howard University is a historically black college (b), so the information in paragraph 8 about increased health coverage for African-Americans is relevant. Second, students preparing for careers as medical providers do have a special interest in healthcare laws (c).

13. D: The copy of Secretary Burwell's tweet about progress achieved by the ACA (p4) involves Twitter, a social networking website (a). The video of her speech, which the post references in paragraph 14, involves YouTube, a video-based social networking website. The tweet for readers to copy and post (paragraph 16, with the posting link below), also involves Twitter (c). The link to subscribe to updates (p15) *directly* involves submitting a phone number and email address on a website to receive text messages and emails. Though these updates might *then* include links to social networking sites, subscribing *LEAST directly* involves them.

14. A: In paragraph 6, the Secretary cites evidence of the ACA's effectiveness, including the lowest unemployment rate since April of 2008—i.e., seven years and five months before the date of this blog post. Other statistics cited include the lowest yearly uninsured rate "on record" EVER—NOT over five years (b), 13.1 million jobs added in more than *five and a half years* ("over 66 straight months") of consecutive job growth—NOT four years (c), and the fact that the predicted "part-time economy" was NOT created (d) as critics had warned it would be.

15. B: The research study statistics cited (paragraph 8) indicate a proportionately greater impact of the ACA for African-American adults in that their rate of uninsured has dropped by more than 10 percent, while it has dropped by c. 7.7 percent for the total population. Hence decreases are not equal for both groups (a). African-American adults' uninsured rate has not dropped *less* than that of the total population (c). The Secretary identifies c. 17.6 million Americans altogether gaining coverage, but never mentions numbers comparing African-American and total population *increases* in *insured* rates (d).

16. A: In paragraph 9, she says that the ACA is improving healthcare, regardless of where people buy their health insurance (a)—not only if they get it through the Marketplace (b). Improvements in coverage quality she cites here include not only new protections for patients and consumers (c), but also preventive services, which were NOT always required free of charge (d) before the ACA's passage.

17. C: In p11, the Secretary identifies three main goals for the coming year: to make the consumers' experiences with the Marketplace better (d), to assure existing customers are retained (b), and to raise the numbers of new enrollments (a). She does NOT include further lowering health insurance premiums (c) as an HHS goal. (The ACA has already significantly lowered premiums overall; and for some consumers depending on income, pre-existing conditions, etc., by as much as 90 percent.)

18. A: In paragraph 16, a prepared tweet has been offered for readers to post on Twitter containing two hashtags, #ACAToday and #ACAisWorking. The phrase in the second hashtag best expresses the speech excerpts' main idea: the Affordable Care Act is effective. (So does paragraph 7, but this is not a question choice.) The title (b) and paragraph 1 (c) both remind consumers of the date when Open Enrollment begins, which is important, but not the main idea of the Secretary's speech. The statistics presented in paragraph 8 (d) give evidence *supporting* the main idea.

19. B: The Secretary represents health in positive terms as "the foundation of our lives." She emphasizes health's importance and positive impacts by representing national progress in negative terms, i.e., of the negative impacts of inadequate healthcare: "Until we know all Americans have a chance to find affordable coverage, quality care, and the tools to make the best decisions for their *health, we will struggle as a nation to move forward.*" This is reversed in (c). Health and national progress are not both represented in positive (a) or negative (d) terms.

20. A: In "You can read Secretary Burwell's full remarks here: http://www.hhs.gov/about/leadership/secretary/speeches/2015/access-affordability-quality-progress-aca.html," the word "here" is a link to an online printed copy of the entire speech to read. The link in paragraph 14 (b) is to a YouTube video of the speech, not a print copy. The second link in paragraph 13 (c) is to follow Secretary Burwell on Twitter to be notified of her future tweets, not read her speech. The third link in paragraph 13 (d) is to join the conversation on Twitter about the speech, not read it.

21. D: By referring to legendary Biblical figures, O. Henry emphasizes Jim and Della's respective pride by exaggerating their value of each possession through comparisons, saying each possession's glory would exceed those of Biblical royalty (a). He also adds humor by placing such royalty incongruously in the context (b) of the couple's situation: "Had the Queen of Sheba lived in the flat across the airshaft," and "Had King Solomon been the janitor, with all his treasures piled up in the basement." However, the story does not have a Biblical setting (c).

22. C: The author uses "brown" in paragraph 2 to describe Della's "beautiful hair... rippling and shining like a cascade of brown waters." In paragraph 3, he describes "her old brown jacket... her old brown hat." By associating the color brown with dazzling beauty first, but then with the old, dull, worn clothes of a poor owner, he thus achieves a distinct contrast—not comparison (a). Alliteration (b) repeats sounds across different, adjacent, and nearby words—not the same word across paragraphs. Neither the beautiful brown hair nor the old brown outerwear is emphasized (d); rather, the two are contrasted.

23. A: The description best shows poverty's effects upon Jim. While it introduces Jim such that readers might feel they knew something about him, it is too brief for the vivid, highly detailed description authors use to "paint a picture" so readers feel they almost know the character personally (b). While it elicits sympathy for Jim, this is not at the expense of sympathy for Della (c): O. Henry elicits sympathy for both throughout the story. Jim's thinness, seriousness, lack of gloves, and too-old overcoat were effects of poverty, not marriage to Della (d), whom he loved dearly.

24. B: Jim's stunned expression signified not just shock at Della's haircut (a), nor captivation at her beauty (c), but rather his initial inability to comprehend that Della had removed the reason—her hair—for his gift—the combs. He was not still experiencing disbelief at the cost of this gift (d).

25. C: By describing Jim's extended incredulity, O. Henry did not mean that Jim was literally dimwitted (a), that his previously described thinness indicated starvation impairing his thinking (b), or that Jim's general character could not cope with anything unexpected (d). Instead, he was showing Jim having difficulty reconciling Della's actions with his own (c), which contradicted/defeated each other, unbeknownst to both. Jim himself confirms this later (paragraph 18): "If you'll unwrap that package you may see why you had me going a while at first."

26. D: The story's plot prominently features situational irony, wherein actions have unexpected and/or contradictory results. Tragic irony (a) involves a tragic character's committing some error of which s/he is unaware, but the audience is. Verbal irony (b) involves contradiction between the intended and stated meaning of spoken words, as in sarcasm. Dramatic irony (c), similar to tragic irony, involves a character's speech or deeds having significance s/he is unaware of, but the audience is.

27. C: O. Henry cleverly manipulates words to show that Della's hair had even more beauty and value than the combs she had long coveted: he describes her hair as "the tresses that should have *adorned the... adornments*"—in other words, although the combs were designed to decorate hair, Della's hair was so beautiful it would have decorated the combs. He only describes the combs' beauty and value in choice (a), Della's past unrequited desire for them in choice (b), and how the beauty of the hair and the combs matched in choice (d).

28. D: Foreshadowing is a literary device that hints at or predicts what will occur later in the story. It creates suspense, dramatic tension, and anticipation for the reader. Quotation (d) does not hint so much as overtly predict; it is the only choice similar to foreshadowing. The other choices are all examples of similes (an explicit comparison using "like" or "as"), i.e., "like a cascade of brown waters" (a), "as immovable as a setter" (b), and "like a little singed cat" (c).

29. C: Jim's response once the irony of the situation sinks in can best be characterized as resilient because he understood that his and Della's love for each other was more important than any material gifts they could give each other. He did not act heartbroken or resigned (a). He may have been disappointed, but his behavior (paragraph 25) was too positive to indicate acceptance of a harsh reality (b). He cannot be said to have been unsurprised (d) considering his temporary "trance" until he understood the situation.

30. B: O. Henry describes Jim and Della as "the magi" because they both were more motivated by love and a desire to give that was greater than a desire to receive, and thus "wisest" in their selflessness. The comparison is not limited to bearing gifts like the magi (a). His description of them as "foolish children" (c), along with his storytelling as having "lamely related to you the uneventful chronicle" of their having "unwisely sacrificed" in the same sentence, uses understatement to emphasize the opposite meanings. Their Christmas gifts were not for the "Babe in the manger" like the magi's (d).

31. B: Andersen states it was New Year's Eve (paragraphs 1, 4, 12). A brand new start is significant because, in a sense, the girl did embark on a new kind of existence, as Andersen suggests. Although the girl envisions a Christmas tree (p7-8) and refers to it (p11), the story is not set on Christmas Eve (a). Despite visions of feasts and food, it is not on Thanksgiving (c); moreover, Andersen was Danish, and Europeans did not celebrate the American holiday of Thanksgiving. Though themes of rebirth and relief from cold would be appropriate, Easter (d) is also incorrect.

32. D: From the description of her uncovered head (a) and feet (c) while walking outside on the street when it was "most terribly cold," snowing, and getting dark, the reader can *infer* that the little girl suffered from poverty. However, the author's description of her as "a poor little girl" (b) requires no inference on the part of the reader, because it explicitly states that she was in fact poor.

33. C: In paragraph 2 (b), Andersen describes the little girl as carrying matches, and states that no one had bought anything from her all day. In paragraph 5 (d), he more explicitly writes that "she had not sold any matches." Paragraph 1 (a) establishes and describes the setting and character, but does not include any evidence that she was trying to sell matches.

34. D: The child was not homeless (a): "to go home she did not venture, for she had not sold any matches and could not bring a farthing of money: from her father she would certainly get blows (c), and at home it was cold too, for above her she had only the roof, through which the wind whistled (b), even though the largest cracks were stopped up with straw and rags" (paragraph 5).

35. A: Freezing cold, she imagined the first match's light and warmth as from a big cast-iron stove; starving, she imagined the second match revealed a feast inside the wall. Though she was cold and hungry, there is no textual evidence supporting delirium (b). Andersen emphasizes the externalization of the character's internal wishes and fantasies; he never attributes magical powers to the fire (c). The vision of her grandmother was more likely at the moment before dying (d) than the others, when she could still light more matches.

36. B: Descriptive writing provides many sensory details, drawing readers in to feel they are experiencing it themselves. Andersen's description makes the character's visions more real to readers, and likewise her devastation at their loss when the flames die. This is its primary effect, not showing the author's writing skills (a). The vivid imagery does not distract readers from the sad tale (c) but emphasizes it by contrasting the visions with reality. The visions—the dancing goose, the Christmas tree even greater than one she had seen—were from the girl's imagination, not her past (d).

37. B: "Someone is just dead!" foreshadows the death at the story's end. The falling star (a) is the author's device to enable this foreshadowing. She imagined the Christmas tree, and when the match went out, so did her vision of its lights; but when "she saw them now as stars in heaven," those stars were real, not imagined (c). From Andersen's use of past perfect ("had loved," "had told") and "who was now no more," the grandmother was deceased already, not dying at that moment (d).

38. A: Andersen establishes (paragraph 9) that her grandmother was "the only person who had loved her, and who was now no more," so she was not alive (d). Her being the only one who had loved the little girl means her parents did not; moreover, they were not gone (b), as her mother (paragraph 1) and blows "from her father" (p5) are referenced. The grandmother being the only one who had loved her also eliminates everybody (c) else having loved her.

39. B: To observers, the bundle of burnt matches was evidence only that the girl had been trying to warm herself, but they could not know she was also trying to keep "her grandmother near her." Because she had both motivations, choice (a) is incorrect. People attributing the burnt matches to attempts to get warm could only affirm her external behavior, but not her internal need (c) to continue seeing her grandmother's spirit. Though people apparently felt pity upon finding her dead, they never demonstrated this while she was living (d).

40. B: Andersen intended the ending as happy: death freed the child from cold, hunger, anxiety, and loneliness, attaining "brightness," "joy," "splendor," and reunion with her beloved grandmother; both "were with God." Her "rosy cheeks and a smiling mouth" were evidence she died happy; nobody suspected or "even dreamed" "what beautiful things she had seen"; that "with her grandmother, she had entered on the joys of a new year." It is not simply a sad ending (a); her final status IS told (c); given the rest of the story, the ending is NOT unexpected (d).

Practice Test #5

Practice Questions

Questions 1 to10 pertain to the following scenario:

10 Tips Nutrition Education Series

Choosing Healthy Meals as You Get Older

MyPlate 10 healthy eating tips for people age 65+

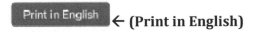 ← **(Print in English)**

Making healthy food choices is a smart thing to do — no matter how old you are! Your body changes through your 60s, 70s, 80s, and beyond. Food provides nutrients you need as you age. Use these tips to choose foods for better health at each stage of life.

1. Drink plenty of liquids
With age, you may lose some of your sense of thirst. Drink water often. Lowfat or fat-free milk or 100 percent juice also helps you stay hydrated. Limit beverages that have lots of added sugars or salt. Learn which liquids are better choices.

2. Make eating a social event
Meals are more enjoyable when you eat with others. Invite a friend to join you or take part in a potluck at least twice a week. A senior center or place of worship may offer meals that are shared with others. There are many ways to make mealtimes pleasing.

3. Plan healthy meals
Find trusted nutrition information fromChooseMyPlate.gov (http://www.choosemyplate.gov/) and the National Institute on Aging. Get advice on what to eat, how much to eat, and which foods to choose, all based on the Dietary Guidelines for Americans. Find sensible, flexible ways to choose and prepare tasty meals so you can eat foods you need.

4. Know how much to eat
Learn to recognize how much to eat so you can control portion size. MyPlate's SuperTracker (https://www.supertracker.usda.gov/) shows amounts of food you need. When eating out, pack part of your meal to eat later. One restaurant dish might be enough for two meals or more.

5. Vary your vegetables
Include a variety of different colored vegetables to brighten your plate. Most vegetables are a low-calorie source of nutrients. Vegetables are also a good source of fiber.

6. Eat for your teeth and gums

Many people find that their teeth and gums change as they age. People with dental problems sometimes find it hard to chew fruits, vegetables, or meats. Don't miss out on needed nutrients! Eating softer foods can help. Try cooked or canned foods like unsweetened fruit, low-sodium soups, or canned tuna.

7. Use herbs and spices

Foods may seem to lose their flavor as you age. If favorite dishes taste different, it may not be the cook! Maybe your sense of smell, sense of taste, or both have changed. Medicines may also change how foods taste. Add flavor to your meals with herbs and spices.

8. Keep food safe

Don't take a chance with your health. A food-related illness can be life threatening for an older person. Throw out food that might not be safe. Avoid certain foods that are always risky for an older person, such as unpasteurized dairy foods. Other foods can be harmful to you when they are raw or undercooked, such as eggs, sprouts, fish, shellfish, meat, or poultry.

9. Read the Nutrition Facts label

Make the right choices when buying food. Pay attention to important nutrients to know as well as calories, fats, sodium, and the rest of the Nutrition Facts label. Ask your doctor if there are ingredients and nutrients you might need to limit or to increase.

10. Ask your doctor about vitamins or supplements

Food is the best way to get nutrients you need. Should you take vitamins or other pills or powders with herbs and minerals? These are called dietary supplements. Your doctor will know if you need them. More may not be better. Some can interfere with your medicines or affect your medical conditions.

MYPLATE MOMENTS

John, 83, Georgia
I love this website and knowing that all the kids are learning on it. I could eat carrots all day!!

Rhett, 14, Tennessee
I used to be a little on the chubby side (188 lbs) and I loved basketball but I was too slow. I found this website and started eating healthy and now I weigh 134 lbs and am very happy with my body. AND... I'm the best freshman basketball player on my team.

Tabbetha, 48, South Carolina
My husband and I began our healthy eating lifestyle in April 2015. As of September 2015, my husband has lost about 50 lbs and I have lost 20 lbs. But even better than that, my husband's blood pressure is normal now!

Last Updated: Sep 1, 2015

- See more at: http://www.choosemyplate.gov/choosing-healthy-meals-you-get-older

1. For what audience is this page of tips designed?
    a. For people of every age
    b. Teens and young adults
    c. Retirement ages and up
    d. Middle-aged adults only

2. Why would eating tips be different for people in different age groups?
    a. Our bodies change in multiple ways as we age.
    b. Our bodies only need fewer calories with age.
    c. Our bodies only need more protein as we age.
    d. Our bodies alter less than behavior as we age.

3. What logical inference could you draw most from the button below the title and subtitles of this text?
    a. This text can only be printed in English.
    b. This text must be translated to print it.
    c. This text is available in many languages.
    d. This text can also be printed in Spanish.

4. According to its information, why does this page advise its audience to drink plenty of liquids?
    a. Because it is the best advice for every age
    b. Because aging can decrease sense of thirst
    c. Because people dehydrate more with age
    d. Because older people forget to drink them

5. What is a key ingredient whose *main* purpose is making mealtimes more appealing to aging individuals?
    a. Including a variety of brighter colors
    b. Sharing mealtimes with other people
    c. Eating foods that are softer for chewing
    d. Taking some food home when eating out

6. What advice do these tips give people about seasonings in foods?
    a. Seniors can add spices and herbs to foods as needed.
    b. Aging makes sense of smell and taste more sensitive.
    c. Certain medications will make foods taste spicier.
    d. Seniors should avoid herbs to prevent upset stomachs.

7. What can you conclude from the information in tip 8?
    a. Food-borne illnesses threaten life equally at all ages.
    b. Animal proteins are the most harmful if overcooked.
    c. Not pasteurizing dairy foods allows bacteria to grow.
    d. Seniors should economize by keeping foods longer.

8. According to this text, what should the target audience do to inform their food purchases?
    a. Consult both package Nutrition Facts and their doctors
    b. Just reading the Nutrition Facts thoroughly is sufficient
    c. They should disregard food labels and ask their doctors
    d. Double vitamin and mineral RDAs but halve the calories

9. Which inference or conclusion is most accurate according to the material in the text?
    a. All seniors need supplements for malabsorption of nutrients from foods.
    b. Scientists have never found that supplements affect medical conditions.
    c. Some nutritional supplements can interfere with the action of medicines.
    d. All seniors should avoid supplements because they interact with medication.

10. From the nature of the comments in the "MyPlate Moments" box, what can they best be called?
    a. Common nutritional problems
    b. Complaints regarding this site
    c. An informational supplement
    d. Testimonials for this website

Questions 11 to20 pertain to the following scenario:

THE WEATHER PREDICTION CENTER

COLLEGE PARK, MD

STORM SUMMARY MESSAGE

1   STORM SUMMARY NUMBER 15 FOR SOUTHERN PLAINS AND LOWER MISSISSIPPI
VALLEY HEAVY RAINFALL
NWS WEATHER PREDICTION CENTER COLLEGE PARK MD
1000 PM CDT SUN OCT 25 2015

2   ...A MULTI-DAY HEAVY RAINFALL AND FLASH FLOOD EVENT CONTINUES TO
PUSH EASTWARD ACROSS EAST TEXAS AND THE LOWER MISSISSIPPI
VALLEY...

3   FLASH FLOOD WATCHES...WARNINGS...AND FLOOD ADVISORIES ARE IN
EFFECT ALONG THE IMMEDIATE GULF COAST FROM EXTREME EAST TEXAS TO
THE FLORIDA PANHANDLE AS WELL AS INLAND LOUISIANA AND
MISSISSIPPI.

4   FOR A DETAILED GRAPHICAL DEPICTION OF THE LATEST
WATCHES...WARNINGS AND ADVISORIES...PLEASE SEE WWW.WEATHER.GOV

5   AT 900 PM CDT...A SURFACE LOW WITH A CENTRAL PRESSURE OF 1001
MB...29.56 INCHES...WAS LOCATED ABOUT 100 MILES SOUTH OF LAKE
CHARLES...LOUISIANA. AN OCCLUDED FRONT WAS DRAPED OVER THE SURFACE
LOW...WITH A WARM FRONT THAT WAS MOVING INLAND ACROSS COASTAL
LOUISIANA. DEEP TROPICAL MOISTURE ALOFT WAS STREAMING INTO THE
LOWER MISSISSIPPI VALLEY AHEAD OF AN UPPER LEVEL SYSTEM THAT WAS
MOVING TOWARD THE LOWER MISSISSIPPI VALLEY. THIS MOISTURE AND
INSTABILITY WAS CONTRIBUTING TO AN ENVIRONMENT CONDUCIVE FOR HEAVY
RAINFALL. NATIONAL WEATHER SERVICE RADARS AND SURFACE OBSERVATIONS
INDICATED AN AREA OF MODERATE TO HEAVY RAINFALL AFFECTING
SOUTHEAST TEXAS...LOUISIANA...AND SOUTHERN MISSISSIPPI. LIGHT TO
MODERATE RAIN BEGAN TO MOVE INTO WESTERN ALABAMA AND THE WESTERN
PORTION OF THE FLORIDA PANHANDLE.

6   ...SELECTED STORM TOTAL RAINFALL IN INCHES FROM 700 AM CDT
WED OCT 21 THROUGH 900 PM CDT SUN OCT 25...

7   ...ARKANSAS...
WALDO 4.2 S   6.18
CAMDEN 6.3 N   4.55
TEXARKANA RGNL ARPT   4.50
HOPE 0.9 SSW   4.42
HOPE 12.2 S   3.62
FOUKE 5.3 ENE   3.14
MOUNT IDA   2.99
PINE BLUFF/GRIDER FIELD   1.58
LITTLE ROCK/ADAMS FIELD   1.22

8   ...LOUISIANA...
BARKSDALE AFB/BOSSIER CITY   6.37
NEW ORLEANS/MOISANT   6.17
SHREVEPORT DOWNTOWN ARPT   3.78
BATON ROUGE 3.5 E   3.60
SICILY ISLAND 3.3 WNW   3.55
BIENVILLE 0.5 S   3.52
FERRIDAY 1.1 NNW   3.48
SHREVEPORT 6.7 S   3.14
BATON ROUGE/RYAN MUNI ARPT   3.11
WAKEFIELD 0.9 WNW   3.05
NEW ORLEANS/LAKEFRONT   2.83
NEW IBERIA/ACADIANA   2.77
ENGLAND AFB/ALEXANDRIA   2.69
FORT POLK   2.48
WHITE BAYOU NEAR ZACHARY   2.28
LAFAYETTE RGNL ARPT   2.19
LAKE CHARLES MUNI ARPT   1.93

9   ...MISSISSIPPI...
MCCOMB/LEWIS FIELD   4.21
NATCHEZ/HARDY   2.93
GLOSTER 1.9 SSW   2.37
VICKSBURG/TALLULAH ARPT   2.09

10   ...TEXAS...
POWELL 1.0 SW   20.15
CORSICANA/CAMPBELL FIELD   20.07
COOLIDGE 5 N   20.00
RICHLAND CHAMBERS RESERVOIR   19.72
GRAPEVINE   18.67
ASH CREEK NEAR MALONE   18.53
CAYUGA   18.30
TRINITY RIVER AT TRINIDAD   17.43
KERENS 3 NW   16.11
SOUTHLAKE 2 W   15.52
BRANDON   14.02
CEDAR CREEK RESERVOIR   13.17
FAYETTEVILLE 5 W   12.79
RICHLAND CREEK NEAR MERTENS   12.28
MIDDLE SULPHUR R   11.67
WACO 1.4 S   11.39

```
ANDERSON MILL 2 SSE                    11.00
CADDO MILLS 4 ESE                      10.86
HOUSTON 1 NNE                           9.38
ARLINGTON MUNI ARPT                     8.93
DALLAS/REDBIRD ARPT                     8.45
DALLAS/LOVE FIELD                       8.37
DALLAS/FORT WORTH INTL ARPT             7.67
COLLEGE STATION 2.1 NNE                 7.60
WACO-MADISON COOPER                     7.53
FORT HOOD/GRAY AAF                       6.99
FORT WORTH NAS                          6.71
AUSTIN 10.7 N                           6.66
HOUSTON/INTERCONTINENTAL                6.37
GALVESTON/SCHOLES                       6.07
AUSTIN CITY                             5.77
SAN ANTONIO 3 SSE                       5.71
SAN ANTONIO INTL ARPT                   4.46
BROWNSVILLE INTL ARPT                   4.42
CORPUS CHRISTI 6.5 WSW                  4.29
BEAUMONT/PORT ARTHUR                    3.34
```

11   ...SELECTED STORM TOTAL RAINFALL IN INCHES WHERE THE EVENT
HAS
ENDED...

12   ...COLORADO...

```
TYRONE 6 SE                             2.51
TRINIDAD 2 ENE                          2.29
THATCHER 7 SSE                          2.22
STONINGTON 9 SE                         2.13
TIMPAS 13 S                             1.82
TWO BUTTES 12 NE                        1.70
HOEHNE 3 ESE                            1.53
DENVER INTL ARPT                        1.46
CAMPO 4 SW                              1.45
THATCHER 11 SSE                         1.23
RYE 2 W                                 1.14
COLORADO CITY 7 E                       1.08
SWISSVALE 3 SW                          1.05
WESTON 6 ESE                            1.04
```

13   ...KANSAS...

```
GARDEN CITY REG ARPT                    2.28
DODGE CITY WFO                          1.92
LIBERAL MUNI ARPT                       1.78
```

14   ...NEW MEXICO...

```
ARTESIA 4 NNE                           2.84
PORTALES 1 SW                           2.75
GASCON 1 WNW                            2.62
CLOVIS 3 ENE                            2.35
ROSWELL 4 WNW                           2.25
SEDILLO 2 WNW                           1.78
GILA 3 NE                               1.72
CHAMA                                   1.65
MAYHILL 1 NNE                           1.60
SANTA FE CO. MUNI ARPT                  1.58
```

```
      LAS VEGAS MUNI ARPT                          1.52
      CLINES CORNER                                1.48
      ALBUQUERQUE 6 E                              1.38
      CLIFF 6 NE                                   1.34


      15      ...OKLAHOMA...
      COLEMAN 4.6 WNW                              4.86
      COLBERT 2.2 SSW                              4.80
      PENNINGTON CREEK NEAR REAGAN                 4.47
      MARIETTA 2.8 SW                              4.42
      MCGEE CREEK RESERVOIR NEAR FARRIS            3.63
      BLUE RIVER                                   3.48
      GUYMON MUNI ARPT                             3.27
      FORGAN 10 NW                                 2.80
      LITTLE BEAVER CREEK NEAR DUNCAN              2.29
      MCALESTER REGIONAL ARPT                      2.21
      JIMMY CREEK NEAR MEERS                       2.19
      FOURCHE MALINE NEAR RED OAK                  2.09
      OKLAHOMA CITY                                1.35


      16      FAVORABLE CONDITIONS FOR HEAVY RAINFALL AND FLASH FLOODING
      WILL
      CONTINUE OVER THE NEXT FEW DAYS AS THE UPPER LEVEL SYSTEM
      TRANSPORTS DEEP MOISTURE ACROSS THE LOWER MISSISSIPPI VALLEY AND
      THE DEEP SOUTH. THROUGH MONDAY...RAINFALL AMOUNTS BETWEEN 2 TO 5
      INCHES...WITH LOCALLY HIGHER AMOUNTS...WILL BE POSSIBLE ACROSS
      SOUTHEAST TEXAS...THE LOWER MISSISSIPPI VALLEY AND THE DEEP
      SOUTH.
      DUE TO ALL THE HEAVY RAINFALL...FLASH FLOODING WILL CONTINUE TO
      BE
      A CONCERN FROM EAST TEXAS TO THE FLORIDA PANHANDLE.


      17      THE NEXT STORM SUMMARY WILL BE ISSUED BY THE WEATHER
      PREDICTION
      CENTER AT 400 AM CDT. PLEASE REFER TO YOUR LOCAL NATIONAL WEATHER
      SERVICE OFFICE FOR ADDITIONAL INFORMATION ON THIS EVENT.


      FANNING
```

Last Updated: 1021 PM EDT SUN OCT 25 2015

11. To what region does this story summary apply?
    a. For College Park, Maryland
    b. The lower Mississippi Valley
    c. East Texas, Southern Plains
    d. For (b) and (c) but not for (a)

12. Which of the following weather service notices were NOT in effect at the time of this report?
    a. Flooding advisories
    b. Hurricane watches
    c. Flash flood watches
    d. Flash flood warning

13. In which direction was the referenced weather system moving?
    a. East
    b. West
    c. North
    d. South

14. For which places were flood advisories, flash flood watches, and flash flood warnings issued at the time of this message?
    a. For only the Gulf Coast portions of all of the states being affected by the rains
    b. For only the inland portions of all of the states that were affected by the rains
    c. For only inland Louisiana and Mississippi, but larger areas along the Gulf Coast
    d. For only the inland parts of East Texas and Florida, and Mississippi's Gulf Coast

15. At 9:00 p.m. Central Daylight time, where was a surface low-pressure system identified?
    a. Louisiana
    b. Alabama
    c. Florida
    d. Texas

16. Of the following, which existed, but readers not knowledgeable of meteorology must infer?
    a. Unstable weather
    b. Tropical moisture
    c. A warm front
    d. A cold front

17. How are the storm's total rainfall measurements ordered in the *first* list in this summary?
    a. Descending order by city within each state
    b. By state and then only by city within the state
    c. Ascending order and city within every state
    d. Alphabetical order by city within each state

18. What is the purpose of the *second* list of total inches of rainfall?
    a. To show some rainfall amounts that came before storms
    b. To show some rainfall amounts in areas after the storms
    c. To show some rainfall amounts in places without storms
    d. To show some rainfall amounts, comparing as no storms

19. Which of the following best identifies the purpose of this storm summary message?
    a. To summarize a weather event that had already happened in the area identified
    b. To summarize recent, describe current, and predict future weather event details
    c. To forecast a severe weather event that was just about to take place in the area
    d. To warn people in the identified areas of a possible weather event in the future

20. Of the following, which most accurately describes the word choice "favorable conditions" as it is used in this text?
    a. It is used in an objective sense here, meaning conditions conducive to the weather forecast.
    b. It is used with a positive connotation, meaning weather conditions are now more favorable.
    c. It is used here specifically to characterize the conditions that are predicted to end the storm.
    d. It is used in a subjective sense here, meaning conditions that only certain persons will favor.

Questions 21 to30 pertain to the following scenario:

Regret
by Kate Chopin (1894)

1   Mamzelle Aurélie possessed a good strong figure, ruddy cheeks, hair that was changing from brown to gray, and a determined eye. She wore a man's hat about the farm, and an old blue army overcoat when it was cold, and sometimes top-boots.

2   Mamzelle Aurélie had never thought of marrying. She had never been in love. At the age of twenty she had received a proposal, which she had promptly declined, and at the age of fifty she had not yet lived to regret it.

3   So she was quite alone in the world, except for her dog Ponto, and the negroes who lived in her cabins and worked her crops, and the fowls, a few cows, a couple of mules, her gun (with which she shot chicken-hawks), and her religion.

4   One morning Mamzelle Aurélie stood upon her gallery, contemplating, with arms akimbo, a small band of very small children who, to all intents and purposes, might have fallen from the clouds, so unexpected and bewildering was their coming, and so unwelcome. They were the children of her nearest neighbor, Odile, who was not such a near neighbor, after all.

5   The young woman had appeared but five minutes before, accompanied by these four children. In her arms she carried little Elodie; she dragged Ti Nomme by an unwilling hand; while Marcéline and Marcélette followed with irresolute steps.

6   Her face was red and disfigured from tears and excitement. She had been summoned to a neighboring parish by the dangerous illness of her mother; her husband was away in Texas--it seemed to her a million miles away; and Valsin was waiting with the mule-cart to drive her to the station.

7   "It's no question, Mamzelle Aurélie; you jus' got to keep those youngsters fo' me tell I come back. Dieu sait, I would n' botha you with 'em if it was any otha way to do! Make 'em mine you, Mamzelle Aurélie; don' spare 'em. Me, there, I'm half crazy between the chil'ren, an' Léon not home, an' maybe not even to fine po' maman alive encore!"--a harrowing possibility which drove Odile to take a final hasty and convulsive leave of her disconsolate family.

8   She left them crowded into the narrow strip of shade on the porch of the long, low house; the white sunlight was beating in on the white old boards; some chickens were scratching in the grass at the foot of the steps, and one had boldly mounted, and was stepping heavily, solemnly, and aimlessly across the gallery. There was a pleasant odor of pinks in the air, and the sound of negroes' laughter was coming across the flowering cotton-field.

9   Mamzelle Aurélie stood contemplating the children. She looked with a critical eye upon Marcéline, who had been left staggering beneath the weight of the chubby Elodie. She surveyed with the same calculating air Marcélette mingling her

silent tears with the audible grief and rebellion of Ti Nomme. During those few contemplative moments she was collecting herself, determining upon a line of action which should be identical with a line of duty. She began by feeding them.

10   If Mamzelle Aurélie's responsibilities might have begun and ended there, they could easily have been dismissed; for her larder was amply provided against an emergency of this nature. But little children are not little pigs; they require and demand attentions which were wholly unexpected by Mamzelle Aurélie, and which she was ill prepared to give.

11   She was, indeed, very inapt in her management of Odile's children during the first few days. How could she know that Marcélette always wept when spoken to in a loud and commanding tone of voice? It was a peculiarity of Marcélette's. She became acquainted with Ti Nomme's passion for flowers only when he had plucked all the choicest gardenias and pinks for the apparent purpose of critically studying their botanical construction.

12   "'Tain't enough to tell 'im, Mamzelle Aurélie," Marcéline instructed her; "you got to tie 'im in a chair. It's w'at maman all time do w'en he's bad: she tie 'im in a chair." The chair in which Mamzelle Aurélie tied Ti Nomme was roomy and comfortable, and he seized the opportunity to take a nap in it, the afternoon being warm.

13   At night, when she ordered them one and all to bed as she would have shooed the chickens into the hen-house, they stayed uncomprehending before her. What about the little white nightgowns that had to be taken from the pillow-slip in which they were brought over, and shaken by some strong hand till they snapped like ox-whips? What about the tub of water which had to be brought and set in the middle of the floor, in which the little tired, dusty, sunbrowned feet had every one to be washed sweet and clean? And it made Marcéline and Marcélette laugh merrily-- the idea that Mamzelle Aurélie should for a moment have believed that Ti Nomme could fall asleep without being told the story of Croque-mitaine or Loup-garou, or both; or that Elodie could fall asleep at all without being rocked and sung to.

14   "I tell you, Aunt Ruby," Mamzelle Aurélie informed her cook in confidence; "me, I'd rather manage a dozen plantation' than fo' chil'ren. It's terrassent! Bonté! Don't talk to me about chil'ren!"

15   "'Tain' ispected sich as you would know airy thing 'bout 'em, Mamzelle Aurélie. I see dat plainly yistiddy w'en I spy dat li'le chile playin' wid yo' baskit o' keys. You don' know dat makes chillun grow up hard-headed, to play wid keys? Des like it make 'em teeth hard to look in a lookin'-glass. Them's the things you got to know in the raisin' an' manigement o' chillun."

16   Mamzelle Aurélie certainly did not pretend or aspire to such subtle and far-reaching knowledge on the subject as Aunt Ruby possessed, who had "raised five an' bared (buried) six" in her day. She was glad enough to learn a few little mother-tricks to serve the moment's need.

17 Ti Nomme's sticky fingers compelled her to unearth white aprons that she had not worn for years, and she had to accustom herself to his moist kisses--the expressions of an affectionate and exuberant nature. She got down her sewing-basket, which she seldom used, from the top shelf of the armoire, and placed it within the ready and easy reach which torn slips and buttonless waists demanded. It took her some days to become accustomed to the laughing, the crying, the chattering that echoed through the house and around it all day long. And it was not the first or the second night that she could sleep comfortably with little Elodie's hot, plump body pressed close against her, and the little one's warm breath beating her cheek like the fanning of a bird's wing.

18 But at the end of two weeks Mamzelle Aurélie had grown quite used to these things, and she no longer complained.

19 It was also at the end of two weeks that Mamzelle Aurélie, one evening, looking away toward the crib where the cattle were being fed, saw Valsin's blue cart turning the bend of the road. Odile sat beside the mulatto, upright and alert. As they drew near, the young woman's beaming face indicated that her homecoming was a happy one.

20 But this coming, unannounced and unexpected, threw Mamzelle Aurélie into a flutter that was almost agitation. The children had to be gathered. Where was Ti Nomme? Yonder in the shed, putting an edge on his knife at the grindstone. And Marcéline and Marcélette? Cutting and fashioning doll-rags in the corner of the gallery. As for Elodie, she was safe enough in Mamzelle Aurélie's arms; and she had screamed with delight at sight of the familiar blue cart which was bringing her mother back to her.

21 The excitement was all over, and they were gone. How still it was when they were gone! Mamzelle Aurélie stood upon the gallery, looking and listening. She could no longer see the cart; the red sunset and the blue-gray twilight had together flung a purple mist across the fields and road that hid it from her view. She could no longer hear the wheezing and creaking of its wheels. But she could still faintly hear the shrill, glad voices of the children.

22 She turned into the house. There was much work awaiting her, for the children had left a sad disorder behind them; but she did not at once set about the task of righting it. Mamzelle Aurélie seated herself beside the table. She gave one slow glance through the room, into which the evening shadows were creeping and deepening around her solitary figure. She let her head fall down upon her bended arm, and began to cry. Oh, but she cried! Not softly, as women often do. She cried like a man, with sobs that seemed to tear her very soul. She did not notice Ponto licking her hand.

21. From the description in the first three paragraphs, how would you best summarize the nature of the main character?
 a. She was a lonely fifty-year-old spinster.
 b. She was a strong, independent farmer.
 c. She was an aging and regretful woman.
 d. She was single with big circle of friends.

22. Based on the textual evidence, what can readers most accurately infer about this story's setting?
   a. It is set on a farm and could be anywhere in the rural Southern USA.
   b. It is set on a farm and is most likely in rural Louisiana's Cajun country.
   c. It is set on a farm and most likely in the New England area of the USA.
   d. It is set on a farm and is probably in Mexican-influenced South Texas.

23. In which paragraph does the author use descriptive writing to engage most of the senses?
   a. Paragraph 7
   b. Paragraph 19
   c. Paragraph 8
   d. Paragraph 21

24. Where in the story does Chopin subtly foreshadow the change in the character's feelings that is depicted at the end and named in the title?
   a. In paragraph 2
   b. In paragraph 3
   c. In paragraph 18
   d. It does not exist

25. In identifying Mamzelle Aurélie's state of preparation for the children, by which choice of wording does the author create both humor and contrast?
   a. "Her larder was amply provided against an emergency of this nature."
   b. "They require and demand attentions... wholly unexpected."
   c. "Attentions... which she was ill prepared to give."
   d. "But little children are not little pigs."

26. Upon first being left with the children, what was Mamzelle Aurélie's approach to caring for them?
   a. Neglectful
   b. Abusive
   c. Dutiful
   d. Loving

27. After Marcéline has "instructed" Mamzelle Aurélie to apply the mother's punishment of tying Ti Nomme in a chair, how does the author treat this situation?
   a. She shows the character's humanity in her refusal to do this.
   b. She makes it rather non-punitive and humorous in outcome.
   c. She shows the character's dislike for children in her behavior.
   d. She makes it into an example of why she never had children.

28. Which of the following best fits the main idea of this story?
   a. Mamzelle Aurélie finally stopped regretting being childless after caring for children.
   b. Mamzelle Aurélie felt even more regret than she always did over her childlessness.
   c. Mamzelle Aurélie only came to regret childlessness after having and losing children.
   d. Mamzelle Aurélie never regretted being childless and still did not after the children.

29. Why does the author write that Mamzelle Aurélie "cried like a man" at the end?
    a. Because she had always lived her life like a man in many other ways
    b. Because her grief was too strong to cry in a more feminine soft way
    c. Because she was not upset enough to cry hysterically, like a woman
    d. Because both (a) and (b) inform this action, but (c) is a contradiction

30. What is the full significance of the story's final sentence?
    a. Mamzelle Aurélie's newfound realization distracted her from the companion she had.
    b. Mamzelle Aurélie was so accustomed to Ponto's licking her hand, she never noticed it.
    c. Mamzelle Aurélie was simply so aggrieved that she could not notice anything external.
    d. Mamzelle Aurélie could no longer appreciate her dog's company after having children.

Questions 31 to40 pertain to the following scenario:

II. INTRODUCTION

1   ". . . a safe and secure homeland must mean more than preventing terrorist attacks from being carried out. It must also ensure that the liberties of all Americans are assured, privacy is protected, and the means by which we interchange with the world — through travel, lawful immigration, trade, commerce, and exchange — are secured. Ultimately, homeland security is about effectively managing risks to the Nation's security." ~ Quadrennial Homeland Security Review Report, 2010

2   **Homeland Security Risks**
The United States homeland security environment is complex and filled with competing requirements, interests, and incentives that must be balanced and managed effectively to ensure the achievement of key national objectives. The safety, security, and resilience of the Nation are threatened by an array of hazards, including acts of terrorism, malicious activity in cyberspace, pandemics, manmade accidents, transnational crime, and natural disasters. At the same time, homeland security organizations must manage risks[2] associated with workforce management, acquisitions operations, and project costs. Collectively, these external and internal risks have the potential to cause loss of life, injuries, negative psychosocial impact, environmental degradation, loss of economic activity, reduction of ability to perform mission essential functions, and loss of confidence in government capabilities.

3   It is the role of DHS and its partners to understand and manage these myriad homeland security risks. We live in a dynamic and uncertain world where the past does not serve as a complete guide to the future. In addition, the systems that provide the functions essential for a thriving society are increasingly intricate and interconnected. This means that potential disruptions to a system are not fully understood and can have large and unanticipated cascading effects throughout American security. Compounding this complexity is the fact that future trends— such as technological advancements, global climate change, asymmetric threats, and the evolving nature of Nation-states—have the potential to significantly alter the homeland security risk landscape in unexpected ways. Yet such emerging trends hold promise as well as peril and should be understood and managed.

4   [2]Throughout this document, risk is defined as "the potential for an unwanted outcome resulting from an incident, event, or occurrence, as determined by its likelihood and the associated consequences." DHS Risk Lexicon, 2010 Edition.

5   Sound Decision Making

Establishing the capability and capacity to identify, understand, and address such complex challenges and opportunities is the crux of risk management. Risk management is an approach for making and implementing improved homeland security decisions. "Risk management is the process for identifying, analyzing, and communicating risk and accepting, avoiding, transferring, or controlling it to an acceptable level considering associated costs and benefits of any actions taken." - DHS Risk Lexicon, 2010 Edition

6   Risk Management Fundamentals

To improve decision making, leaders in DHS and their partners in the homeland security enterprise must practice foresight and work to understand known and uncertain risks, as best they can, in order to make sound management decisions. These leaders need to consider the risks facing the homeland to make appropriate resource tradeoffs and align management approaches. Addressing these risks and promoting security is a shared responsibility that depends on unity of effort among Federal, state, local, tribal and territorial governments, the private sector, non-governmental organizations, and the citizenry as a whole.

7   The Value of Risk Management

The Secretary of Homeland Security has established the requirement for DHS to build and promote an integrated approach to homeland security risk management, working with partners across the homeland security enterprise. The Department's role in establishing integrated risk management is to build security, safety, and resilience across domains by connecting efforts to prevent terrorism and enhance security, secure and manage our borders, enforce and administer our immigration laws, safeguard and secure cyberspace, ensure resilience to disasters, and provide essential support in assuring national and economic security.

8   Improved homeland security depends on connecting information about risks, activities, and capabilities and using this information to guide prevention, protection, response, and recovery efforts. The establishment of sound risk management practices across DHS and the homeland security enterprise will help protect and enhance national interests, conserve resources, and assist in avoiding or mitigating the effects of emerging or unknown risks. At the organizational level, the application of risk management will complement and augment strategic and operational planning efforts, policy development, budget formulation, performance evaluation and assessments, and reporting processes.

9   Risk management will not preclude adverse events from occurring; however, it enables national homeland security efforts to focus on those things that are likely to bring the greatest harm, and employ approaches that are likely to mitigate or prevent those incidents. Furthermore, the American people, resources, economy, and way of life are bolstered and made more resilient by anticipating, communicating, and preparing for hazards, both internal and external, through comprehensive and deliberate risk management.

10   Risk management is not an end in and of itself, but rather part of sound organizational practices that include planning, preparedness, program evaluation, process improvement, and budget priority development. The value of a risk management approach or strategy to decision makers is not in the promotion of a particular course of action, but rather in the ability to distinguish between various choices within the larger context. Establishing the infrastructure and organizational culture to support the execution of homeland security risk management is a critical requirement for achieving the Nation's security goals. Risk management is essential for homeland security leaders in prioritizing competing requirements and enabling comprehensive approaches to measure performance and detail progress.

11   **Resilience and Risk Management**
One of the foundational concepts of homeland security is the need to build resilient systems, communities, and institutions that are robust, adaptable and have the capacity for rapid recovery. Resilience and risk management are mutually reinforcing concepts. Risk management contributes to the achievement of resilience by identifying opportunities to build resilience into planning and resourcing to achieve risk reduction in advance of a hazard, as well as enabling the mitigation of consequences of any disasters that do occur.

31. According to the opening quotation, which of the following applies to homeland security?
    a. Its entire extent is to the prevention of terrorist attacks.
    b. Protecting privacy supersedes Constitutional freedoms.
    c. Ensuring American freedoms trumps protecting privacy.
    d. It includes ensuring that our global interactions are safe.

32. Which accurately represents what the passage says about risks to our homeland security?
    a. They are much more likely to cause deaths and injuries than to affect Americans psychosocially.
    b. By interfering with necessary government actions, they can reduce citizen trust in government.
    c. The potential of damaging the economy is more important than for damaging the environment.
    d. Hazards like terrorism, natural and manmade disasters, crime, and diseases offer the only risks.

33. To what does "risk[2]" in paragraph 2 refer?
    a. A footnote with a definition in paragraph 4
    b. An end note not excerpted here
    c. No further information is offered
    d. A footnote with a comment in paragraph 3

34. Of the following, which most accurately describes the relationship of the last sentence in paragraph 3 to the rest of the paragraph?
    a. It provides a summary in one sentence of all the information detailed in prior sentences.
    b. It intensifies all the previously identified negative aspects of the homeland security risks.
    c. It changes what precedes it by identifying positive as well as negative aspects of the risks.
    d. It provides support for understanding and managing risks because they afford only peril.

35. According to the textual evidence, what can you conclude about the relationship between homeland security decisions and risk management?
    a. Homeland security decisions are made in an effort to inform managing risks.
    b. Homeland security decisions improve the implementation of managing risks.
    c. Homeland security decisions comprise an approach toward risk management.
    d. Homeland security decisions are informed by the risk management approach.

36. What purpose does the passage excerpted here accomplish?
    a. It identifies the major principles of homeland security risk management.
    b. It outlines a comprehensive approach to risk management for the DHS.
    c. It presents basics of risks, decisions, and management, but not applications.
    d. It describes all steps in the homeland security risk management process.

37. What best represents the point of view of the authors of this passage?
    a. Effective risk management will prevent all adverse occurrences.
    b. Effective risk management is not a means to an end but an end in itself.
    c. Effective risk management will support the American way of life.
    d. Effective risk management is best focused on separate domains.

38. Among the following positive effects cited for solid, integrated risk management across the Department of Homeland Security, which one is NOT identified in this passage as a result on the organizational level?
    a. The conservation of resources
    b. The development for policies
    c. The establishment of budgets
    d. The processes used to report

39. What relationship does resilience (i.e., the ability to recover readily) have to risk management, according to this text?
    a. Resilience is a quality that is necessary to enable risk management.
    b. Resilience and risk management reciprocally reinforce each other.
    c. Resilience is a quality that is furthered by sound risk management.
    d. Resilience and risk management act in parallel, but do not interact.

40. What is correct about the authors' position regarding the value of risk management to leaders?
    a. It shows them which specific action plans to pursue.
    b. It can be executed with or without an infrastructure.
    c. It will succeed irrespective of organizational cultures.
    d. It helps them sort and prioritize competitive options.

Constructed Response

Read the passages and examine the graphic below, and then answer the essay questions that follow.

PASSAGE 1

If we could first know where we are and whither we are tending, we could better judge what to do and how to do it. We are now far into the fifth year since a policy was initiated with the avowed object and confident promise of putting an end to slavery agitation. Under the operation of that policy, that agitation has not only not ceased but has constantly augmented. In my opinion, it will not cease until a crisis shall have been reached and passed. "A house divided against itself cannot stand." I believe this government cannot endure, permanently, half slave and half free. I do not expect the Union to be dissolved; I do not expect the house to fall; but I do expect it will cease to be divided. It will become all one thing, or all the other. Either the opponents of slavery will arrest the further spread of it and place it where the public mind shall rest in the belief that it is in the course of ultimate extinction, or its advocates will push it forward till it shall become alike lawful in all the states, old as well as new, North as well as South.

Excerpt from Abraham Lincoln's speech, "A House Divided" (1858)

PASSAGE 2

The next question propounded to me by Mr. Lincoln is, can the people of a Territory in any lawful way, against the wishes of any citizen of the United States, exclude slavery from their limits prior to the formation of a State Constitution? I answer emphatically, as Mr. Lincoln has heard me answer a hundred times from every stump in Illinois, that in my opinion the people of a Territory can, by lawful means, exclude slavery from their limits prior to the formation of a State Constitution. Mr. Lincoln knew that I had answered that question over and over again. He heard me argue the Nebraska bill on that principle all over the State in 1854, in 1855, and in 1856, and he has no excuse for pretending to be in doubt as to my position on that question. It matters not what way the Supreme Court may hereafter decide as to the abstract question whether slavery may or may not go into a Territory under the Constitution, the people have the lawful means to introduce it or exclude it as they please, for the reason that slavery cannot exist a day or an hour anywhere, unless it is supported by local police regulations. Those police regulations can only be established by the local legislature, and if the people are opposed to slavery they will elect representatives to that body who will by unfriendly legislation effectually prevent the introduction of it into their midst. If, on the contrary, they are for it, their legislation will favor its extension. Hence, no matter what the decision of the Supreme Court may be on that abstract question, still the right of the people to make a slave Territory or a free Territory is perfect and complete under the Nebraska bill. I hope Mr. Lincoln deems my answer satisfactory on that point.

Excerpt from Stephen Douglas's Freeport Doctrine speech at Freeport, Illinois. (1858)

GRAPHIC AND ACCOMPANYING TEXT

If there was ever a single-issue candidate for high office, it was Abraham Lincoln. In 1854, slavery, specifically the threatened spread of slavery into the Western territories, dominated his thoughts, and the issue set him afire. His voice took on new urgency, his message greater clarity, and he would entertain no compromise. Lincoln considered Illinois Senator Stephen A. Douglas's concept of "popular sovereignty"—allowing the territories to determine their own policy on slavery—a denial of the responsibility of the Congress to uphold the United States Constitution. Lincoln's guiding beacon was the statement in the Declaration of Independence that "all men are created equal." By upholding that principle, with all of its implications, Abraham Lincoln set the course for his own destiny and that of the United States.

1. Write an essay about 100-200 words long comparing and contrasting the two passages excerpted from the debates. Identify which specific claims each makes. Evaluate how sufficient, pertinent, and valid the evidence each supplies in support of each claim. Give examples from both passages in support of your evaluations. Write for an adult, educated audience and, except when quoting from the provided sources, write in your own words. Edit your final draft to comply with all standard American English writing conventions.

2. In roughly 100-200 words, write an essay that explains how the information accompanying the graphic either supports or refutes one of the passages. Give examples from the passage you choose and the graphic's accompanying information to support what you explain. Target an adult, educated audience. Other than quoting the supplied sources, write in your own words. Edit your final draft to be consistent with all standard American English writing conventions.

3. Compose an essay about 400-600 words long in which you fully develop an argument supporting a claim evaluating the relative merits of each argument for local vs. national slavery legislation in the context of the historical period. Comment on how each speaker's respective writing style supports or does not support his claims. Your essay must also include: (1) a claim showing your knowledge and comprehension of the subject; (2) reasoning that is logical, valid, and refers to and elaborates upon the arguments in the supplied sources; (3) enough pertinent evidence from all three sources to support your claim; and (4) at least one potential counterclaim you can predict and your response to it. Aim your writing to address an adult, educated audience. Establish a suitable tone, a style compatible with the subject matter, precision and clarity in your word choice at the beginning, and sustain them throughout your essay. Other than quoting supplied sources, write using your own words. Edit your final draft of the essay to meet all standard American English writing conventions.

Answers and Explanations

1. C: The second subtitle below the title specifies "for people age 65+." Therefore these particular eating tips are not for all ages (a), for adolescents and young adults (b), or only for those in middle adulthood (d). They are specifically designed for people aged 65—a typical retirement age—and older (c).

2. A: Our bodies do not only need fewer calories (b) or more protein (c) as we age, and they do not change less than our behaviors (d); either or both may change. Our aging bodies change in a variety of ways: ability to absorb vitamin D decreases, hunger and thirst may diminish, muscle mass typically decreases while fatty tissue increases in some and decreases in others, etc.

3. D: The most logical inference you could draw from the "Print in English" button at the top is that the article is also available to print in Spanish because Spanish is the most common non-English language in which media are made available today in America. If it could only be printed in English (a), there would be no reason to add "in English" after "Print." It needs no translation (b) as it is already in English. It is not as likely the article is available in many languages (c).

4. B: Although the advice to drink plenty of liquids is typically good advice for all ages (a), this is not the reason given in the text; it is because aging can decrease the ability to sense thirst (b), and if so we need to compensate for that. There is no information about people dehydrating more with age (c) or forgetting to drink liquids (d) when they are older.

5. B: These tips contain advice (tip 5) to include a variety of different, brightly colored vegetables (a), but the *main* purpose is because vegetables are typically high-fiber and low-calorie, and offer different nutrients indicated by their colors. Eating softer foods (c) is advised (tip 6), but the *main* reason is to prevent dental problems from interfering with nutrition. Taking home food from restaurants (d) is advised (tip 4), but the *main* reason is portion control to avoid overeating. Making eating social (b) is advocated (tip 2) for making mealtimes more appealing.

6. A: Tip 7 advises aging people to compensate for changes in sense of smell and taste by adding herbs and spices to foods as needed; smell and taste more likely become *less* sensitive with aging, not more (b). Some medications can decrease sensation of food flavor or alter its quality, but particular medications are not known to make foods taste spicier (c) and the text does not say this. It advises seniors to use herbs to add flavor, not avoid them; some very "hot" spices can cause an upset stomach, but herbs typically do not (d).

7. C: From the information in tip 8, you can conclude that food-borne and food-related illnesses are *more* life-threatening to older people (a); that animal proteins are most harmful if *under*cooked (b) or raw; that bacteria can grow in dairy foods that are not pasteurized (c), which always present risks to older people; and that, rather than taking chances with their health (e.g., to economize), seniors should throw away food if it may be unsafe (d).

8. A: The text advises older readers both to read the Nutrition Facts on food packages and to ask their doctors about nutrients and ingredients to increase or limit. Just reading food labels is not enough (b) because aging changes people's nutritional needs. However, asking the doctor alone (c) is also not enough: to follow physician advice, patients must read Nutrition Facts to choose foods conforming to it. This text never suggests choice (d), which is very unsound advice. Nutritional needs vary individually; doctors, nutritionists, and dietitians determine them using bloodwork results.

9. C: While outside material shows seniors often less efficiently absorb some nutrients from foods like vitamin D, this text neither states that all seniors do, nor that all seniors need supplements (a). Neither should they all avoid them (d); the text directs readers to consult their doctors, who will know. Tip 10 states some supplements can affect medical conditions (b), so readers can infer or conclude scientists *have* found this because this authoritative government source is science-based. It also says some supplements *can* interfere with medicines (c).

10. D: The box of "MyPlate Moments" does not describe common nutritional problems (a) and does not contain complaints about the website (b) or additional information to supplement (c) the dietary tips above it. Rather, it contains testimonials (d) from people who have used the website and are reporting the positive results they have achieved by following its healthy eating tips.

11. D: This storm summary applies to the Southern Plains (c) and the lower Mississippi Valley (b) according to paragraph 1, and East Texas (c) according to p2. It does NOT apply to College Park, Maryland (a); this is where the Weather Prediction Center (WPC) of the National Center for Environmental Protection (NCEP), which issues such storm summaries and weather forecasts, is located.

12. B: According to the text, flood advisories (a), flash flood watches (c), and flash flood warnings (d) were all in effect for certain regions at the time of this report. However, there were NOT any hurricane watches (b) in effect at that time; the storms involved heavy rain and flooding in some places due to the heavy rains, but no hurricane was involved.

13. A: The text states (paragraph 2) that the weather system was moving eastward, not in a westward (b), northward (c), or southward (d) direction. Some readers might assume this because weather generally moves in an easterly direction, but the text also confirms it.

14. c: The advisories, watches, and warnings were issued for the Gulf Coast from "extreme East Texas to the Florida panhandle as well as Inland Louisiana and Mississippi" (paragraph 3). Thus neither the Gulf Coast portions of all states affected (a) nor all inland portions of all states affected (b) were included; the inland parts of East Texas and Florida (d) were NOT included.

15. A: The "surface low" (low barometric pressure) system was identified "about 100 miles south of Lake Charles, Louisiana" (paragraph 5). Moderate to heavy rainfall was identified in Texas (d). Light to moderate rain was identified as beginning to move into western Alabama (b) and the westerly part of the Florida (c) panhandle, but these were not the locations of the surface low at the time.

16. D: The text (paragraph 5) explicitly names "instability" (a) contributing to conditions promoting heavy rainfall, as well as "deep tropical moisture" (b) and "a warm front" moving across the Louisiana coast inland. However, it does not explicitly name a cold front (d); readers not knowledgeable of meteorology must infer this from the information that "An occluded front was draped over the surface low." An occluded front develops when a cold front catches up with a warm front and they meet.

17. A: The *first* list arranges the total inches of rainfall by each state affected, and then in descending order, i.e., from most to fewest inches, by city within each state. Hence the order is not only by state and city (b); it is not ascending (c), i.e., from fewest to most inches, but vice versa; and only the states are in alphabetical order, not the cities within them (d).

18. B: The second list is provided to show how much rain fell in areas where the weather event was already over—not to show how much rain fell before the event (a), not to show how much rain fell in areas where it did not occur (c), and not to compare amounts of rainfall in storm areas to areas with no storms at all (d).

19. B: The purpose of this storm summary was not to summarize weather that had already occurred (a), to forecast an imminent severe weather event (c), or to warn people that such a weather event was possible in the future (d). It was to summarize what had already taken place during an ongoing weather event, describe current weather conditions during this event, and predict future weather conditions during this event (b).

20. A: This text uses the term objectively: in meteorology, "favorable conditions" means conditions that are conducive to whatever weather events are being forecast, i.e., "favorable conditions for heavy rainfall and flash flooding will continue over the next few days" (paragraph 16). It does not carry the positive connotation of "better" as the word "favorable" does in other contexts (b). It does not refer to conditions favorable to the storms' ending (c), but to their continuing. It is used objectively, not subjectively, and has nothing to do with any particular persons' favor (d).

21. B: Chopin's description of Mamzelle Aurélie expresses her character succinctly: her "strong figure, ruddy cheeks" and "determined eye" depict her as strong, vital, and determined (paragraph 1). Her never having been in love or considered marriage, having "promptly declined" a proposal at 20, and that by 50 "she had not yet lived to regret it" (p2)—which contradicts choice (c)—all demonstrate her independence. She was alone (p3), but is not described as lonely (a); she does not have a big circle of friends (d).

22. B: Nearly all characters' names are French (and two children's stories' titles); their dialogue contains French vocabulary words and expressions like "Dieu sait" (God knows), "maman," "encore" (still), "terrassent" (bringing down/slaying), "Bonté!" (Good heavens!), etc. Only Louisiana has parishes (paragraph 6). The farm setting and Cajun pidgin English dialects spoken indicate the setting. In fact, this story was first published in Chopin's collection entitled *A Night in Acadia.* There is no textual evidence to support a setting in New England (c) or Texas (d)—Texas "seemed... a million miles away" (p6). Evidence locates it more specifically than choice (a).

23. C: Paragraph 7 (a) is nearly all dialogue, plus one narrative independent clause at the end, with no description. Paragraph 19 (b) uses description, but with only visual details. Paragraph 8 (c) includes details engaging the senses of vision, hearing, and smell. Paragraph 21 (d) uses description that engages the senses of vision and hearing.

24. A: Regarding Mamzelle Aurélie's having declined a marriage proposal when young, paragraph 2 ends with, "she had not yet lived to *regret* it." By echoing the title word, Chopin subtly foreshadows the change in emotion from never regretting her life alone to regretting it after the children's departure. Paragraph 3 (b) describes her "quite alone in the world," but not regretful. Paragraph 18 (c) summarizes her having become accustomed to child-related things she had previously complained about. This emotional change is from exasperation to acceptance, not from self-sufficiency to regret. Because choice (a) is correct, choice (d) is incorrect.

25. D: By establishing contrast through comparison ("little children are not little pigs"), Chopin also lends humor to the main character's situation: she had plenty of food to feed the children (a), which is neither funny nor a problem; and as a farmer, she knew how to feed animals. However, children needed more care than just being fed, which she had not anticipated (b) when they arrived, and being childless and living alone, was unprepared to offer them (c).

26. C: Mamzelle Aurélie did not neglect (a) or abuse (b) the children initially, but neither did she approach their care lovingly (d), as she had never had children and found their arrival "unexpected," "bewildering," and "unwelcome" (paragraph 4). Instead, she was "determining upon a line of action which should be identical with a line of *duty*. She began by feeding them" (p9). While this was not all the children needed, it was certainly a primary duty.

27. B: Mamzelle Aurélie does not refuse to tie Ti Nomme in a chair (paragraph 12). However, she does defeat the purpose of punishing by tying him in a chair so "roomy and comfortable" that "he seized the opportunity to take a nap in it, the afternoon being warm." This also lends humor to an action which otherwise could have seemed abusive. The character's actions do not show a dislike for children (c). The author does not make this episode an example for the character's childlessness (d).

28. C: Mamzelle Aurélie did NOT regret being childless or unmarried at the beginning of the story (cf. paragraph 2), and did NOT stop regretting it after caring for children (a). Therefore she did not always feel regret (b). She only came to regret not having children after having the experience of caring for children temporarily (c). The story depicts a major change in her outlook when she felt regret after their departure, so choice (d) is also incorrect.

29. D: The author's characterization of Mamzelle Aurélie is of a woman who had always been more independent and self sufficient than most women in the late 19th century; her behaviors were more like a man's in many ways, and her crying like a man is consistent with this. But at the same time, Chopin uses this description to show how strong Mamzelle Aurélie's grief was (b)—too strong to cry "softly, as women often do." She makes this clear by modifying "cried like a man" with "sobs that seemed to tear her very soul." Hence (c) contradicts the rest.

30. A: When Mamzelle Aurélie did not notice Ponto licking her hand, it was not merely because she was so habituated to it (b), was too upset to notice anything outside herself (c), or because her appreciation of her dog was permanently ruined by the experience of caring for children (d). It was because her realization of regret for the first time over being childless not only brought profound grief, but additionally distracted her from the companion she did have (a). Ponto's companionship is significant as the first exception named to Mamzelle Aurélie's aloneness (paragraph 3).

31. D: The opening quotation makes clear that preventing terrorist attacks is NOT the entire extent of homeland security (paragraph 1), which also involves protecting privacy (b) and ensuring Americans' freedoms (c)—both EQUALLY, not one more than the other—and moreover, ensuring that our interactions with the rest of the world "through travel, lawful immigration, trade, commerce, and exchange" are safe (d).

32. B: Paragraph 2 identifies not only deaths and injuries, but also "negative psychosocial impact" as homeland security risks (a); and "reduction of ability to perform mission essential functions, and loss of confidence in government capabilities." Readers can infer the former to cause the latter. Additional potential consequences include "environmental degradation, loss of economic activity"; neither is deemed more important (c). Terrorism, natural disasters, manmade accidents, global

crime, and cyber-attacks are NOT the only risks (d): this paragraph points out that employee management-related, asset-acquiring operations-related, and project expense-related risk management are also homeland security jobs.

33. A: The word "risk" with the superscript number 2 refers to a footnote, which is reproduced in this passage (in a smaller font) and labeled as paragraph 4; this footnote provides the definition of risk that is used throughout the document from which this passage is excerpted. Because the footnote is included in this excerpt, the number does not refer to an end note later in the text not excerpted (b). Because it is, choice (c) is incorrect. The footnote provides a definition, not a comment; and it appears in paragraph 4, not paragraph 3 (d).

34. C: This paragraph explains some emergent trends presenting challenges to managing the complexities of homeland security risks. Its last sentence does not summarize the rest (a), and it does not make these trends seem worse (b). Instead, it counters the daunting nature of the risks described by identifying the "*promise as well as peril*" (d) they involve, citing these as reasons for understanding and managing them.

35. D: As paragraph 5 explains, risk management is an approach that informs and improves homeland security decisions—not the other way around. Homeland security decisions are not made first to inform risk management (a), to improve risk management implementation (b), or as an approach toward managing risks (c).

36. C: This passage is from a 31-page document meant to be "the capstone doctrine" for Department of Homeland Security (DHS) risk management. The excerpted portion introduces some basics, including identifying risks, explaining sound decision-making, and identifying the value of risk management. However, it does NOT include applications for risk management, which follow it in the complete text. Additional parts of the full text NOT included in this passage cover major DHS risk management principles (a) and tenets, a comprehensive approach to DHS risk management (b), and the steps in the DHS risk management process (d).

37. C: The authors state, "Risk management will not preclude adverse events from occurring" (paragraph 9), so choice (a) is incorrect. "Risk management is not an end in and of itself" (p10), hence choice (b) is incorrect. Instead, it is a part of "sound organizational practices that include planning, preparedness, program evaluation, process improvement, and budget priority development." They describe such practices as bolstering America's way of life (c) as well as its people, economy, and resources (p9). They also emphasize the Department of Homeland Security's *integrated* approach *across* domains (p7-8) to risk management (d).

38. A: The authors identify developing policy (b), establishing budgets (c), and reporting processes (d) as well as operational and strategic planning and performance evaluation as benefits of applying risk management on the organizational level. They identify conserving resources (a) along with protecting national interests and preventing or limiting risk effects as benefits on the national and general level rather than the organizational level.

39. B: As explained in paragraph 11, resilience and risk management have a reciprocally reinforcing relationship. A fundamental homeland security concept is building resilience in institutions, communities, and systems; risk management helps develop resilience by incorporating it into prevention, resource, and recovery planning. The relationship is not unidirectional, either with resilience required for risk management only (a) or risk management promoting resilience only (c). The two DO interact (d).

40. D: The authors believe that risk management strategies and approaches do NOT show leaders which actions to take (a); rather, they find the value to decision-makers of risk management is in helping them differentiate among and prioritize different and competing needs and options. They also find both the necessary infrastructure (b) and organizational culture (c) "critical" to meeting goals for national security (paragraph 10).

Secret Key #1 - Time is Your Greatest Enemy

Pace Yourself

Wear a watch. At the beginning of the test, check the time (or start a chronometer on your watch to count the minutes), and check the time after every few questions to make sure you are "on schedule."

If you are forced to speed up, do it efficiently. Usually one or more answer choices can be eliminated without too much difficulty. Above all, don't panic. Don't speed up and just begin guessing at random choices. By pacing yourself, and continually monitoring your progress against your watch, you will always know exactly how far ahead or behind you are with your available time. If you find that you are one minute behind on the test, don't skip one question without spending any time on it, just to catch back up. Take 15 fewer seconds on the next four questions, and after four questions you'll have caught back up. Once you catch back up, you can continue working each problem at your normal pace.

Furthermore, don't dwell on the problems that you were rushed on. If a problem was taking up too much time and you made a hurried guess, it must be difficult. The difficult questions are the ones you are most likely to miss anyway, so it isn't a big loss. It is better to end with more time than you need than to run out of time.

Lastly, sometimes it is beneficial to slow down if you are constantly getting ahead of time. You are always more likely to catch a careless mistake by working more slowly than quickly, and among very high-scoring test takers (those who are likely to have lots of time left over), careless errors affect the score more than mastery of material.

Secret Key #2 - Guessing is not Guesswork

You probably know that guessing is a good idea - unlike other standardized tests, there is no penalty for getting a wrong answer. Even if you have no idea about a question, you still have a 20-25% chance of getting it right.

Most test takers do not understand the impact that proper guessing can have on their score. Unless you score extremely high, guessing will significantly contribute to your final score.

Monkeys Take the Test

What most test takers don't realize is that to insure that 20-25% chance, you have to guess randomly. If you put 20 monkeys in a room to take this test, assuming they answered once per question and behaved themselves, on average they would get 20-25% of the questions correct. Put 20 test takers in the room, and the average will be much lower among guessed questions. Why?
1. The test writers intentionally write deceptive answer choices that "look" right. A test taker has no idea about a question, so picks the "best looking" answer, which is often wrong. The monkey has no idea what looks good and what doesn't, so will consistently be lucky about 20-25% of the time.
2. Test takers will eliminate answer choices from the guessing pool based on a hunch or intuition. Simple but correct answers often get excluded, leaving a 0% chance of being correct. The monkey has no clue, and often gets lucky with the best choice.

This is why the process of elimination endorsed by most test courses is flawed and detrimental to your performance- test takers don't guess, they make an ignorant stab in the dark that is usually worse than random.

$5 Challenge

Let me introduce one of the most valuable ideas of this course- the $5 challenge:

You only mark your "best guess" if you are willing to bet $5 on it.

You only eliminate choices from guessing if you are willing to bet $5 on it.

Why $5? Five dollars is an amount of money that is small yet not insignificant, and can really add up fast (20 questions could cost you $100). Likewise, each answer choice on one question of the test will have a small impact on your overall score, but it can really add up to a lot of points in the end.

The process of elimination IS valuable. The following shows your chance of guessing it right:

If you eliminate wrong answer choices until only this many remain:	Chance of getting it correct:
1	100%
2	50%
3	33%

However, if you accidentally eliminate the right answer or go on a hunch for an incorrect answer, your chances drop dramatically: to 0%. By guessing among all the answer choices, you are GUARANTEED to have a shot at the right answer.

That's why the $5 test is so valuable- if you give up the advantage and safety of a pure guess, it had better be worth the risk.

What we still haven't covered is how to be sure that whatever guess you make is truly random. Here's the easiest way:

Always pick the first answer choice among those remaining.
Such a technique means that you have decided, **before you see a single test question**, exactly how you are going to guess- and since the order of choices tells you nothing about which one is correct, this guessing technique is perfectly random.

This section is not meant to scare you away from making educated guesses or eliminating choices- you just need to define when a choice is worth eliminating. The $5 test, along with a pre-defined random guessing strategy, is the best way to make sure you reap all of the benefits of guessing.

Secret Key #3 - Practice Smarter, Not Harder

Many test takers delay the test preparation process because they dread the awful amounts of practice time they think necessary to succeed on the test. We have refined an effective method that will take you only a fraction of the time.

There are a number of "obstacles" in your way to succeed. Among these are answering questions, finishing in time, and mastering test-taking strategies. All must be executed on the day of the test at peak performance, or your score will suffer. The test is a mental marathon that has a large impact on your future.

Just like a marathon runner, it is important to work your way up to the full challenge. So first you just worry about questions, and then time, and finally strategy:

Success Strategy

1. Find a good source for practice tests.
2. If you are willing to make a larger time investment, consider using more than one study guide- often the different approaches of multiple authors will help you "get" difficult concepts.
3. Take a practice test with no time constraints, with all study helps "open book." Take your time with questions and focus on applying strategies.
4. Take a practice test with time constraints, with all guides "open book."
5. Take a final practice test with no open material and time limits

If you have time to take more practice tests, just repeat step 5. By gradually exposing yourself to the full rigors of the test environment, you will condition your mind to the stress of test day and maximize your success.

Secret Key #4 - Prepare, Don't Procrastinate

Let me state an obvious fact: if you take the test three times, you will get three different scores. This is due to the way you feel on test day, the level of preparedness you have, and, despite the test writers' claims to the contrary, some tests WILL be easier for you than others.

Since your future depends so much on your score, you should maximize your chances of success. In order to maximize the likelihood of success, you've got to prepare in advance. This means taking practice tests and spending time learning the information and test taking strategies you will need to succeed.

Never take the test as a "practice" test, expecting that you can just take it again if you need to. Feel free to take sample tests on your own, but when you go to take the official test, be prepared, be focused, and do your best the first time!

Secret Key #5 - Test Yourself

Everyone knows that time is money. There is no need to spend too much of your time or too little of your time preparing for the test. You should only spend as much of your precious time preparing as is necessary for you to get the score you need.

Once you have taken a practice test under real conditions of time constraints, then you will know if you are ready for the test or not.

If you have scored extremely high the first time that you take the practice test, then there is not much point in spending countless hours studying. You are already there.

Benchmark your abilities by retaking practice tests and seeing how much you have improved. Once you score high enough to guarantee success, then you are ready.

If you have scored well below where you need, then knuckle down and begin studying in earnest. Check your improvement regularly through the use of practice tests under real conditions. Above all, don't worry, panic, or give up. The key is perseverance!

Then, when you go to take the test, remain confident and remember how well you did on the practice tests. If you can score high enough on a practice test, then you can do the same on the real thing.

General Strategies

The most important thing you can do is to ignore your fears and jump into the test immediately- do not be overwhelmed by any strange-sounding terms. You have to jump into the test like jumping into a pool- all at once is the easiest way.

Make Predictions

As you read and understand the question, try to guess what the answer will be. Remember that several of the answer choices are wrong, and once you begin reading them, your mind will immediately become cluttered with answer choices designed to throw you off. Your mind is typically the most focused immediately after you have read the question and digested its contents. If you can, try to predict what the correct answer will be. You may be surprised at what you can predict.

Quickly scan the choices and see if your prediction is in the listed answer choices. If it is, then you can be quite confident that you have the right answer. It still won't hurt to check the other answer choices, but most of the time, you've got it!

Answer the Question

It may seem obvious to only pick answer choices that answer the question, but the test writers can create some excellent answer choices that are wrong. Don't pick an answer just because it sounds right, or you believe it to be true. It MUST answer the question. Once you've made your selection, always go back and check it against the question and make sure that you didn't misread the question, and the answer choice does answer the question posed.

Benchmark

After you read the first answer choice, decide if you think it sounds correct or not. If it doesn't, move on to the next answer choice. If it does, mentally mark that answer choice. This doesn't mean that you've definitely selected it as your answer choice, it just means that it's the best you've seen thus far. Go ahead and read the next choice. If the next choice is worse than the one you've already selected, keep going to the next answer choice. If the next choice is better than the choice you've already selected, mentally mark the new answer choice as your best guess.

The first answer choice that you select becomes your standard. Every other answer choice must be benchmarked against that standard. That choice is correct until proven otherwise by another answer choice beating it out. Once you've decided that no other answer choice seems as good, do one final check to ensure that your answer choice answers the question posed.

Valid Information

Don't discount any of the information provided in the question. Every piece of information may be necessary to determine the correct answer. None of the information in the question is there to throw you off (while the answer choices will certainly have information to throw you off). If two seemingly unrelated topics are discussed, don't ignore either. You can be confident there is a relationship, or it wouldn't be included in the question, and you are probably going to have to determine what is that relationship to find the answer.

Avoid "Fact Traps"

Don't get distracted by a choice that is factually true. Your search is for the answer that answers the question. Stay focused and don't fall for an answer that is true but incorrect. Always go back to the question and make sure you're choosing an answer that actually answers the question and is not just a true statement. An answer can be factually correct, but it MUST answer the question asked. Additionally, two answers can both be seemingly correct, so be sure to read all of the answer choices, and make sure that you get the one that BEST answers the question.

Milk the Question

Some of the questions may throw you completely off. They might deal with a subject you have not been exposed to, or one that you haven't reviewed in years. While your lack of knowledge about the subject will be a hindrance, the question itself can give you many clues that will help you find the correct answer. Read the question carefully and look for clues. Watch particularly for adjectives and nouns describing difficult terms or words that you don't recognize. Regardless of if you completely understand a word or not, replacing it with a synonym either provided or one you more familiar with may help you to understand what the questions are asking. Rather than wracking your mind about specific detailed information concerning a difficult term or word, try to use mental substitutes that are easier to understand.

The Trap of Familiarity

Don't just choose a word because you recognize it. On difficult questions, you may not recognize a number of words in the answer choices. The test writers don't put "make-believe" words on the test; so don't think that just because you only recognize all the words in one answer choice means that answer choice must be correct. If you only recognize words in one answer choice, then focus on that one. Is it correct? Try your best to determine if it is correct. If it is, that is great, but if it doesn't, eliminate it. Each word and answer choice you eliminate increases your chances of getting the question correct, even if you then have to guess among the unfamiliar choices.

Eliminate Answers

Eliminate choices as soon as you realize they are wrong. But be careful! Make sure you consider all of the possible answer choices. Just because one appears right, doesn't mean that the next one won't be even better! The test writers will usually put more than one good answer choice for every question, so read all of them. Don't worry if you are stuck between two that seem right. By getting down to just two remaining possible choices, your odds are now 50/50. Rather than wasting too much time, play the odds. You are guessing, but guessing wisely, because you've been able to knock out some of the answer choices that you know are wrong. If you are eliminating choices and realize that the last answer choice you are left with is also obviously wrong, don't panic. Start over and consider each choice again. There may easily be something that you missed the first time and will realize on the second pass.

Tough Questions

If you are stumped on a problem or it appears too hard or too difficult, don't waste time. Move on! Remember though, if you can quickly check for obviously incorrect answer choices, your chances of guessing correctly are greatly improved. Before you completely give up, at least try to knock out a couple of possible answers. Eliminate what you can and then guess at the remaining answer choices before moving on.

Brainstorm

If you get stuck on a difficult question, spend a few seconds quickly brainstorming. Run through the complete list of possible answer choices. Look at each choice and ask yourself, "Could this answer the question satisfactorily?" Go through each answer choice and consider it independently of the other. By systematically going through all possibilities, you may find something that you would otherwise overlook. Remember that when you get stuck, it's important to try to keep moving.

Read Carefully

Understand the problem. Read the question and answer choices carefully. Don't miss the question because you misread the terms. You have plenty of time to read each question thoroughly and make sure you understand what is being asked. Yet a happy medium must be attained, so don't waste too much time. You must read carefully, but efficiently.

Face Value

When in doubt, use common sense. Always accept the situation in the problem at face value. Don't read too much into it. These problems will not require you to make huge leaps of logic. The test writers aren't trying to throw you off with a cheap trick. If you have to go beyond creativity and make a leap of logic in order to have an answer choice answer the question, then you should look at the other answer choices. Don't overcomplicate the problem by creating theoretical relationships or explanations that will warp time or space. These are normal problems rooted in reality. It's just that the applicable relationship or explanation may not be readily apparent and you have to figure things out. Use your common sense to interpret anything that isn't clear.

Prefixes

If you're having trouble with a word in the question or answer choices, try dissecting it. Take advantage of every clue that the word might include. Prefixes and suffixes can be a huge help. Usually they allow you to determine a basic meaning. Pre- means before, post- means after, pro - is positive, de- is negative. From these prefixes and suffixes, you can get an idea of the general meaning of the word and try to put it into context. Beware though of any traps. Just because con is the opposite of pro, doesn't necessarily mean congress is the opposite of progress!

Hedge Phrases

Watch out for critical "hedge" phrases, such as likely, may, can, will often, sometimes, often, almost, mostly, usually, generally, rarely, sometimes. Question writers insert these hedge phrases to cover every possibility. Often an answer choice will be wrong simply because it leaves no room for exception. Avoid answer choices that have definitive words like "exactly," and "always".

Switchback Words

Stay alert for "switchbacks". These are the words and phrases frequently used to alert you to shifts in thought. The most common switchback word is "but". Others include although, however, nevertheless, on the other hand, even though, while, in spite of, despite, regardless of.

New Information

Correct answer choices will rarely have completely new information included. Answer choices typically are straightforward reflections of the material asked about and will directly relate to the question. If a new piece of information is included in an answer choice that doesn't even seem to relate to the topic being asked about, then that answer choice is likely incorrect. All of the information needed to answer the question is usually provided for you, and so you should not have to make guesses that are unsupported or choose answer choices that require unknown information that cannot be reasoned on its own.

Time Management

On technical questions, don't get lost on the technical terms. Don't spend too much time on any one question. If you don't know what a term means, then since you don't have a dictionary, odds are you aren't going to get much further. You should immediately recognize terms as whether or not you know them. If you don't, work with the other clues that you have, the other answer choices and terms provided, but don't waste too much time trying to figure out a difficult term.

Contextual Clues

Look for contextual clues. An answer can be right but not correct. The contextual clues will help you find the answer that is most right and is correct. Understand the context in which a phrase or statement is made. This will help you make important distinctions.

Don't Panic

Panicking will not answer any questions for you. Therefore, it isn't helpful. When you first see the question, if your mind goes blank, take a deep breath. Force yourself to mechanically go through the steps of solving the problem and using the strategies you've learned.

Pace Yourself

Don't get clock fever. It's easy to be overwhelmed when you're looking at a page full of questions, your mind is full of random thoughts and feeling confused, and the clock is ticking down faster than you would like. Calm down and maintain the pace that you have set for yourself. As long as you are on track by monitoring your pace, you are guaranteed to have enough time for yourself. When you get to the last few minutes of the test, it may seem like you won't have enough time left, but if you only have as many questions as you should have left at that point, then you're right on track!

Answer Selection

The best way to pick an answer choice is to eliminate all of those that are wrong, until only one is left and confirm that is the correct answer. Sometimes though, an answer choice may immediately look right. Be careful! Take a second to make sure that the other choices are not equally obvious. Don't make a hasty mistake. There are only two times that you should stop before checking other answers. First is when you are positive that the answer choice you have selected is correct. Second is when time is almost out and you have to make a quick guess!

Check Your Work

Since you will probably not know every term listed and the answer to every question, it is important that you get credit for the ones that you do know. Don't miss any questions through careless mistakes. If at all possible, try to take a second to look back over your answer selection and make sure you've selected the correct answer choice and haven't made a costly careless mistake (such as marking an answer choice that you didn't mean to mark). This quick double check should more than pay for itself in caught mistakes for the time it costs.

Beware of Directly Quoted Answers

Sometimes an answer choice will repeat word for word a portion of the question or reference section. However, beware of such exact duplication – it may be a trap! More than likely, the correct choice will paraphrase or summarize a point, rather than being exactly the same wording.

Slang

Scientific sounding answers are better than slang ones. An answer choice that begins "To compare the outcomes…" is much more likely to be correct than one that begins "Because some people insisted…"

Extreme Statements

Avoid wild answers that throw out highly controversial ideas that are proclaimed as established fact. An answer choice that states the "process should be used in certain situations, if…" is much more likely to be correct than one that states the "process should be discontinued completely." The first is a calm rational statement and doesn't even make a definitive, uncompromising stance, using a hedge word "if" to provide wiggle room, whereas the second choice is a radical idea and far more extreme.

Answer Choice Families

When you have two or more answer choices that are direct opposites or parallels, one of them is usually the correct answer. For instance, if one answer choice states "x increases" and another answer choice states "x decreases" or "y increases," then those two or three answer choices are very similar in construction and fall into the same family of answer choices. A family of answer choices is when two or three answer choices are very similar in construction, and yet often have a directly opposite meaning. Usually the correct answer choice will be in that family of answer choices. The "odd man out" or answer choice that doesn't seem to fit the parallel construction of the other answer choices is more likely to be incorrect.

Special Report: How to Overcome Test Anxiety

The very nature of tests caters to some level of anxiety, nervousness or tension, just as we feel for any important event that occurs in our lives. A little bit of anxiety or nervousness can be a good thing. It helps us with motivation, and makes achievement just that much sweeter. However, too much anxiety can be a problem; especially if it hinders our ability to function and perform.

"Test anxiety," is the term that refers to the emotional reactions that some test-takers experience when faced with a test or exam. Having a fear of testing and exams is based upon a rational fear, since the test-taker's performance can shape the course of an academic career. Nevertheless, experiencing excessive fear of examinations will only interfere with the test-takers ability to perform, and his/her chances to be successful.

There are a large variety of causes that can contribute to the development and sensation of test anxiety. These include, but are not limited to lack of performance and worrying about issues surrounding the test.

Lack of Preparation

Lack of preparation can be identified by the following behaviors or situations:

- Not scheduling enough time to study, and therefore cramming the night before the test or exam
- Managing time poorly, to create the sensation that there is not enough time to do everything
- Failing to organize the text information in advance, so that the study material consists of the entire text and not simply the pertinent information
- Poor overall studying habits

Worrying, on the other hand, can be related to both the test taker, or many other factors around him/her that will be affected by the results of the test. These include worrying about:

- Previous performances on similar exams, or exams in general
- How friends and other students are achieving
- The negative consequences that will result from a poor grade or failure

There are three primary elements to test anxiety. Physical components, which involve the same typical bodily reactions as those to acute anxiety (to be discussed below). Emotional factors have to do with fear or panic. Mental or cognitive issues concerning attention spans and memory abilities.

Physical Signals

There are many different symptoms of test anxiety, and these are not limited to mental and emotional strain. Frequently there are a range of physical signals that will let a test taker know that he/she is suffering from test anxiety. These bodily changes can include the following:

- Perspiring
- Sweaty palms
- Wet, trembling hands
- Nausea
- Dry mouth
- A knot in the stomach
- Headache
- Faintness
- Muscle tension
- Aching shoulders, back and neck
- Rapid heart beat
- Feeling too hot/cold

To recognize the sensation of test anxiety, a test-taker should monitor him/herself for the following sensations:

- The physical distress symptoms as listed above
- Emotional sensitivity, expressing emotional feelings such as the need to cry or laugh too much, or a sensation of anger or helplessness
- A decreased ability to think, causing the test-taker to blank out or have racing thoughts that are hard to organize or control

Though most students will feel some level of anxiety when faced with a test or exam, the majority can cope with that anxiety and maintain it at a manageable level. However, those who cannot are faced with a very real and very serious condition, which can and should be controlled for the immeasurable benefit of this sufferer.

Naturally, these sensations lead to negative results for the testing experience. The most common effects of test anxiety have to do with nervousness and mental blocking.

Nervousness

Nervousness can appear in several different levels:

- The test-taker's difficulty, or even inability to read and understand the questions on the test
- The difficulty or inability to organize thoughts to a coherent form
- The difficulty or inability to recall key words and concepts relating to the testing questions (especially essays)
- The receipt of poor grades on a test, though the test material was well known by the test taker

Conversely, a person may also experience mental blocking, which involves:

- Blanking out on test questions
- Only remembering the correct answers to the questions when the test has already finished

Fortunately for test anxiety sufferers, beating these feelings, to a large degree, has to do with proper preparation. When a test taker has a feeling of preparedness, then anxiety will be dramatically lessened.

The first step to resolving anxiety issues is to distinguish which of the two types of anxiety are being suffered. If the anxiety is a direct result of a lack of preparation, this should be considered a normal reaction, and the anxiety level (as opposed to the test results) shouldn't be anything to worry about. However, if, when adequately prepared, the test-taker still panics, blanks out, or seems to overreact, this is not a fully rational reaction. While this can be considered normal too, there are many ways to combat and overcome these effects.

Remember that anxiety cannot be entirely eliminated, however, there are ways to minimize it, to make the anxiety easier to manage. Preparation is one of the best ways to minimize test anxiety. Therefore the following techniques are wise in order to best fight off any anxiety that may want to build.

To begin with, try to avoid cramming before a test, whenever it is possible. By trying to memorize an entire term's worth of information in one day, you'll be shocking your system, and not giving yourself a very good chance to absorb the information. This is an easy path to anxiety, so for those who suffer from test anxiety, cramming should not even be considered an option.

Instead of cramming, work throughout the semester to combine all of the material which is presented throughout the semester, and work on it gradually as the course goes by, making sure to master the main concepts first, leaving minor details for a week or so before the test.

To study for the upcoming exam, be sure to pose questions that may be on the examination, to gauge the ability to answer them by integrating the ideas from your texts, notes and lectures, as well as any supplementary readings.

If it is truly impossible to cover all of the information that was covered in that particular term, concentrate on the most important portions, that can be covered very well. Learn these concepts as best as possible, so that when the test comes, a goal can be made to use these concepts as presentations of your knowledge.

In addition to study habits, changes in attitude are critical to beating a struggle with test anxiety. In fact, an improvement of the perspective over the entire test-taking experience can actually help a test taker to enjoy studying and therefore improve the overall experience. Be certain not to overemphasize the significance of the grade - know that the result of the test is neither a reflection of self worth, nor is it a measure of intelligence; one grade will not predict a person's future success.

To improve an overall testing outlook, the following steps should be tried:

- Keeping in mind that the most reasonable expectation for taking a test is to expect to try to demonstrate as much of what you know as you possibly can.
- Reminding ourselves that a test is only one test; this is not the only one, and there will be others.
- The thought of thinking of oneself in an irrational, all-or-nothing term should be avoided at all costs.
- A reward should be designated for after the test, so there's something to look forward to. Whether it be going to a movie, going out to eat, or simply visiting friends, schedule it in advance, and do it no matter what result is expected on the exam

Test-takers should also keep in mind that the basics are some of the most important things, even beyond anti-anxiety techniques and studying. Never neglect the basic social, emotional and biological needs, in order to try to absorb information. In order to best achieve, these three factors must be held as just as important as the studying itself.

Study Steps

Remember the following important steps for studying:

- Maintain healthy nutrition and exercise habits. Continue both your recreational activities and social pass times. These both contribute to your physical and emotional well being.
- Be certain to get a good amount of sleep, especially the night before the test, because when you're overtired you are not able to perform to the best of your best ability.
- Keep the studying pace to a moderate level by taking breaks when they are needed, and varying the work whenever possible, to keep the mind fresh instead of getting bored.
- When enough studying has been done that all the material that can be learned has been learned, and the test taker is prepared for the test, stop studying and do something relaxing such as listening to music, watching a movie, or taking a warm bubble bath.

There are also many other techniques to minimize the uneasiness or apprehension that is experienced along with test anxiety before, during, or even after the examination. In fact, there are a great deal of things that can be done to stop anxiety from interfering with lifestyle and performance. Again, remember that anxiety will not be eliminated entirely, and it shouldn't be.

Otherwise that "up" feeling for exams would not exist, and most of us depend on that sensation to perform better than usual. However, this anxiety has to be at a level that is manageable.

Of course, as we have just discussed, being prepared for the exam is half the battle right away. Attending all classes, finding out what knowledge will be expected on the exam, and knowing the exam schedules are easy steps to lowering anxiety. Keeping up with work will remove the need to cram, and efficient study habits will eliminate wasted time. Studying should be done in an ideal location for concentration, so that it is simple to become interested in the material and give it complete attention. A method such as SQ3R (Survey, Question, Read, Recite, Review) is a wonderful key to follow to make sure that the study habits are as effective as possible, especially in the case of learning from a textbook. Flashcards are great techniques for memorization. Learning to take good notes will mean that notes will be full of useful information, so that less sifting will need to be done to seek out what is pertinent for studying. Reviewing notes after class and then again on occasion will keep the information fresh in the mind. From notes that have been taken summary sheets and outlines can be made for simpler reviewing.

A study group can also be a very motivational and helpful place to study, as there will be a sharing of ideas, all of the minds can work together, to make sure that everyone understands, and the studying will be made more interesting because it will be a social occasion.

Basically, though, as long as the test-taker remains organized and self confident, with efficient study habits, less time will need to be spent studying, and higher grades will be achieved.

To become self confident, there are many useful steps. The first of these is "self talk." It has been shown through extensive research, that self-talk for students who suffer from test anxiety, should be well monitored, in order to make sure that it contributes to self confidence as opposed to sinking the student. Frequently the self talk of test-anxious students is negative or self-defeating, thinking that everyone else is smarter and faster, that they always mess up, and that if they don't do well, they'll fail the entire course. It is important to decreasing anxiety that awareness is made of self talk. Try writing any negative self thoughts and then disputing them with a positive statement instead. Begin self-encouragement as though it was a friend speaking. Repeat positive statements to help reprogram the mind to believing in successes instead of failures.

Helpful Techniques

Other extremely helpful techniques include:

- Self-visualization of doing well and reaching goals
- While aiming for an "A" level of understanding, don't try to "overprotect" by setting your expectations lower. This will only convince the mind to stop studying in order to meet the lower expectations.
- Don't make comparisons with the results or habits of other students. These are individual factors, and different things work for different people, causing different results.
- Strive to become an expert in learning what works well, and what can be done in order to improve. Consider collecting this data in a journal.
- Create rewards for after studying instead of doing things before studying that will only turn into avoidance behaviors.
- Make a practice of relaxing - by using methods such as progressive relaxation, self-hypnosis, guided imagery, etc - in order to make relaxation an automatic sensation.
- Work on creating a state of relaxed concentration so that concentrating will take on the focus of the mind, so that none will be wasted on worrying.
- Take good care of the physical self by eating well and getting enough sleep.
- Plan in time for exercise and stick to this plan.

Beyond these techniques, there are other methods to be used before, during and after the test that will help the test-taker perform well in addition to overcoming anxiety.

Before the exam comes the academic preparation. This involves establishing a study schedule and beginning at least one week before the actual date of the test. By doing this, the anxiety of not having enough time to study for the test will be automatically eliminated. Moreover, this will make the studying a much more effective experience, ensuring that the learning will be an easier process. This relieves much undue pressure on the test-taker.

Summary sheets, note cards, and flash cards with the main concepts and examples of these main concepts should be prepared in advance of the actual studying time. A topic should never be eliminated from this process. By omitting a topic because it isn't expected to be on the test is only setting up the test-taker for anxiety should it actually appear on the exam. Utilize the course syllabus for laying out the topics that should be studied. Carefully go over the notes that were made in class, paying special attention to any of the issues that the professor took special care to emphasize while lecturing in class. In the textbooks, use the chapter review, or if possible, the chapter tests, to begin your review.

It may even be possible to ask the instructor what information will be covered on the exam, or what the format of the exam will be (for example, multiple choice, essay, free form, true-false). Additionally, see if it is possible to find out how many questions will be on the test. If a review sheet or sample test has been offered by the professor, make good use of it, above anything else, for the preparation for the test. Another great resource for getting to know the examination is reviewing tests from previous semesters. Use these tests to review, and aim to achieve a 100% score on each of the possible topics. With a few exceptions, the goal that you set for yourself is the highest one that you will reach.

Take all of the questions that were assigned as homework, and rework them to any other possible course material. The more problems reworked, the more skill and confidence will form as a result. When forming the solution to a problem, write out each of the steps. Don't simply do head work. By doing as many steps on paper as possible, much clarification and therefore confidence will be formed. Do this with as many homework problems as possible, before checking the answers. By checking the answer after each problem, a reinforcement will exist, that will not be on the exam. Study situations should be as exam-like as possible, to prime the test-taker's system for the experience. By waiting to check the answers at the end, a psychological advantage will be formed, to decrease the stress factor.

Another fantastic reason for not cramming is the avoidance of confusion in concepts, especially when it comes to mathematics. 8-10 hours of study will become one hundred percent more effective if it is spread out over a week or at least several days, instead of doing it all in one sitting. Recognize that the human brain requires time in order to assimilate new material, so frequent breaks and a span of study time over several days will be much more beneficial.

Additionally, don't study right up until the point of the exam. Studying should stop a minimum of one hour before the exam begins. This allows the brain to rest and put things in their proper order. This will also provide the time to become as relaxed as possible when going into the examination room. The test-taker will also have time to eat well and eat sensibly. Know that the brain needs food as much as the rest of the body. With enough food and enough sleep, as well as a relaxed attitude, the body and the mind are primed for success.

Avoid any anxious classmates who are talking about the exam. These students only spread anxiety, and are not worth sharing the anxious sentimentalities.

Before the test also involves creating a positive attitude, so mental preparation should also be a point of concentration. There are many keys to creating a positive attitude. Should fears become rushing in, make a visualization of taking the exam, doing well, and seeing an A written on the paper. Write out a list of affirmations that will bring a feeling of confidence, such as "I am doing well in my English class," "I studied well and know my material," "I enjoy this class." Even if the affirmations aren't believed at first, it sends a positive message to the subconscious which will result in an alteration of the overall belief system, which is the system that creates reality.

If a sensation of panic begins, work with the fear and imagine the very worst! Work through the entire scenario of not passing the test, failing the entire course, and dropping out of school, followed by not getting a job, and pushing a shopping cart through the dark alley where you'll live. This will place things into perspective! Then, practice deep breathing and create a visualization of the opposite situation - achieving an "A" on the exam, passing the entire course, receiving the degree at a graduation ceremony.

On the day of the test, there are many things to be done to ensure the best results, as well as the most calm outlook. The following stages are suggested in order to maximize test-taking potential:

- Begin the examination day with a moderate breakfast, and avoid any coffee or beverages with caffeine if the test taker is prone to jitters. Even people who are used to managing caffeine can feel jittery or light-headed when it is taken on a test day.
- Attempt to do something that is relaxing before the examination begins. As last minute cramming clouds the mastering of overall concepts, it is better to use this time to create a calming outlook.
- Be certain to arrive at the test location well in advance, in order to provide time to select a location that is away from doors, windows and other distractions, as well as giving enough time to relax before the test begins.
- Keep away from anxiety generating classmates who will upset the sensation of stability and relaxation that is being attempted before the exam.
- Should the waiting period before the exam begins cause anxiety, create a self-distraction by reading a light magazine or something else that is relaxing and simple.
- During the exam itself, read the entire exam from beginning to end, and find out how much time should be allotted to each individual problem. Once writing the exam, should more time be taken for a problem, it should be abandoned, in order to begin another problem. If there is time at the end, the unfinished problem can always be returned to and completed.

Read the instructions very carefully - twice - so that unpleasant surprises won't follow during or after the exam has ended.

When writing the exam, pretend that the situation is actually simply the completion of homework within a library, or at home. This will assist in forming a relaxed atmosphere, and will allow the brain extra focus for the complex thinking function.

Begin the exam with all of the questions with which the most confidence is felt. This will build the confidence level regarding the entire exam and will begin a quality momentum. This will also create encouragement for trying the problems where uncertainty resides.

Going with the "gut instinct" is always the way to go when solving a problem. Second guessing should be avoided at all costs. Have confidence in the ability to do well.

For essay questions, create an outline in advance that will keep the mind organized and make certain that all of the points are remembered. For multiple choice, read every answer, even if the correct one has been spotted - a better one may exist.

Continue at a pace that is reasonable and not rushed, in order to be able to work carefully. Provide enough time to go over the answers at the end, to check for small errors that can be corrected.

Should a feeling of panic begin, breathe deeply, and think of the feeling of the body releasing sand through its pores. Visualize a calm, peaceful place, and include all of the sights, sounds and sensations of this image. Continue the deep breathing, and take a few minutes to continue this with closed eyes. When all is well again, return to the test.

If a "blanking" occurs for a certain question, skip it and move on to the next question. There will be time to return to the other question later. Get everything done that can be done, first, to guarantee all the grades that can be compiled, and to build all of the confidence possible. Then return to the weaker questions to build the marks from there.

Remember, one's own reality can be created, so as long as the belief is there, success will follow. And remember: anxiety can happen later, right now, there's an exam to be written!

After the examination is complete, whether there is a feeling for a good grade or a bad grade, don't dwell on the exam, and be certain to follow through on the reward that was promised...and enjoy it! Don't dwell on any mistakes that have been made, as there is nothing that can be done at this point anyway.

Additionally, don't begin to study for the next test right away. Do something relaxing for a while, and let the mind relax and prepare itself to begin absorbing information again.
From the results of the exam - both the grade and the entire experience, be certain to learn from what has gone on. Perfect studying habits and work some more on confidence in order to make the next examination experience even better than the last one.

Learn to avoid places where openings occurred for laziness, procrastination and day dreaming.

Use the time between this exam and the next one to better learn to relax, even learning to relax on cue, so that any anxiety can be controlled during the next exam. Learn how to relax the body. Slouch in your chair if that helps. Tighten and then relax all of the different muscle groups, one group at a time, beginning with the feet and then working all the way up to the neck and face. This will ultimately relax the muscles more than they were to begin with. Learn how to breathe deeply and comfortably, and focus on this breathing going in and out as a relaxing thought. With every exhale, repeat the word "relax."

As common as test anxiety is, it is very possible to overcome it. Make yourself one of the test-takers who overcome this frustrating hindrance.

Additional Bonus Material

Due to our efforts to try to keep this book to a manageable length, we've created a link that will give you access to all of your additional bonus material.

Please visit http://www.mometrix.com/bonus948/nystcealst to access the information.